ROUTLEDGE LIBRARY EDITIONS:
SEMANTICS AND SEMIOLOGY

Volume 4

DESCRIPTIONS IN CONTEXT

DESCRIPTIONS IN CONTEXT

CLEO A. CONDORAVDI

LONDON AND NEW YORK

First published in 1997 by Garland Publishing, Inc.

This edition first published in 2017
by Routledge
2 Park Square, Milton Park, Abingdon, Oxon OX14 4RN

and by Routledge
711 Third Avenue, New York, NY 10017

Routledge is an imprint of the Taylor & Francis Group, an informa business

© 1997 Cleo A. Condoravdi

All rights reserved. No part of this book may be reprinted or reproduced or utilised in any form or by any electronic, mechanical, or other means, now known or hereafter invented, including photocopying and recording, or in any information storage or retrieval system, without permission in writing from the publishers.

Trademark notice: Product or corporate names may be trademarks or registered trademarks, and are used only for identification and explanation without intent to infringe.

British Library Cataloguing in Publication Data
A catalogue record for this book is available from the British Library

ISBN: 978-1-138-69750-8 (Set)
ISBN: 978-1-315-52029-2 (Set) (ebk)
ISBN: 978-1-138-69699-0 (Volume 4) (hbk)
ISBN: 978-1-138-69741-6 (Volume 4) (pbk)
ISBN: 978-1-315-52189-3 (Volume 4) (ebk)

Publisher's Note
The publisher has gone to great lengths to ensure the quality of this reprint but points out that some imperfections in the original copies may be apparent.

Disclaimer
The publisher has made every effort to trace copyright holders and would welcome correspondence from those they have been unable to trace.

DESCRIPTIONS IN CONTEXT

CLEO A. CONDORAVDI

GARLAND PUBLISHING, Inc.
NEW YORK & LONDON / 1997

Copyright © 1997 Cleo A. Condoravdi
All rights reserved

Library of Congress Cataloging-in-Publication Data

Condoravdi, Cleo A., 1962–
  Descriptions in context / Cleo A. Condoravdi.
    p.   cm. — (Outstanding dissertations in linguistics)
  A revision of the author's thesis (Ph. D.)—Yale University, 1994.
  Includes bibliographical references and index.
  ISBN 0-8153-2871-0 (alk. paper)
  1. Definiteness (Linguistics). 2. Semantics. 3. Grammar, Comparative and general—Number. I. Title. II. Series.
P299.D43C66 1997
401'.43—dc21
                                                97-2202

Printed on acid-free, 250-year-life paper
Manufactured in the United States of America

Contents

PREFACE		IX
1	INTRODUCTION	3
2	BARE PLURALS AND GENERICITY	5
	1 Introduction	5
	2 Genericity and the Readings of Bare Plurals	6
	2.1 Genericity	6
	2.2 Bare Plurals	8
	3 The Kind Analysis	9
	3.1 Basic Outline	9
	3.2 Arguments for a Unified Treatment	17
	3.2.1 Bare Plurals Are Unambiguous	18
	3.2.2 Bare Plurals and Indefinite NP's	19
	3.2.3 A Generic Operator and Bare Plurals	26
	3.3 Limits and Limitations of Uniformity	31
	3.4 Summary	33
	4 The Indefiniteness Analysis	33
	4.1 Basic Outline	33
	4.2 Individual-Level and Stage-Level Predicates	37
	4.3 The Generic Operator	39
	4.3.1 Implicit Domain Restrictions	39
	4.3.2 Modal Dimension	41
	4.4 Conclusion	45
	Appendix	46
	Notes	47
3	FUNCTIONAL READING OF BARE PLURALS	55
	1 Introduction	55
	2 The Functional Reading of Bare Plurals	57
	2.1 Initial Observations	57
	2.2 Functional Reading with Individual-Level Predicates	58

	2.2.1	Genericity and the Functional Reading	59
	2.2.2	Contextual Restrictions	67
2.3	Functional Reading with Stage-Level Predicates		70
2.4	Other Indefinites		73
2.5	Excluding a Purely Pragmatic Account		74
	2.5.1	The Implicature Approach	75
	2.5.2	The Referentiality Approach	79
2.6	Functional Reading in Quantified Contexts		81
	2.6.1	Dependent Functional Reading	82
	2.6.2	Quantificational and Modal Subordination	87
2.7	The Presupposition of Existence		89
	2.7.1	Simple Cases	90
	2.7.2	Projection of the Existential Presupposition	92
	2.7.3	Functional Reading with Adverbs of Quantity	95
2.8	Overview		100

3 An Operator Analysis   102
   3.1 Degenerate Genericity   103
   3.2 Degenerate Genericity and the Functional Reading   106
      3.2.1 Implicit Contextual Restrictions   107
      3.2.2 Implication of Existence   114
      3.2.3 Scopal Interaction   115
   3.3 Stage-Level Predicates   121
   3.4 Positive Contextual Sensitivity   123
   3.5 Summary   129
4 Conclusion   130
Notes   130

4   STRONG AND WEAK NOVELTY   141

1 Introduction   141
2 The Dynamic View on Meaning   143
   2.1 Assertions and Contextual Update   143
   2.2 Presuppositions and Contextual Admittance   152
3 The Novelty-Familiarity Theory of Definiteness and Indefiniteness   157
   3.1 Files as Information States   157
   3.2 Informativeness of Files   159
   3.3 The Felicity Conditions of Definites and Indefinites   162
   3.4 The Truth Conditions for Definites and Indefinites   165
4 The Functional Reading   168
   4.1 Weakly and Strongly Novel NP's   168

4.2 Contextually Salient Functions	172
4.3 Negative Contextual Sensitivity	174
4.4 Strong and Weak Novelty and NP Strength	175
4.5 Existential Force and Strong vs. Weak Novelty	177
4.6 Maximality	178
4.7 Consequences of the Existential Presupposition	179
4.7.1 Positive Contextual Sensitivity	179
4.7.2 Dependent Functional Reading	180
5 Conclusion	181
Notes	182
BIBLIOGRAPHY	187
INDEX	199

Preface

This is a slightly revised version of my dissertation, submitted to Yale University in 1994. The references have been updated, some stylistic changes were made throughout the text, and some clarificatory comments were added in chapter 2. Since the dissertation was finished, my thinking about some of the issues involved has changed but not in ways that affect the central claims of this work.

Acknowledgments. I would like to thank the members of my committee, Donka Farkas, Bill Ladusaw, Annie Zaenen, and Larry Horn, for their advice and encouragement through the course of this work. My advisor, Donka Farkas, has followed its development from vague hunches, to formed ideas, to a spelled out proposal with insight and enthusiasm. She has been very generous with ideas, suggestions, comments, support, and, not least, hospitality during my trips to Santa Cruz. Both the general argument and the specific workings of details owe a lot to our discussions. I hope that, after all the versions she has seen, this one is closer to the simplicity and explicitness she was urging all along. Many thanks to Bill Ladusaw and Annie Zaenen for readily agreeing to serve on my committee. Bill has a surprising way of turning a marginal point into a decisive one, of redirecting the focus of an argument and of bringing out what is essential in a proposal, often with one well-chosen phrase. I am very glad for having had the opportunity to discuss with him much of the material in this thesis. Annie's faith in me has made a big difference in more ways than I can say and, more tangibly, this thesis is much the better for her involvement with it. She never failed to detect a weakness or a hole in an argument, even in an area that is not her own, but also to acknowledge that some point had finally become convincing. Thanks to Larry Horn for many useful comments on a near-final draft and for taking care of the logistics of submitting from afar.

Tony Davis and Chris Piñón have been wonderful friends throughout this time and have contributed in no small ways. They have ungrudgingly read countless versions of various parts and their critical comments helped clarify my claims and improve the style in which they are presented. Tony was always ready to listen to an idea, to help sort out the central from the peripheral or sharpen an example, and brought sanity and rationality in moments of panic. Chris's skeptical scrutiny and meticulous attention to detail were invaluable checks for hasty conclusions or uncalled-for optimism. I have greatly enjoyed and benefited from our discussions, in the confines of my office or the expanse of the Stanford hills.

I am lucky that Sandro Zucchi, Henriëtte de Swart and Kees van Deemter were at Stanford during various stages of this work. I would like to thank them for the interest they took in my work and the challenging questions they asked. Discussions with David Israel, a maven on just about everything, have always proved revealing both in the short and in the long run. I am also grateful to Mark Gawron, Eric Jackson, Sam Bayer, and Louise McNally for discussions and comments that shaped the direction of this work early on. Thanks to Henriëtte de Swart and Paul Kiparsky for thorough and detailed comments on draft versions of chapters 2 and 3 that led to considerable improvements and to András Kornai for a close reading of a pre-final version of chapter 2.

Finally, many thanks to Annie Zaenen, Ivan Sag, Geoff Nunberg, John Perry, and Dikran Karagueuzian, who have made it possible for me to be at CSLI before and after the dissertation was completed, and to Tom Burke for his expert technical help in preparing the book manuscript.

Descriptions in Context

1
Introduction

This work is a contribution to the semantics of definite and indefinite descriptions. I take as a starting point the presuppositional theory of definiteness and indefiniteness proposed by Heim. Heim's theory shares with more traditional approaches a conception of definiteness as a simple binary opposition. I show that there exists a special type of indefinites that have an interpretation commonly associated with definites.

More specifically, in the novelty/familiarity theory of indefinite and definite NP's that Heim (1982) develops, there is a one-to-one correspondence between the definiteness of an NP and the felicity conditions it is associated with. Indefinite NP's are associated with a novelty condition for their index, definite NP's are associated with familiarity conditions for their index and their descriptive content.

I argue that the felicity conditions associated with indefinite NP's can vary. In addition to indefinite NP's that always assert existence, there are indefinites that may presuppose existence. Bare plurals in English exemplify this special type.

I develop a more fine-grained theory of novelty within the framework of File Change Semantics. The theory accounts for the full range of readings of the special type of indefinites, explains why their additional interpretations appear in a precisely circumscribed range of contexts and gives a unified characterization of indefiniteness within which the parameters of difference between regular and special indefinites can be naturally formulated. Formally, the analysis I propose allows the felicity conditions of a given noun phrase to interact with its file change potential to the following effect. The admissible contexts can be partitioned into those that entail *in part* the information added by the processing of the noun phrase and those that either fully entail that information (for definites) or do not entail any part of that information (for indefinites). Definites and indefinites of the traditionally recognized kind are then those that, given their felicity conditions, would have as admissible contexts only those of the latter type. Indefinites of the newly discovered type are those whose admissible contexts, given their felicity conditions, would be contexts of the former kind.

More generally, this work can be seen as providing an empirical argument in favor of a dynamic theory of meaning and against the more traditional truth-conditional theory of meaning with its strict separation between semantics and pragmatics and its restricted conception of context-dependency.

The empirical evidence is of a new kind—most of the evidence in the literature concerns anaphoric binding—and helps sort out two ideas. One is the idea that NP's should be distinguished according to whether they are inherently quantificational or not, allowing the semantic scope of non-quantificational NP's to extend beyond their syntactic scope. It was meant to account for donkey and intersentential anaphora and the variable quantificational force of indefinites. The other is to view meaning as a dynamic notion, an idea that can be characterized with the motto: the meaning of a sentence is the way in which it changes a given body of information. These two ideas, which came together in the work of Kamp and Heim, have been very influential and have guided a large part of recent work in semantics. Since, however, one way of implementing the first idea is in terms of the general setup that dynamic semantics provides, they are also often conflated. That they are independent of each other was already demonstrated by Heim (1982), with the difference in the semantic systems of chapters II and III of that work. The same point has also manifested itself implicitly in the direction of subsequent work that has adopted the former but has rejected the latter, such as Kratzer (1995) and Diesing (1990, 1992a). The facts and the analysis I present argue in favor of *both* ideas.

2
Bare Plurals and Genericity

1. INTRODUCTION

This chapter provides the background on bare plurals and genericity necessary for the discussion of the following chapters. It contains an overview of the familiar problems posed by bare plurals and generics and of two influential analyses that have so far been proposed. Its main focus are the empirical and theoretical motivations behind each analysis and the crucial assumptions underlying it.

The semantics of bare plurals is inextricably linked to the semantics of genericity and therefore they must be treated as interdependent in any analysis. Bare plural NP's pose a particular challenge because of their apparently divergent behavior. On the surface, at least, they can be interpreted as indefinite descriptions, as quantificational NP's with varying force, or as expressions referring to kinds, individuals of a special sort. The basic question then is whether they are ambiguous and, if so, in how many ways.

The central issue concerning the linguistic analysis of genericity is whether the regularity expressed by generic sentences should be built into their semantics as a generalization/quantification of some sort.[1] I will distinguish two kinds of approaches to generics: *direct generalization approaches*, which specify the truth conditions of generic sentences in terms of quantification, and *inferred generalization approaches*, which specify the truth conditions of generic sentences in some other way.

I will concentrate on Carlson's (1977b) classic kind analysis and on the indefiniteness analysis along the lines of Heim (1982), Gerstner & Krifka (1987), Krifka (1987), Krifka et al. (1995) and Wilkinson (1988a, 1991). Carlson's analysis is an inferred generalization approach to generics that takes bare plurals to be expressions denoting kinds. The indefiniteness analysis is a direct generalization approach that takes bare plurals to be indefinite descriptions with ordinary individuals in their denotation. Other approaches combining features of these two will be mentioned along the way.

Although Carlson's theory and the indefiniteness theory differ in terms of the semantics they give to genericity and to bare plurals, they are similar in making a clear separation between the meaning of a generic statement, which the semantics they propose is supposed to capture, and the kind of reasoning or action that belief of a generic statement may give rise to, which they consider as outside the purview of a semantic analysis.[2]

In section 2 I give a brief overview of the problems raised by generics and bare plurals. In section 3 I present and discuss the kind analysis and in section 4 I present and discuss the indefiniteness analysis. I will ultimately side with the indefiniteness analysis of bare plurals and the direct generalization approach to generics and these two positions are crucial for the material to follow in this book. However, given the uniformity, intuitive appeal and great empirical coverage of Carlson's analysis, I will present it in some detail and will show that some of the arguments he provided in favor of a kind analysis can be turned around as motivating the indefiniteness analysis of bare plurals and the direct generalization approach to generics.

2. GENERICITY AND THE READINGS OF BARE PLURALS

2.1 *Genericity*

Generic sentences express regularities and non-accidental generalizations, which among other things play an important role in reasoning. On the basis of a generic statement we can draw inferences, albeit defeasible, about particular occurrences or particular objects. The generalizations can be either descriptive or normative. The linguistic means of expressing genericity are varied: there is nominal and verbal genericity, and often no special expression is designated as exclusively generic. Thus definite and indefinite descriptions may have a generic use in addition to their usual uses; similarly, often the same tense can be used in an episodic and in a generic context.

The sentences in [1] are all intuitively identified as generic sentences, yet the source of genericity, the means used to express it, and the inferences it supports about particular instantiations are different in each case.

[1]   a. *Punica granatum* is an Old World tree.
      b. The 3-R4* generation robot will soon be antiquated.
      c. A pirate ship flies a black flag.
      d. Pomegranates have a crowned end.
      e. In this place one whistles a lullaby to show approval.

[1a] contains the name of a biological species and asserts something about the origin of that species. Members of the species planted in America are not, strictly speaking, Old World trees, rather they are descendants of trees that originated in the Old World. In [1b] the definite description also identifies a kind whose instantiations satisfy the descriptive content of the NP. [1b] is similar to [1a] in that the conditions placed on a kind for it to be considered antiquated are different from those placed on its particular instantiations. For example, the kind could be antiquated well before any one of its instantiations. Thus, in [1a] and [1b] the NP denotes a kind and the predicates can be meaningfully predicated of both a kind and an individual of the usual sort but the conditions under which these properties can be said to hold of a kind and of an individual are quite different.

[1c]–[1e] are more complicated. Do apparently indefinite descriptions identify a kind as well, and is that the source of genericity in [1c] and [1d]? The question becomes particularly vexing with respect to [1e], where it is unclear what the relevant kind should be. Moreover, it seems that, in contrast to [1a] and [1b], the truth or falsity of [1c]–[1e] has something to do with whether particular instances of pomegranates, pirate ships or people who are in this place have the relevant property. [1c]–[1e] seem to express a generalization about actual and potential entities satisfying the descriptive content of the singular indefinite, that of the bare plural, or the property of being in this place, respectively. For descriptive purposes, I will follow Link (1988, 1995) and use the term *proper kind predication* for cases like [1a] and [1b] and the term *derived kind predication* for cases like [1c]–[1e].

Generic generalizations have two hallmarks that distinguish them from actual, universal generalizations: they are not sensitive to the way things actually are but they *are* sensitive to alternative ways things might be or ought to be. As a consequence, generic generalizations are at the same time weaker and stronger than the corresponding actual accidental generalizations. They are weaker in that they tolerate exceptions, that is they can be true even on the face of exceptional cases. For example, [1d] is true even though, as it happens, there exist pomegranates whose crowned end has been chopped off. In fact, [1d] could still be true even if the crowned end of all pomegranates in existence were to be chopped off. They are stronger in that their truth does not depend simply on actual instantiations.[3] For example, it does not suffice for [1c] to be true that all the pirate ships in existence fly a black flag since this could happen as matter of accident, without any such convention in place. Therefore, actual generalizations are not necessarily generic.

2.2 Bare Plurals

In some cases a bare plural uncontroversially denotes a kind. In [2a], for example, the bare plural must denote a kind since the predicate *be extinct* can apply only to kinds and not to ordinary individuals. In addition, bare plurals exhibit both a generic or (quasi-)universal reading and an existential reading, each one of which is related to the kind of reading the whole sentence receives. The universal reading is tied to a generic or habitual generalization reading for the whole sentence. The existential reading is tied to an episodic reading for the whole sentence. [2b] and [2c], in which the bare plural appears to have universal and quasi-universal force,[4] respectively, express a characteristic property of dogs in general, while [2d], in which the bare plural appears to have existential force, is about an instance of barking by some dogs.

[2] a. Dinosaurs are extinct.
     b. Dogs are mammals.
     c. Dogs bark.
     d. Dogs barked last night outside my window.

Moreover, while the bare plural can get the universal/generic reading with all predicates, the existential reading is confined to a subclass of predicates (all episodic and a few stative predicates).

Observing these correlations, Carlson (1977a, 1977b) argued that the bare plural itself is not ambiguous, its different readings being the result of the semantics of the predicates it combines with. Subsequent work has in part accepted Carlson's arguments for a unified treatment of some of the readings of the bare plural but has sought it elsewhere, guided by different assumptions on the origin of genericity. Specifically, it has sought a unified treatment for the existential and generic readings of [2d], [2b] and [2c] but not of the one involving reference to kinds, as in [2a].

3. THE KIND ANALYSIS

3.1 Basic Outline

Carlson, in a series of works (1977a, 1977b, 1979, 1982), provides a uniform analysis of bare plurals, in which they rigidly denote kinds.[5] The multitude of their readings is derived from the different types of predications they appear in. Central to the analysis is the ontological assumption that the domain of individuals must be enriched to include kinds and the semantic assumption that the source of genericity resides in the intensionality of individuals.[6]

Carlson proposes that kinds are individuals in their own right which have different realizations (or manifestations) relative to different points of evaluation (i.e., worlds and times). In that sense they are intensional individuals. Following a proposal of Gabbay & Moravcsik (1973), Carlson goes a step further in assuming that ordinary individuals are also intensional in that they too have different realizations relative to different points of evaluation.[7]

The semantic proposal consists of two main claims. The first claim is that the regularity or generalization expressed by a generic statement is essentially indirect and, crucially, not part of its truth conditions: a generic statement attributes a property to an individual which can then be inferred to be "inherited" by a certain number of its extensional manifestations. A property of a kind is inherited by some of its realizations, and a property of an object is inherited by some of its spatio-temporal manifestations, but these conditions do not constitute part of the truth conditions of a generic statement. As Carlson (1977b:109) puts it: "Instead of asking the wrong question ('What is the generic quantifier?'), we are now asking the right question ('How can we infer quantification from generic sentences?')."[8] The second claim, crucially connected to the first, is that a generic sentence comprises simply a predication, albeit one of the right type. As Carlson (1979:65) states: "generic attribution is considered to be nothing more than attribution of a predicate to an individual, rather than to a stage of that individual."

Within the model structure proposed by Carlson kinds, objects and stages are all basic entities of the model. Kinds and objects are the intensional individuals, stages their spatio-temporal manifestations. NP's may denote kinds or objects but no NP denotes stages. The three types of entities are related by two realization relations: R relates stages to individuals (objects and kinds), R' relates objects to kinds. Meaning Postulates ensure that kinds, objects, stages and the realization relations satisfy the conditions in [3] (see Carlson (1977b:414–416) for a complete list of Meaning Postulates and their exact formulation).[9]

[3] a. every stage is the stage of some individual (object or kind)
b. different objects cannot have the same stages
c. if a stage realizes some object and that object realizes some kind, then the stage realizes that kind
d. a stage realizing a kind is also a stage of an object realizing that kind
e. individuals with a stage realization in some world exist in that world
f. any two kinds with exactly the same realizations in all worlds are identical.

A stipulated equivalence between kinds and their object realizations allows for a correspondence between the kind denoted by a kind-denoting NP and the intension of the common noun (CN) predicate of the NP. Namely, if the NP denotes the kind k, the intension of the CN and the set of sets defined by $\lambda x R'(x, k)$ at each point of evaluation are identical. In other words, at every world and every time, the set of objects satisfying the descriptive content of the NP will be exactly the same as the set of objects which (at that world and that time) realize the kind denoted by the NP. Thus, the translation of the bare plural NP *dogs* is as in [4].[10]

[4] $\lambda P\check{}P(\iota x^k \ (\Box \ \forall z^o \ (dog'(z^o) \leftrightarrow R'(z^o, x^k))))$

The denotation of the bare plural then is the property set of the unique kind whose realizations relative to every point of evaluation are exactly those belonging to the extension of the CN *dog* relative to that point of evaluation. Given the meaning postulate described in [3f], uniqueness is guaranteed for all models. Thus, the equivalence between kinds and their object realizations that is built into the translation of bare plurals and the meaning postulate guaranteeing uniqueness make bare plurals rigid designators.

In accord with the tripartite split of entities into stages, objects and kinds, predicates are sorted according to whether they take stages, objects or kinds as arguments. Individual-level predicates take individuals (i.e., kinds or objects) as arguments, stage-level predicates take stages of individuals as arguments. Individual-level predicates and stage-level predicates denote properties of different types of entities; giving a predicate an argument of the wrong type results in sortal incorrectness.

Empirically, it appears that the same predicate (corresponding to a full VP) can have both an episodic and a characteristic property reading, or, in terms of the analysis, it can apply both to objects and to kinds. Based on that evidence the finer typology in [5] emerges.[11]

[5] a. predicates that can apply only to kinds
   (strictly kind-level predicates)
   b. predicates that can apply both to objects and to kinds but not to stages
   (strictly individual-level predicates)
   c. predicates that can apply to stages, objects and kinds and have a characteristic property reading
   d. predicates that can apply to stages, objects and kinds but do not have a characteristic property reading

Strictly kind-level predicates can be either stative (e.g., *be extinct, constitute a species*) or episodic (e.g., *become extinct, populate*).[12] Bare plurals construed with such predicates are intuitively understood as referring to a kind. Strictly individual-level predicates are always stative and have a characteristic property reading. They are comprised of *be* plus an adjectival predicate or a predicative NP (e.g., *be intelligent, be a bore*).[13] Bare plurals construed with such predicates have a generic/(quasi-)universal reading. Predicates of the category [5c] are episodic when applied to stages, while they express a characteristic property when applied to objects or kinds; they comprise all verbal predicates except for *be* (e.g., *bark*). Bare plurals construed with such predicates have an existential reading when the predicate is episodic (as in [2d]) and a generic reading when the predicate has a characteristic property interpretation (as in [2c]). Finally, predicates of the category in [5d] are comprised of *be* plus an adjectival predicate or a predicative PP (e.g., *be available, be in the corner*). Bare plurals construed with such predicates have an existential reading.[14] Schematically, the generalizations are summarized in [6], where individuals comprise both objects and kinds.

[6]

Type of Predicate	Type of Argument	Interpretation of Predicate	Interpretation of Bare Plural
[5a]: *extinct*	kinds	stative or episodic	kind-referring
[5b]: *intelligent*	individuals	characteristic property (stative)	universal
[5c]: *bark*	stages individuals	episodic characteristic property	existential universal
[5d]: *available*	stages or individuals	stative (but not characteristic property)	existential

Carlson's analysis captures these generalizations by distinguishing between basic and derived predicates within the system of Intensional Logic (IL), into which expressions of English are mapped by the translation mapping. Derived predicates are derived from basic predicates in two ways: (a) a stage-level predicate is mapped to an individual-level predicate containing existential quantification over stages, (b) appropriate generalization operators raise the level of a given predicate creating an intensional context. There are no derived stage-level predicates. Derived predicates of the first kind are needed so as to make a basically stage-level predicate capable of composing with an individual-denoting NP. If α' is a stage-level predicate of (the sorted) type $<e^s,t>$, then $\lambda x^i \exists y^s [R(y^s, x^i) \& \alpha'(y^s)]$ is an individual-level predicate of (the sorted) type $<e^i,t>$. Derived predicates of the second kind characterize the characteristic property reading associated with the majority of generic statements. Gn is the generalization operator mapping stage-level predicates to individual-level predicates and Gn' the generalization operator mapping object-level predicates to kind-level. Both Gn and Gn' are intensional VP operators. More precisely, if α' is a predicate of type $<e^s,t>$ or $<e^o,t>$, then application of the generalization operators Gn or Gn' results in the predicates $Gn(\hat{}\alpha')$ and $Gn'(\hat{}\alpha')$, which are of type $<e^i,t>$ and $<e^k,t>$, respectively.

Basic predicates and derived predicates of the first type give rise to predications unmediated by a generalization operator; derived predicates of the second type give rise to mediated predications, which create an intensional context for the VP.[15] Unmediated predications arise when basically object-level predicates combine with object-denoting NP's,[16] when basically kind-level predicates combine with kind-denoting NP's, or when individual-level predicates with existential quantification over stages combine with individual-denoting NP's.[17] Mediated predications arise when an individual-level predicate derived from a basically stage-level predicate combines with an individual-denoting NP,[18] or when a kind-level predicate derived from a basically object-level predicate combines with a kind-denoting NP. All individual-level predicates with stage-level counterparts are derived from the latter either via the mapping described in (a) above or via the generalization operator *Gn*. Most kind-level predicates with object-level counterparts are derived from the latter via the generalization operator *Gn'*. Exceptions are predicates like *be popular, be well-known*, etc., which do not give rise to a generic reading with singular indefinites. These are assumed by Carlson to be both basically object-level and kind-level. The typology of predicates according to their surface distribution outlined in [5] and [6] corresponds to the classification within the system of IL given in [7].

[7]   a. basically kind-level:
be-extinct', populate', be-popular'
b. i. basically object-level:
be-intelligent', be-popular'
ii. derived kind-level:
Gn'(^*be-intelligent'*)
c. i. basically stage-level:
smoke'
ii. derived individual-level with existential quantification over stages:
$\lambda x^i \exists y^s [R(y^s, x^i) \& smoke'(y^s)]$
iii. individual-level derived via a generalization operator:
Gn(^*smoke'*)
d. i. basically stage-level:
be-available'
ii. derived individual-level with existential quantification over stages:
$\lambda x^i \exists y^s [R(y^s, x^i) \& be\text{-}available'(y^s)]$

Predicates of the categories [7ci] and [7di] do not correspond directly to the translation of any natural language predicate. Natural language predicates that are stage-level need to compose with individual-denoting NP's, hence their translation is always a derived predicate.

Carlson can analyze bare plurals and other generic NP's as uniformly kind-denoting by having (i) a sufficiently rich ontology, (ii) constraints on models (meaning postulates) which regulate the elements of the ontology, (iii) predicates selecting for the sorts of entities they can apply to, (iv) mappings from basic predicates to predicates which can apply to entities of a different sort.

A kind-denoting NP, such as a bare plural, always combines with a kind-level predicate; different readings for the NP arise depending on whether the predicate is basic or derived, and, if derived, on whether it is mediated by a generalization operator or not. If the predicate is basic or mediated by a generalization operator (categories [7a], [7bii], [7ciii]), then there is no quantification either over objects or over stages in the semantics. If the predicate is derived but unmediated (categories [7cii] and [7dii]), then there is quantification over stages in the semantics.

Thus the apparent universal force of the bare plural, arising when the kind-level predicate it combines with is derived from an object-level predicate or has an object-level counterpart but is not derived from it (e.g., *be popular, be well-known,*) is not captured in the semantics. The intuition that there is quantification over (unexceptional) objects satisfying the descriptive content of the bare plural is attributed to pragmatic inferencing.

Distinguishing predicates such as *be popular, be well-known* from the rest is an artifact of Carlson's analysis, which tries to capture the fact that singular generic indefinites do not have a generic reading with such predicates. Carlson analyzes singular generic indefinites as kind-denoting but assumes that they combine only with derived kind-level predicates. While this also correctly excludes basically kind-level predicates like *extinct* from applying to them, it is a rather ad hoc way of accounting for the difference between bare plurals and the singular generic indefinite (see Farkas (1985)).

The existential reading of the bare plural, arising when the kind-level predicate is derived from a stage-level predicate, is attributed to the existential quantification over stages of individuals built into the translation of such predicates. The apparent existential quantification over objects satisfying the descriptive content of the NP is the result, on the one hand, of the semantics, which gives us existential quantification over stages, and, on the other, of the meaning postulates spelled out in [3d] and [3e] above, which guarantee that the relevant stage also realizes an object existing in the actual world and realizing the same kind.

The analysis, moreover, predicts that bare plurals will not have an existential reading with basically individual-level predicates, thus correctly capturing a very important and otherwise mysterious generalization.

Specifically, [2a], [2b], [2c], [2d] receive the translations in [8a], [8b], [8c] and [8d], respectively (ignoring tense and adverbial modifiers). A bare plural, analyzed as denoting a unique kind, receives the translation $\lambda P\check{\ }P(a^k)$, where a^k is a constant picking out a kind-level entity.[19] The predicate *extinct* is basically kind-level, hence [8a] involves an unmediated predication. The predicate *mammal* is basically object-level and can be raised to kind-level; hence [8b] involves a mediated predication. The predicate *bark* is basically stage-level and can either be raised to object-level or kind-level via a generalization operator or simply by mapping to an individual-level predicate and introducing existential quantification over stages; hence [8c] involves a mediated predication and a generic reading for the bare plural, while [8d] involves an unmediated predication and an existential reading for the bare plural.

[8] a. $\lambda P\check{\ }P(din)(\hat{\ }extinct') \Rightarrow$
       $extinct'(din)$
    b. $\lambda P\check{\ }P(dog)(\hat{\ }Gn'(\hat{\ }mammal')) \Rightarrow$
       $Gn'(\hat{\ }mammal')(dog))$
    c. $\lambda P\check{\ }P(dog)(\hat{\ }Gn(\hat{\ }bark')) \Rightarrow$
       $Gn(\hat{\ }bark')(dog))$
    d. $\lambda P\check{\ }P(dog)(\hat{\ }\lambda y^i\ \exists x^s\ (R(x^s,d)\ \&\ bark'(x^s))) \Rightarrow$
       $\exists x^s\ (R(x^s,dog)\ \&\ bark'(x^s))$

Relative to a given world and time, [8a] is true iff the individual kind dinosaurs is in the set of kind-level entities that are extinct in that world and that time, [8b] is true iff the individual kind dogs is in the set of kind-level entities that are mammals in that world and that time, [8c] is true iff the individual kind dogs is in the set of kind-level entities that bark in that world and that time, and [8d] is true in a given world and time iff the kind dogs has stage realizations in that world and that time which are in the set of stage-level entities that bark.[20] The truth conditions make *no* reference to how many object or stage realizations of a kind possess the property denoted by the predicate in order for the predicate to be truthfully predicated of a kind. In a given model and relative to a given point of evaluation a kind is either in the denotation of a kind-level predicate or not, and that is independent of how many stage or object realizations of that kind, if any at all, are in the denotation of the equivalent stage or object-level predicate, either in that point of evaluation or in any other point of evaluation. This is what makes this analysis fall within the category of inferred generalization approaches.[21]

Since the truth of derived kind-level predications does not depend on the truth of object-level predications in any way, the analysis sidesteps the problem of exceptions and captures the distinction between generic and actual generalizations. Generic generalizations, in contrast to actual generalizations, are only apparent, involving in reality a kind-level predication. But, in doing so, the analysis has a serious shortcoming in that it does not capture the distinction between different kinds of generic generalizations, such as descriptive, dispositional, and normative generalizations. While the operators Gn and Gn' are supposed to capture all the different kinds of generic generalizations, they cannot discriminate among them. In the same way that the truth of a kind-level predication relative to a given point of evaluation does not depend on the truth of the corresponding object-level predication relative to any point of evaluation, similarly, it does not depend on the truth of the kind-level predication relative to any other point of evaluation. But this is precisely what we need if we are to capture normative generalizations.[22] This shortcoming is serious, as different types of generic generalizations must be distinguished since they are not always truth-conditionally equivalent. For example, a descriptive generalization might be true without the corresponding normative generalization being true as well, as in [9a], and vice versa, as in [9b].

[9] a. People around here shoot at each other indiscriminately.
    b. A country with rich natural resources shares them with its neighbors.

Carlson runs into further problems with respect to dispositional and normative generalizations because of two meaning postulates he posits requiring that if $Gn(\hat{\ }\alpha')$ can be truthfully predicated of some individual and that individual has at least some (past) stages then α' can be truthfully predicated of at least one stage. This might be true of descriptive generalizations but it is certainly not true of normative generalizations. For example, 'In chess bishops move diagonally' may be true in the actual world even if no bishop has ever moved diagonally because, say, no game of chess has ever actually been played (although the rules of the game are in place) or every game of chess has been played incorrectly.

It is important to note that an inferred generalization approach to generics is independent of a uniform analysis for the bare plural. For example, one could have a direct generalization approach to generics (at least those that do not involve proper kind predication) and a uniform analysis for the bare plural as kind-denoting. This is the position taken by Farkas (1985), who assumes that there is a generic operator quantifying over object realizations of the kind denoted by the bare plural, and by Schubert & Pelletier (1988, 1989), who assume that bare plurals denote kinds and have a meaning postulate requiring the existence of an object realizing the kind in every world.[23] Similarly, one could have a uniform analysis of the generic readings of the bare plural and a separate analysis for its existential reading.

3.2 Arguments for a Unified Treatment

Carlson designed his theory to provide a uniform analysis of generics and a unified analysis of the different readings of bare plurals. All generic sentences involve the attribution of an individual-level property to an individual (object or kind) and a bare plural always denotes a kind. This approach was justified by the following three claims, which he defended in great detail:

(1) The ambiguity resides in the predicate and not in the NP.
(2) On their existential reading bare plurals are not indefinite NP's.
(3) The generic reading of the bare plural is not due to a generic operator.

If they are indeed correct, (1) and (2) jointly support a unified analysis of the existential and the generic reading of bare plurals, and (3) an inferred generalization approach to generics. In sections 3.2.1, 3.2.2, and 3.2.3 I discuss the evidence which led Carlson to these claims. I have tried to bring an updated perspective with respect to the arguments supporting (2) and (3), so I present them in a way that does not always follow Carlson's organization or characterization. I will argue that a critical reexamination of the evidence leads to different conclusions from the ones Carlson drew. In some cases, the evidence is compatible either with the assumption that the bare plural is kind-denoting or with the assumption that it is an indefinite description. In other cases, the evidence in fact favors the assumption of the indefiniteness of the bare plural and of the presence of an operator in generics.

3.2.1 Bare Plurals are Unambiguous

Let us take for granted that some predicates can denote either episodic or characteristic properties. If, in addition, bare plurals were ambiguous between an existential and a generic reading, then there would, in principle, be four possible readings resulting from the combination of a bare plural with such a predicate, as schematized in [10]. Correspondingly, for those predicates that can denote only characteristic properties (basically individual-level predicates) there would in principle be two possibilities, those in [10a] and [10c].

[10] a. generic NP — characteristic property
      b. existential NP — episodic property
      c. existential NP — characteristic property
      d. generic NP — episodic property

Of these, Carlson points out, only [10a] and [10b] actually occur. Consider the sentences in [11].

[11] a. Dinosaurs ate kelp.
      b. Dinosaurs were intelligent.

[11a] has a reading corresponding to [10a], according to which all (at least all unexceptional) dinosaurs had the characteristic property of eating kelp, and a reading corresponding to [10b], according to which some dinosaurs ate kelp on one particular occasion. The readings corresponding to [10c] and [10d] are lacking: there is no reading according to which some dinosaurs had the characteristic property of eating kelp, nor is there a reading in which there was an instance of kelp eating by all (unexceptional) dinosaurs.[24] Similarly, [11b] has only a reading corresponding to [10a], according to which all (unexceptional) dinosaurs had the characteristic property of being intelligent. There is no reading corresponding to [10c], according to which there were some dinosaurs that were intelligent.

As we have seen, the reading of [11a] corresponding to [10a] is the result of a derived mediated predication, of the type specified in [7ciii], and the reading corresponding to [10b] is the result of a derived unmediated predication, of the type specified in [7cii]. Given the typology in [7] and taking *eat kelp* to be a basically stage-level predicate, there are no other possibilities. The reading of [11b] corresponding to [10a] is the result of a derived mediated predication, of the type specified in [7bii]. Given [7] and the fact that *be intelligent* is a basically individual-level predicate, no other possibilities exist.

While Carlson is correct in claiming that the readings of type [10c] and [10d] are missing, another generalization that he makes, namely that a bare plural subject cannot have an existential reading in a generic sentence, is too restrictive. Cases exemplified by [12] (originally discussed in Milsark (1974)) constitute a serious problem for his analysis, which predicts that the only reading available for [12a] is one equivalent to [12c]. In fact [12b] is also a possible reading, and the only plausibly true one in this case.[25]

[12] a. Typhoons arise in this part of the Pacific.
      b. In this part of the Pacific there arise typhoons.
      c. In general, typhoons arise in this part of the Pacific.

Notice, moreover, that [12a] (with the existential reading for the bare plural) and [12b] are interpreted as generic while they contain no NP in them that is kind-denoting, which can then give rise to a kind-level predication.[26] Given the overall architecture of the theory there is no way of accommodating such cases since the predicate can either be derived via a generalization operator, thus giving a generic reading to the bare plural, or have existential quantification over stages, giving an existential reading to the bare plural and an episodic reading for the whole sentence.

3.2.2 Bare Plurals and Indefinite NP's

In support of the claim that bare plurals are not indefinites, even on their existential reading, Carlson brings three types of arguments: (a) scopal restrictions, (b) anaphoric properties, (c) similarity with definite, kind-denoting NP's.

a. Scopal Restrictions

When interpreted existentially, bare plurals always have narrow scope with respect to sentential operators (e.g., negation), count nominal quantifiers, attitudinal predicates and partitive quantifiers. For example, while the singular indefinite can have both narrow and wide scope with respect to negation, thus allowing for a non-contradictory reading of [13a], the bare plural has only narrow scope with respect to negation, allowing only for a contradictory reading of [13b].

[13] a. A cat attacked John and a cat did not attack John.

b. Cats attacked John and cats did not attack John.

Since the existential reading for bare plurals arises as a result of existential quantification over stages introduced within the translation of the VP predicate, the analysis allows only for translations in which the existential quantification has narrow scope with respect to every other operator. If the bare plural were analyzed as an indefinite, Carlson's argument goes, then the existential quantifier associated with it would scope freely with respect to other operators resulting in more readings than are actually attested.

The facts about scope have since been widely discussed and sometimes disputed so I will not devote too much attention to them here (see Kratzer (1980), Link (1984), Wilkinson (1988a), Rooth (1995)). The interaction between bare plurals and partitive quantifiers (labelled *differentiated scope phenomenon* by Carlson) is well-known from studies on aspect. The facts pointing to a difference between bare plurals and indefinites NP's in terms of their aspectual properties, while robust, cannot be taken as a definitive argument against the bare plural's being indefinite since they can be accounted for in a different manner than assuming existential quantification introduced by the predicate over stage realizations of a kind. See, e.g., Krifka (1989), Verkuyl (1989), Moltmann (1991). Similarly, a more in-depth analysis of the other scopal restrictions might reveal that they are a by-product of some other property of bare plurals and are therefore consistent with the position that bare plurals are indefinite NP's.

b. Anaphora

The argument from anaphora can be summarized as follows: bare plurals are not indefinite NP's because pronouns anaphoric on them have a wider range of readings than pronouns anaphoric on indefinites. In what follows I look more closely at Carlson's analysis of anaphora with the aim of showing that not assuming that bare plurals are indefinite at least on their existential reading misses certain important generalizations.

Pronouns outside the syntactic (c-command) scope of their indefinite antecedents are interpreted as E-type, that is as synonymous with a definite description: consider the synonymy of [14a] and [14b]. Carlson notes that pronouns with bare plural antecedents have an additional interpretation. They can be interpreted as E-type, as in [14c], but they can also be interpreted as pronouns of laziness standing for a description identical to that of their bare plural antecedent.[27] This is illustrated by [14d], which has a reading corresponding to that of [14e] (in other words, Mary need not have sold the strawberries I grew). In contrast, [14f], in which the pronoun has an indefinite antecedent, does not have such a reading.

[14] a. I bought some strawberries yesterday. Mary washed them.
b. I bought some strawberries yesterday. Mary washed the strawberries I bought yesterday.
c. I bought strawberries yesterday. Mary washed them.
d. I grew strawberries. Mary sold them.
e. I grew strawberries. Mary sold strawberries.
f. I grew some strawberries. Mary sold them.
g. # Strawberries are fragrant. I bought them yesterday.

Carlson assumes that pronouns in general receive two translations.[28] The interpretation of the antecedent ultimately influences the range of readings for the pronoun. He analyzes E-type pronouns along the lines of Cooper (1979) as implicit Russellian definite descriptions. Their translation, $\lambda P\ (\exists x^i\ (\forall y^i\ (\check{}Q(z^s))(y^i) \leftrightarrow x^i = y^i))\ \&\ \check{}P(x^i))$, involves two free variables, which must be given a value of the appropriate type by the context of use. The relation variable Q can pick as its value the realization relation R that relates stages to individuals when that is contextually available; the stage-level variable z^s can then be assigned as its value the contextually available stage-level entity that is an argument of R. For example, the pronoun in [14c] picks out those individuals that are strawberries and have a stage-level realization that was bought by me yesterday. The existence of such individuals is guaranteed by the first sentence of [14c] since for that sentence to be true there must be stages of the kind strawberries that were bought by me yesterday. The meaning postulate described in [3d] guarantees that these are also stages of an object realizing the same kind. The second sentence of [14c] then asserts of those individuals that they also have a stage-level realization that was washed by Mary.

A pronoun may also translate as the set of properties associated with some individual entity: $\lambda P\check{}P(x^i)$. It is this translation that results in a pronoun of laziness interpretation if the antecedent is a bare plural. The context must make available a unique individual-level entity which can be given as the value of the free variable x^i. In [14d], where the first sentence contains a kind-denoting NP, the pronoun appears in a context which makes available a unique individual-level entity. The free variable in the translation of the pronoun is assigned as value the kind-level entity denoted by the bare plural *strawberries*.

Although a pronoun always has the option of translating as the set of properties associated with some individual entity, whether a true pronoun of laziness reading will arise depends on whether its antecedent is kind-denoting or object-denoting. If the antecedent is object-denoting, either translation for the pronoun would amount to the same reading. For example, in the context of the first sentence of [14f], where the NP introduces existential quantification over objects, the free variable in the translation of the pronoun can be given as value the object-level entity which makes the first sentence true.[29] But any such entity must satisfy both the condition of being a strawberry and of having stages that were grown by me. So, in effect, the pronoun is interpreted as if it were E-type (modulo the origin of existence and uniqueness).[30] In other words, having two different translations for the pronoun does not lead to two distinct interpretations except when the antecedent is kind-denoting.

However, the two interpretations are not always available for a pronoun anaphoric on a bare plural. Carlson observes that such a pronoun can be E-type only if its antecedent is in an episodic context. The pronoun in [14g], whose antecedent occurs with an individual-level predicate, lacks an E-type reading (i.e., the reading according to which I bought the strawberries that are fragrant). This reading is excluded by Carlson on the grounds that the first sentence does not introduce existential quantification over stages and hence there is no contextually available value for the free variables in the translation of the pronoun.[31] However, why should the translation of the pronoun be specified in such a way as to contain a two-place relation variable or a free variable sorted for stages? There is no independent evidence for specifying the adicity of the contextually recoverable property or sortally restricting its arguments. Is there a way of excluding the relevant reading without this stipulation?

Suppose we follow Cooper and take E-type pronouns to translate as $\lambda P\ (\exists x^i\ (\forall y^i\ (\check{}Q)(y^i) \leftrightarrow x^i = y^i)\ \&\ \check{}P(x^i))$, with Q being a property denoting expression that may contain only free variables (of any sort) and parentheses. Then for the pronoun in [14g] we can reconstruct the free property variable as the property of being fragrant and assign to Q the value $Gn'(\hat{}fragrant')$. Since the first sentence of [14g] guarantees the existence of an individual-level entity that is fragrant, namely the kind strawberries, the second sentence would assert that I bought stages of the unique kind that is the kind strawberries and which is fragrant. Nothing will require that the objects whose stages I bought had to be fragrant.[32] In this case, therefore, the E-type interpretation and the pronoun of laziness interpretation would amount to the same thing.

However, when object-level entities are implicated in the truth-conditions of the sentence containing the antecedent, this approach predicts that the pronoun will have a distinct E-type interpretation. Sentences with adverbs of quantification introduce quantification over object realizations of a kind, as we will see in section 3.3, and are therefore predicted to give rise to such a reading for subsequent pronouns. [15a] exemplifies such a case: the first sentence of [15a] would translate as in [15b] and the second as in [15c], assuming we assign to Q as value the property of being fragrant.

[15] a. Strawberries are sometimes fragrant. I bought them yesterday.
b. $\exists z^o(R'(z^o, \text{strawb}) \,\&\, fragrant'(z^o))$
c. $\exists x^o(\forall y^o(fragrant'(y^o) \leftrightarrow x^o = y^o)) \,\&\, \exists z^s(R(z^s, x^o) \,\&\, bought(\text{I}, z^s))$

But then the pronoun will be taken to be synonymous with the definite description 'the fragrant objects (that are strawberries)', contrary to fact. Therefore, unless a sortal restriction is put on the free entity variable, the analysis predicts more readings than are actually available. However, by putting sortal restrictions on the free variables in the translation of E-type pronouns, the analysis seems to stipulate what it should explain, namely, why the interpretation of the predicate that the bare plural antecedent is construed with affects the range of interpretations of the pronoun. In other words, the analysis fails to capture the generalization that a bare plural supports E-type anaphora only if it receives an existential reading, i.e., only when it is in an episodic context.

Moreover, the reverse generalization appears to hold as well: if both the bare plural antecedent and the pronoun are in an episodic context, then the pronoun must be interpreted as E-type.[33] Gerstner and Krifka (1987) have noted the deviance of examples like [16], which can be explained on pragmatic grounds assuming the E-type interpretation is the only possible one for the pronoun.[34]

[16] # John ate apples$_i$ and Mary ate them$_i$ too.

Now, Carlson's analysis can exclude the E-type reading on pragmatic grounds as well (since it would imply that John and Mary ended up eating the same apples) but has no way of ruling out the pronoun of laziness interpetation.

An assumption underlying Carlson's argument from anaphora is that a pronoun may have a kind or generic reading only because its antecedent is kind-denoting. But as various authors (e.g., van Eijck 1983, Wilkinson 1991) have demonstrated, a wide variety of NP's give rise to this kind of anaphora; the best way to analyze it is to treat the pronoun as a pronoun of laziness whose descriptive content is determined on the basis of the CN of its antecedent. The factors determining when such a reading for the pronoun could arise (since it is not always available) is predicted to be uniform for the various types of NP's.[35] Such an approach is of course entirely compatible with treating the bare plural as an indefinite NP, at least on its existential reading. A treatment of the bare plural as an indefinite would then account for the possibility of E-type anaphora with bare plurals. On the other hand, a bare plural involved in a proper kind predication would directly support kind anaphora so we would expect such anaphora to be freer than the one involving a pronoun of laziness interpretation.[36]

c. *Definite Kind-Denoting NP's*

Definite NP's referring to kinds, like *this kind of wolf*, exhibit a parallelism with bare plurals in episodic contexts. Although they have an existential reading (see [17a]), we would not want to analyze them as indefinite NP's. In addition, they have the same properties with respect to scope as bare plurals (see [17b], [17c]).

[17] a. I saw this kind of wolf at the zoo.
b. # I saw this kind of wolf at the zoo and I did not see this kind of wolf at the zoo.
c. John believes that this kind of wolf will appear in his garden.

Carlson concludes that what such NP's share with bare plurals is precisely reference to kinds and takes the parallelism between these two types of superficially dissimilar NP's as further evidence that bare plurals are, despite appearances, disguised definite descriptions of a special sort.

However, one can cast doubt on the claim that definite kind-referring NP's really have an existential reading with episodic predicates. Although [17a] implies that I saw a wolf in the zoo that was a wolf of this kind, it is not beyond doubt that this is in fact part of its truth-conditional meaning. I will not offer an analysis of definite kind-referring NP's here but I will try to establish that, unlike bare plurals, they do not have an existential reading and that, therefore, an episodic predicate does not introduce existential quantification over stages. More generally, I will argue that definite kind-referring NP's do not behave (even superficially) in ways that exactly parallel bare plurals.

Because the implication of existence of an individual that is a realization of a kind is so strong, it is easy to be convinced that the bare plural and the kind-referring NP receive the same interpretation in episodic contexts (except, of course, for the fact that an NP like *this kind of wolf* refers to a subkind of the kind wolf), which according to Carlson's analysis comes about because the predicate introduces quantification over stages of the kind. Nevertheless, there is some subtle evidence that can distinguish between the existential reading of the bare plural and that of a definite kind-referring NP. The former is part of the truth-conditional content of the sentence, the latter is only an implication.[37] Consider [18].

[18]   a. I got rid of weeds from the garden yesterday.
       b. I got rid of this kind of weed from the garden yesterday.

[18a] and [18b] are true under somewhat different circumstances: if I got rid of some weeds but left some still standing, [18a] would be true while [18b] would be false. [18b] requires that I get rid of every single specimen of this kind of weed in the garden, a requirement linked to the fact that *get rid of* is interpreted as a basically kind-level predicate with respect to its second argument in [18b]. So the implication associated with the NP *this kind of N* as to how many realizations of the kind have the relevant property can vary, depending on the lexical semantics of the predicate. This can also be taken as indication that the existential reading of the bare plural in [18a] is not due to the predicate but to the NP itself.

A pronoun anaphoric on an NP like *this kind of N* behaves like a pronoun anaphoric on a definite NP and unlike a pronoun anaphoric on a bare plural. In contrast to [16], [19a] is perfectly acceptable. Moreover, if the episodic predicate which the NP *this kind of N* is an argument of introduced existential quantification over stages, an E-type interpretation for a pronoun anaphoric on that NP would be possible. For example, the pronoun in [19b] would be synonymous with the definite description *the raccoon that I saw yesterday that is a realization of this kind of raccoon* and the continuation with the *although*-clause would not be contradictory. This, however, is not the case: the pronoun is synonymous with the description *this kind of raccoon*, hence the contradiction of the continuation. In [19c], on the other hand, the pronoun is interpreted as E-type and no contradiction arises.[38]

[19] a. John ate this kind of apple and Mary ate it too.
b. I saw this kind of raccoon in the forest. It was magnificent (# although this kind of raccoon is (generally) repulsive).
c. I saw raccoons in the forest. They were magnificent (although raccoons are (generally) repulsive).

This perspective on the apparent existential reading of definite kind-referring NP's in episodic contexts is compatible with the scopal properties of such NP's. The contradictory reading of [17b] is the same as that of any definite in the place of the kind-referring NP and we need not appeal to narrow scope existential quantification to account for it. As for [17c], if there is no existential quantification over realizations of this kind of wolf in the semantics, then no existential quantifier needs to scope with respect to the attitude predicate. John may have a *de re* belief about the kind itself without having a belief about any particular realization of the kind.

3.2.3 *A Generic Operator and Bare Plurals*

Carlson offers a *reductio* argument that bare plurals should not be treated like other quantificational NP's. He explores the consequences of assuming that there is a generic nominal quantifier and then rejects such an assumption for the reasons discussed in (a)–(g) below. A theme common to most of them is that such a quantifier would not resemble any known nominal quantifier in certain significant respects. From this he infers that a direct generalization approach to generics is untenable. In presenting his arguments, my aim is to establish that although he is right on the first point, the second conclusion does not necessarily follow. As we will see in section 4, it is possible to analyze generics as involving a generic quantifier which is not nominal. Moreover, we can construe some of Carlson's evidence as showing that an operator *is* present.

a. *Exceptions*

Although it would appear at first sight that the generic quantifier has the force of a universal quantifier, unlike all other universal quantifiers, it tolerates exceptions, which at times might even outnumber the non-exceptional cases. The intuition about exceptional cases is of course that they are not normal in some relevant respect.[39] Carlson considers appending the restriction 'normal' to a universal quantifier but finds such a move inadequate. For instance, he argues that normality with respect to having a mane would require all normal lions to be male while normality with respect to feeding their young milk would require all normal lions to be female, hence we end up with a contradiction. Or, if all normal dogs are mammals, could an abnormal dog not be a mammal? His criticism against 'all normal,' however, does not take into account the context-dependency of 'normal'; the argument would have force only if the criteria of normality were identical for all properties. There are no universal criteria for normality but this does not mean that there are no criteria for normality relative to a given property.

b. No Fixed Quantificational Force

Not only does the generic quantifier not have universal force, it does not even seem to have a stable quantificational force. Its varied force depends, among other things, on the predicate with which the bare plural is construed since that seems to be responsible to a large extent for determining the criteria of normality, and on external circumstances that seem to vary from case to case. So although few shoplifters actually get prosecuted and few alligators survive long enough to attain their full length, [20a] and [20b] are true, while [20c] is false even though most books are actually paperbacks.

[20]   a. Shoplifters are prosecuted in criminal court.
        b. Alligators grow twenty feet long.
        c. Books are paperbacks.

Furthermore, even if we claimed ambiguity and allowed its force to vary, the generic quantifier could not be identified with any of the known nominal quantifiers since the truth conditions of generic sentences and that with a nominal quantifier are different. For example, while [21b] and [21d] are true, [21a] and [21c] are not.

[21]   a. Seeds do not germinate.
        b. Most seeds do not (in fact) germinate.
        c. Crocodiles die before they get two weeks old.
        d. Most crocodiles (actually) die before they get two weeks old.

This kind of argument, however, is valid only if we try to link the truth of a generic statement to the way things actually are, that is if the generic quantifier is taken to quantify over actual entities. In other words, Carlson has successfully argued against using an extensional operator to account for genericity but this falls short of showing that *no* operator can be used to account for the semantics of genericity.

Carlson takes (a) and (b) to be strong and decisive arguments against a quantificational analysis of generics in general. On the basis of them, he concludes that a quantificational analysis would be "profoundly misdirected" (Carlson 1982:167). However, the real import of the argument is that we should not build quantification over instantiations into the semantics because inferences we get about *actual* instantiations of the generalization vary widely, depending both on the content of the generalization expressed and other background assumptions we bring to bear. In any case, the kind-denoting analysis that Carlson advocates solves this problem only by allowing itself to take no stance on what inferences we can draw from the characteristic property of a kind about its individual instantiations.[40] The analysis not only misses something significant in not connecting in any way the truth of a derived kind predication to the truth of predications about individual instantiations but it does not even give a general answer to what Carlson took to be the right question to ask about generics, namely 'How can we infer quantification from generic sentences?' (Carlson 1977b:109).

c. The Port-Royal Puzzle

The generic quantifier, unlike other nominal quantifiers, is not right monotone. This is known as the Port-Royal Puzzle and is exemplified by [22]: [22a] does not entail [22b], whereas [22c] entails [22d].

[22]   a. Dutchmen are good sailors.
       b. Dutchmen are sailors.
       c. Every Dutchman is a good sailor.
       d. Every Dutchman is a sailor.

Interestingly, Carlson's ultimate analysis of the contrast in [22] does not rely on the monotonicity properties of universally quantifies NP's vs. those of bare plurals. (In a sense, it removes the preconditions for testing monotonicity for bare plurals by relying on the presence of the *Gn'* operator prefixed to the predicate ˆ*good'*(ˆ*sailor'*).) See Carlson (1977b:295ff) and Wilkinson (1991:17ff) for discussion.

d. Interaction with Adverbs of Quantification

If a generic quantifier were associated with the bare plural, then like other nominal quantifiers, it would force a temporal reading for an adverb of quantification. This, however, is not the case; unlike [23a], [23b] has a felicitous reading, according to which many Texans are tall.[41]

[23] a. # Every Texan is often tall.
      b. Texans are often tall.

Points (c) and (d) are the decisive arguments against a nominal generic operator but they are perfectly consistent with, if not providing evidence for, an adverbial generic operator. Research on natural language quantification has shown that quantifiers of natural language belong to two main categories: nominal quantifiers, associated with an NP, and so-called adverbial quantifiers, which are not associated with an NP and whose paradigmatic cases are adverbs of quantification. An implicit quantifier is considered adverbial if it exhibits the semantic properties of overt adverbial quantifiers.

e. Kind-Level Predicates

Bare plurals can co-occur with kind-level predicates, like *extinct*, which cannot take as arguments expressions denoting ordinary individuals. At most, however, this shows that not *all* forms of genericity can be analyzed as involving quantification, not that none can.

f. Scopal Restrictions

Generically interpreted bare plurals exhibit scope restrictions, a fact which can be accounted for if bare plurals are analyzed as rigidly denoting kinds rather than as quantified NP's. The semantics of rigid designation is such that rigid designators always exhibit wide scope with respect to any other operator. Specifically, bare plurals have wide scope with respect to negation and narrow scope in attitudinal contexts.[42] For example, [24a] expresses the (false) generalization that all (normal) pomegranates have the characteristic property of not having a crowned end, rather than the weaker generalization that pomegranates do not have the characteristic property of having a crowned end.[43]

[24]   a. Pomegranates do not have a crowned end.
       b. Bishops should not move diagonally.
       c. Pomegranates do not normally/typically have a crowned end.

However, as seen in [24b] and [24c], both necessity modals and overt generic operators like *normally* or *typically* seem to favor wide scope with respect to negation too, thus favoring the stronger generalization reading even when this leads to falsity.[44] Therefore, the evidence from examples like [24a] could lead either to the conclusion that bare plurals behave like names, or, alternatively, that the implicit generic operator behaves like modals and other overt generic operators in taking wide scope with respect to negation.[45]

With respect to attitudinal contexts the issue is more complicated since the argument based on the absence of a wide scope reading for the bare plural is tied to an extensional version of the hypothesized generic operator. For an example like [25a], Carlson takes wide scope to give rise to the following reading, which he claims is missing: for each entity that is actually a pomegranate John believes of it that it is poisonous. This interpretation is consistent with John's lacking the belief that all pomegranates are poisonous.

[25] John believes that pomegranates are poisonous.

The kind analysis predicts that John has a belief about the kind itself without having a belief that all pomegranates are poisonous or a belief about actual instantiations of the kind.

The generalization operator must indeed have narrow scope with respect to the attitude predicate. In general, adverbial operators do not take scope beyond their clause. Therefore, the property of exhibiting narrow scope with respect to an attitude predicate is shared by modals ([26a]), overt generic operators ([26b]), and adverbs of quantification both on their generic ([26c]) and their temporal reading ([26d]).

[26]   a. John believes that bishops (should) move non-diagonally.
       b. John believes that pomegranates normally/typically have a crowned end.
       c. John believes that pomegranates are always poisonous.
       d. John believes that during last winter Mary always went for a walk at night.

Since only nominal operators within the complement of an attitude predicate can take scope over the attitude predicate, these facts simply establish that the generic operator is not nominal but are perfectly consistent with its being an adverbial operator.

g. Definite Kind-Denoting NP's

Definite NP's referring to kinds, like *this kind of animal*, exhibit a generic reading and yet we would not want to analyze them as involving a generic quantifier. This, however, is not inconsistent with having a generic operator and a kind-denoting NP without the former being contributed by the latter.

3.3 Limits and Limitations of Uniformity

One of the most compelling arguments of Carlson's in favor of the kind analysis is that kinds provide the intensionality necessary for the semantics of genericity without the need to posit any quantification. However, an across-the-board unified analysis of generics as involving no quantification is untenable. Carlson himself has to allow for a "mixed" analysis in which some quantification is built into the semantics. This is necessary for generic sentences with adverbs of quantification. In Carlson's (1979) analysis, (atemporal) adverbs of quantification are VP operators applying to object-level predicates and yielding kind-level predicates. In that respect they are like the generic operator Gn'. They differ, however, from Gn' in that they quantify over object-level realizations of a kind. I will now show that the same kinds of arguments Carlson advances against a generic quantifier, summarized in (a) and (b) in section 3.2.3, can be made with respect to his analysis that postulates a quantifier associated with adverbs of quantification.[46]

Let us take the adverb of quantification *always*, which, treated as a VP operator mapping object-level predicates to kind-level predicates, translates as in [27].

[27] $\lambda P \lambda x^k (\forall y^o (R'(y^o, x^k) \rightarrow {}^{\smile}P(y^o)))$

Although it is incontestable that the adverb has universal force, one could object to positing a universal quantifier in ways that parallel Carlson's arguments against a quantificational analysis of generics by showing that it leads to inadequate predictions about what the domain of quantification and the force of the quantifier are. [28a], for example, translating as [29a], comes out as too weak under this analysis since in order for it to be true in the actual world it suffices that all actual dogs be intelligent. But, intuitively, [28a] expresses something stronger. [28b], on the other hand, translating as [29b], comes out as too strong since it would require of male ducks that are well-bred to lay eggs, whereas, intuitively, [28b] is judged to be true without that strong requirement holding.

[28] a. Dogs are always intelligent.
b. Ducks that are well-bred always lay eggs.

[29] a. $\forall y^o (R'(y^o, d) \rightarrow intelligent'(y^o))$
b. $\forall y^o (R'(y^o, wbd) \rightarrow Gn(\hat{\ } lay\text{-}eggs'(y^o)))$

In other words, once some other operator than the implicit one is introduced, we can avoid neither the modal aspect of genericity nor the requirement for normality. Carlson, on the other hand, is committed to extensionality once an adverb of quantification is present.

Neither can we avoid readjustments in the domain of quantification, resulting in narrowing of the domain, so as to satisfy certain conditions associated with the predicate. Again, Carlson's analysis makes wrong predictions in this respect. For example, [30] comes out as false in Carlson's analysis, given that most shoplifters are never caught, let alone prosecuted.

[30] Shoplifters are always prosecuted in criminal court.

To sum up, Carlson's analysis of adverbs of quantification suffers precisely from the problems he identified with positing an operator for generic sentences. The reason for that is not that the quantificational force of the operator cannot be specified with any precision—adverbs of quantification wear their force on their sleeve—but rather because of the assumed extensionality of the operator. Here the intensionality of individuals is not helpful precisely because the truth conditions make no reference to alternative points of evaluation. If one were to revise this analysis so as to make the adverb of quantification intensional, the need for making the bare plural kind-denoting in these cases would be diminished. Moreover, once we recognize the need for intensionality in the evaluation of sentences with adverbs of quantification, it takes only a small step to make a similar assumption about generic sentences without an overt operator.

3.4 Summary

Carlson concludes that all genericity should be given a uniform analysis, that bare plurals are neither indefinite nor ambiguous, and that generics do not involve a generic quantifier. As we saw, the last point confounds three distinct claims: (*i*) there is no nominal generic operator associated with bare plurals, (*ii*) no extensional semantics would do for generics, (*iii*) there is no quantification over objects at different points of evaluation in the specification of the truth-conditions for generics. (*i*) and (*ii*) are undoubtedly true but (*iii*) is not. In fact, none of the evidence Carlson provided against a direct generalization approach to generics was really evidence in favor of (*iii*).

Some of the crucial facts leading Carlson to these conclusions about genericity and bare plurals can be dealt with within a quantificational approach to generics and a more sophisticated framework for the treatment of indefinites, as we will see in the next section. In contrast to Carlson's claims summarized by (1)–(3) in section 3.2, this approach is committed to (1)'–(3)':

(1)' Ambiguity resides neither in the predicate nor in the NP; the apparent ambiguity results from the presence or absence of a sentential operator and from the interpretation of indefinites within and outside quantificational structures.

(2)' Bare plurals are indefinite both on their existential and generic reading.

(3)' An operator is present in the generic reading of bare plurals but it is not associated with the NP.

4. THE INDEFINITENESS ANALYSIS

4.1 Basic Outline

The indefiniteness analysis brings together the conception of genericity as involving direct generalization and a semantics for bare plurals in which they are treated as ordinary indefinites. The analysis of bare plurals as indefinite NP's proposed by Krifka (1987), Gerstner & Krifka (1987), and Wilkinson(1988a, 1991) relies on the treatment of adverbial operators; and indefinites in Lewis (1975), Kamp (1981) and Heim (1982) and claims that one type of genericity is to be attributed to the presence of an appropriate operator.[47]

The analysis assumes that there are two sources of genericity, one arising from the presence of a sentential dyadic intensional operator, the other from the presence of a kind-denoting term and a kind-level predicate. In that sense it partitions genericity in such a way that one type is amenable to a direct generalization approach and the other type to an inferred generalization approach. Krifka's distinction between I-genericity and D-genericity is precisely along this dimension; moreover, it connects I-genericity to indefiniteness and D-genericity to definiteness.[48]

Bare plurals are claimed to be ambiguous; on one interpretation they denote kinds, and hence can appear within D-generics, on another interpretation they are ordinary indefinites, and hence can appear within I-generics. The singular indefinite is only an ordinary indefinite; hence it can appear only within I-generics. The singular definite generic, on the other hand, is unambiguously kind-denoting; hence it can appear only within D-generics. Thus examples [1a], [1b] and [2a], repeated in [31], involve D-genericity, while [1c], [1d], [1e], [2b] and [2c], repeated in [32], involve I-genericity.

[31] a. *Punica granatum* is an Old World tree.
      b. The 3-R4* generation robot will soon be antiquated.
      c. Dinosaurs are extinct.

[32] a. A pirate ship flies a black flag.
      b. Pomegranates have a crowned end.
      c. In this place one whistles a lullaby to show approval.
      d. Dogs are mammals.
      e. Dogs bark.

From here on I will concentrate on I-genericity.

This analysis of bare plurals and I-genericity makes three basic claims: (*i*) I-genericity involves a sentential dyadic intensional operator; with an interpretation similar to that of adverbs of quantification, (*ii*) bare plurals are indefinites, (*iii*) indefinites are non-quantificational, variable contributing elements. If the bare plural is an indefinite, then its apparent ambiguity between an existential and a generic reading can be seen as a special case of the apparent variable quantificational force of indefinites. Its generic reading is a quantificational reading which comes about when the bare plural is in the restriction of an appropriate operator, such as an adverb of quantification, a modal or an implicit generic operator. When not in the scope of an operator, the bare plural is caught by existential closure; hence its existential reading in episodic sentences. The bifurcation in the readings of bare plurals is, therefore, not a property unique to them but one shared by all indefinite NP's. In this respect, the analysis is in accord with Carlson's conclusion that there is no genuine ambiguity in the semantics of the NP: if we exclude the true kind reading of D-genericity, the variability in the readings of bare plurals is not due to an ambiguity *per se* but is traced to a more basic property of the bare plural. In this case the relevant property is indefiniteness, which interacts with the interpretation of operators and free variables to yield the desired range of interpretations.

The logical form of a generic sentence has the schematic representation in [33].

[33] $G(\phi, \psi)$

If an indefinite is within the restriction ϕ of the generic operator, it will be bound by the operator and will have a generic reading;[49] if it is in the nuclear scope ψ, it will get an existential reading. A bare plural that receives an existential reading in a generic sentence, as in [12], is an instance of the latter case. Whether an indefinite is mapped in the restriction or nuclear scope of the generic operator is not fully determined on the basis of surface syntactic structure, as is clearly demonstrated by [12]. This problem has come to be known as the issue of *semantic partition* (Diesing 1990, 1992a) and is an active issue of current research. In general, the indefiniteness analysis predicts that a given sentence may have several generic readings as a result of different partitionings of its material between the restriction and the nuclear scope. Several factors seem to play a role in determining semantic partition, most notably syntactic structure (Diesing 1990, 1992a, 1992b, Kratzer 1995) and focus (Rooth 1985, 1995, Krifka 1992).

The generic reading of singular and plural indefinites arises when the variable of the indefinites is bound by a generic operator. The plural indefinite and the singular indefinite are thus analyzed in the same way, as contributing an open formula. The open formula corresponding to the indefinites in [34a] and [34b] appears in the restriction of the implicit generic operator G and its free variable is bound by G, as in [35a]. In [34c] and [34d], on the other hand, there is no operator and the variable in the open formula corresponding to the indefinites is subject to existential closure, as in [35b].[50]

[34]   a. Whales are mammals.
       b. A whale is a mammal.
       c. Whales are roaming the coast.

d. A whale is roaming the coast.

[35] a. $G_x\,(whale(x), mammal(x))$
      b. $\exists_x\,(whale(x)\ \&\ roam\text{-}the\text{-}coast(x))$

[35a] is interpreted according to [36], where the generic operator is assumed to have universal force. How this can be reconciled with the tolerance to exceptions will be discussed in section 4.3, where the intensionality of G will be taken into account.[51]

[36] $[\![G_x(whale(x), mammal(x))]\!]^g_{M,c,w} = 1$ iff for every $g' \overset{x}{\approx} g$ such that $[\![whale(x)]\!]^{g'}_{M,c,w} = 1$, $[\![mammal(x)]\!]^{g'}_{M,c,w} = 1$.

A quantificational analysis of generics is consistent with incorporating only a subset of (i)–(iii) above, or with modified formulations of any one of (i)–(iii). This is for two different reasons. One is that an analysis of bare plurals as uniformly kind-denoting can be combined with a direct generalization approach to generics. The other is that the apparent variable quantificational force of indefinites can be captured within a different set of assumptions, which associate an existential quantifier with an indefinite but have an appropriately revised semantics for the existential quantifier and adverbial operators.

Farkas (1985) and Farkas & Sugioka (1983), for instance, operated only with a modified version of (i); they assumed an implicit sentential operator binding variables corresponding to stage or object realizations of the kind denoted by a bare plural. An analysis incorporating (i) and (iii) but treating bare plurals as kind denoting terms is proposed in Rooth (1995), where it is the object realizations of kinds that behave like indefinites.[52] The advantage of preserving a uniform kind denotation for bare plurals is that it allows the same bare plural to support both kind-level and object-level anaphora. The narrow scope properties of bare plurals, however, do not follow anymore once the existential quantification is not part of the semantics of stage-level predicates. Finally, recent analyses analyzing indefinites as dynamic existential quantifiers and adverbs of quantification as generalized quantifiers, such as Chierchia (1992) and de Swart (1996), applied to generics, can be seen as modern incarnations of the (i)–(ii) analysis.[53] [37] gives an overview of the similarities and differences between the different analyses with respect to three significant features. FV-Indef. stands for the analyses taking indefinites to be quantifier-free, Dyn-Indef. for the analyses taking indefinites to be analyzed in terms of a dynamic existential quantifier.

[37]	Direct Generalization	Uniform denotation of bare plurals for kind/generic readings	Uniform analysis of bare plurals in episodic/generic contexts
Carlson	−	+	+
FV-Indef.	+	−	+
Farkas	+	+	−
Rooth	+	+	+
Dyn-Indef.	+	−	+

4.2 Individual-Level and Stage-Level Predicates

Once existential quantification need not be built into the predicate and once the bare plural can be taken to denote ordinary individuals, we get a simplification in the domain of predicates, for we no longer need derived kind-level or derived object-level predicates.[54] Nevertheless, although stages as ontological entities can be dispensed with, we still need to maintain the distinction between stage-level and individual-level predicates since a number of linguistic phenomena are sensitive to it. The two types of predicates have different distributional patterns and influence the interpretation of a variety of linguistic elements. Specifically, stage-level predicates, in contrast to individual-level predicates, permit an existential reading for bare plurals, are acceptable as post-nominal predicates in *there*-insertion sentences (Milsark 1974, Carlson 1977b), allow for a conditional reading as adjuncts and absolutes (Stump 1985) and are acceptable in conditional clauses without necessitating the presence of an indefinite NP (Kratzer 1995).

How the distinction is to be theoretically construed, however, remains an open question. There have been several recent proposals but their degree of overall success remains to be ascertained. For example, Kratzer (1995) proposes that the difference between individual-level and stage-level predicates is in their lexical argument structure: stage-level predicates have an extra Davidsonian argument in their argument structure while individual-level predicates do not. Diesing (1990, 1992a) proposes that the difference between individual-level and stage-level predicates is in the syntactic structure they project to: individual-level predicates project to control structures, stage–level predicates to raising structures. Some discussion of these proposals, to the extent that they are relevant to the material presented there, is to be found in the next chapter.

Assuming we adopt a basic bipartite division of predicates, the correspondence between Carlson's classification and that of the indefiniteness analysis is as follows: basically stage-level and individual-level predicates correspond to stage-level and individual-level predicates, respectively. Derived kind-level predicates correspond to (non-kind-level) individual-level predicates. Derived object-level predicates correspond to stage-level predicates within a quantificational context: a generic sentence containing a stage-level episodic predicate is taken to express a generalization over episodes. The question is whether this is always the case. An interesting issue arises with what Krifka (1988) calls 'unconditional generics,' exemplified by [38b], as opposed to conditional generics, exemplified by [38a].

[38] a. When John hikes in the woods, he always smokes.
b. John smokes.

Is a generic operator involved in [38b]?[55] Krifka (1988) assumes that a generic operator is indeed involved in [38b] whose restriction is contextually recoverable. Kratzer (1988, 1995), on the other hand, distinguishes between derived genericity, brought about by an operator, and intrinsic genericity, residing in the predicate. In derived genericity there is quantification at the sentential level, in intrinsic genericity there is no quantification. The intuitive difference between derived genericity and intrinsic genericity is exemplified in [38], where we have a generalization over episodes in [38a], hence derived genericity, but intrinsic genericity in [38b]. According to Kratzer then, the predicate *smoke* is lexically ambiguous between a stage-level interpretation, as in [38a], and an individual-level interpretation, as in [38b].

All three approaches agree on the truth conditions of a sentence containing a basically individual-level predicate but interesting differences arise with respect to sentences with a basically stage-level predicate that express a generic or habitual generalization. Let us take [39] as our test case.

[39] a. John is a smoker.
b. John always/normally smokes.
c. John smokes.

[39a] contains a basically individual-level predicate and, under all three analyses, it would be true in a given world iff John is in the set of things that are smokers in that world. [39b] contains a derived stage-level predicate and all three analyses specify its truth conditions in terms of quantification: Carlson over stages of John,[56]

Krifka and Kratzer over situations. Carlson and Kratzer would give [39c] truth conditions equivalent to those of [39a],[57] while Krifka would give it truth conditions equivalent to those of [39b]. If the adverb of quantification is taken to have a modal dimension, considering non-actual situations will be crucial in specifying the meaning of [39b] and [39c]. [40] provides a schematic summary.

[40]	Quantification		Modality	
	yes	no	yes	no
Carlson	b	a, c		a, b, c
Kratzer	b	a, c	b	a, c
Krifka	b, c	a	b, c	a

The discussion above shows that the issue of the (non-)uniformity of genericity manifests itself quite independently of bare plurals, in the domain of individual-level predicates.

4.3 The Generic Operator

Carlson argued that no known quantifier could be substituted for the generic quantifier and took that to be a strong argument against a quantificational analysis of generics. How can the quantificational analysis meet this challenge?

Farkas (1985) and Farkas & Sugioka (1983) have claimed that the generic operator is adverbial and Dahl (1975), Heim (1982), Krifka (1988), and Krifka et al. (1995) that it, moreover, has a modal dimension. Coupling this with the analysis of indefinites as involving free variables, we can assume that the generic operator is a universal operator quantifying over pairs of worlds and assignment functions.[58] The restriction of a generic operator may be supplemented by extra conditions in addition to those contributed by the indefinite NP's mapped in the restrictor (Wilkinson 1988a, 1991, Krifka 1988, Krifka et al. (1995)).

The tolerance to exceptions that generics exhibit has at least two sources: implicit restrictions in the domain of quantification and the modal dimension of the operator. Both assumptions are necessary and neither is sufficient without the other.

4.3.1 Implicit Domain Restrictions

If the generic operator is adverbial, then not only material from the subject NP but also material from the VP can enter the restriction of the operator. For example, the articulation of a sentence into a focus–background structure affects the mapping, with focussed material being mapped into the nuclear scope and material in the focus background being mapped into the restriction (Rooth 1985, 1995, Krifka 1992). Moreover, sortal restrictions of the predicate and presuppositions of material in the nuclear scope would be accommodated into the restrictor. Once we have this freedom, a lot of the "criteria of normality" can be incorporated as extra conditions in the restriction of the operator.

For example, as a descriptive generalization, [41] is a generalization about caught shoplifters, not shoplifters at large, since being prosecuted has as an enabling condition having been caught.

[41] Shoplifters are prosecuted in criminal court.

That presuppositions of the predicate implicitly restrict the domain of quantification can be observed with adverbs of quantification, as in [42] from Schubert & Pelletier (1989).

[42] A cat always lands on its feet.

If the implicit conditions for the satisfaction of the predicate are not taken into account, [42] would just be false. But these conditions clearly affect the evaluation of [42] and this is also why [42] implies that sometimes some cats fall, or get dropped, or find themselves in the air in some way.

If the generic operator is adverbial, it would be right monotone only under certain conditions, i.e., if we keep their first argument constant (see de Swart (1991)). The Port-Royal Puzzle can be accounted for keeping this in mind and assuming that part of the VP predicate belongs in the restrictor. In [43a] quantification is over Dutchmen who are sailors, not over Dutchmen, hence [43a] does not entail [43b].[59]

[43]   a. Dutchmen are good sailors.
       b. Dutchmen are sailors.
       c. Dutchmen are always good sailors.
       d. Dutchmen are always sailors.

Notice that a similar case obtains with overt adverbs of quantification; [43c] does not entail [43d]. In the move from [43a] to [43b] we have not kept the first argument constant, since in [43a] we quantify over Dutchmen who are sailors while in [43b] we quantify over Dutchmen. [43c] and [43d] are analogous in this regard.

Implicit domain restrictions arise to satisfy presuppositional requirements of the restrictor. Another source for implicit domain restrictions, namely contextual restrictions, is not available for generic sentences. I will discuss this property in more detail in the next chapter.

4.3.2 Modal Dimension

Positing a modal dimension for the generic operator captures the fact that the existence of actual exceptions does not suffice to make a generic generalization false. The determination of the modal dimension is, as with overt modals, heavily context-dependent. As Kratzer (1977, 1981) argues, modals are unambiguous but context-dependent; they require the context of use to fix two parameters of their interpretation.[60] These two parameters are conversational backgrounds, assigning to each world a set of propositions, and determining in turn a modal base and an ordering source.

The apparent multiple ambiguity that we can detect with generic adverbial quantifiers can thus be explained away if we take into account the context-dependency of the modal base and the ordering source. The question about generics that Carlson took to be misguided, 'What is the generic quantifier?,' is reformulated in this analysis as 'What is the modal base and the ordering source associated with the generic quantifier?'

The generic operator can be interpreted analogously to Kratzer's (1981) human necessity operator. This and alternative intereperations for the generic operator are discussed by Krifka et al. (1995). For an alternative modal treatment see Asher & Morreau (1991, 1995). [44] gives the interpretation of a dyadic human necessity operator, concentrating on the modal aspect of the interpretation of the generic operator (i.e., ϕ and ψ are assumed to contain no free variables to be bound by the operator or by existential closure over the nuclear scope). In the informal exposition below I will simplify and talk of the maximally normal worlds.

[44] $[G(\phi, \psi)]^g_{M,c,w} = 1$, where c determines a modal base R_w and an ordering source $\leq_w$ iff for every $w_1 \in R_w$ such that $[\phi]^g_{M,c,w_1} = 1$, there is $w_2 \in R_w$ such that $w_2 \leq_w w_1$ and for every $w_3 \in R_w$ such that $w_3 \leq_w w_2$, $[\psi]^g_{M,c,w_3} = 1$.

In view of these assumptions about the modal dimension of the generic operator, let us consider, informally, the generalizations expressed by [1c]–[1e], repeated in [45a]–[45c].

[45] a. A pirate ship flies a black flag.
      b. Pomegranates have a crowned end.
      c. In this place one whistles a lullaby to show approval.

[45b] expresses a descriptive generalization. The modal base is circumstantial and the ordering source stereotypical. In constructing the modal base we consider facts about the inherent properties of pomegranates, so the worlds in the modal base are worlds where the biological facts about pomegranates (e.g., their evolutionary history) are identical to those of the actual world. In constructing the ordering source we consider facts which determine an ideal where no mutations have come about and no other external intervention has altered the appearance of pomegranates. The generalization expressed by [45b] is that everything that is a pomegranate in the worlds in the modal base has a crowned end in all those most normal worlds determined by the ordering source. If there exist pomegranates whose crowned end has been chopped off, then the actual world is not among those closest to the ideal and therefore the actual generalization 'every actual pomegranate in existence (right now) has a crowned end' would not be entailed by [45b].

[45a] expresses a descriptive generalization too. The modal base is constructed on the basis of facts having to do with the conventions about the operation of pirate ships and the ordering source on the basis of an ideal where these conventions are upheld and adhered to. [45c] expresses both a descriptive and a normative generalization. The modal base is constructed on the basis of facts having to do with the habits, social rules, or conventions of the people in this place. The ordering source may be stereotypical, whereby it is constructed on the basis of an ideal where people follow their habits, or deontic, whereby it is constructed on the basis of an ideal where people adhere to the social rules. Conventions and social rules induce certain habits and vice versa so that's why both readings appear to be equally prominent.

However, this is not always the case so a descriptive generalization might be true without the corresponding normative generalization being true, as well, and vice versa, as discussed with respect to [9], repeated in [46].

[46] a. People around here shoot at each other indiscriminately.
b. A country with rich natural resources shares them with its neighbors.

Let's assume that the area around here is such that it induces violent habits in people but that violent behavior is neither morally nor legally sanctioned. Then [46a] would be true if interpreted with respect to a circumstantial modal base taking into account facts about the habits and dispositions of the local population and a stereotypical ordering source. But it would be false if interpreted with respect to a circumstantial modal base taking into account facts about what morality or the law prescribes and a deontic ordering source where the ideal is such that what morality or the law prescribes is adhered to. Let us assume in turn that in fact countries carefully protect their natural resources. Then [46b] would be false with respect to a circumstantial modal base taking into account facts about the practice of countries with rich natural resources and a stereotypical ordering source where these practices are followed. [46b] may also have a normative generalization reading: in that case it is interpreted with respect to a modal base determined on the basis of facts having to do with what is considered morally proper behavior and an ordering source which ranks worlds according to their closeness to an ideal where that behavior is realized. The generalization expressed by [46b] is that a country with rich natural resources which it does not share with its neighbors is less close to the ideal of morally desirable behavior than a country with rich natural resources which it shares with its neighbors.

In these cases, both the descriptive and the normative generalization readings correspond to identical logical structures. The difference between the two types of readings has to do with what the modal base and ordering source are taken to be in each case. For example, the logical form of [46b] is as in [47a] and is interpreted according to [47b].

[47] a. $G_{x,y,z}(country(x)$ & $resources(y)$ & $have(x,y)$
& $neighbor(x,z),\ shares(x,y,z))$

b. $[[47a]]^g_{M,c,w} = 1$, where c determines a modal base R_w and an ordering source $\leq_w$ iff for every $g' \stackrel{A}{\approx} g$ where $A = \{x,y,z\}$[61] and for every $w_1 \in R_w$ such that $[country(x)$ & $resources(y)$ & $have(x,y)$ & $neighbor(x,z)]^{g'}_{M,c,w_1} = 1$ there is $w_2 \in R_w$ such that $w_2 \leq_w w_1$ and for every $w_3 \in R_w$ such that $w_3 \leq_w w_2$ $[shares(x,y,z)]^{g'}_{M,c,w_3} = 1$.

In the logical form of [46b] given in [47a] the dependent definite *its neighbors* is accommodated within the restriction and there is symmetric quantification over countries, their neighbors and natural resources. A reading where there is asymmetric quantification over countries and their neighbors is also available but I will not consider it any further here except to note that the familiar problems which arise with respect to conditionals and quantification arise with respect to generics as well.

This analysis of I-genericity also accounts for Dahl's (1975) observation that indefinite NP's are associated with a non-accidental generalization reading, under the assumption that an implicit generic operator is present in [48a] and [48b] but not in [48c].[62]

[48]   a. A member of this club does not drink whisky.
       b. Members of this club do not drink whisky.
       c. The members of this club do not drink whisky.

The interpretation of the generic operator and its context-dependency with respect to a modal base and an ordering source also help predict when a generic generalization would entail the corresponding actual generalization. This would be the case when the modal base and ordering source are determined by the context to be realistic, or when the modal base is realistic and the ordering source trivial. A modal base is realistic if the worlds in the modal base are selected on the basis of their similarity with the actual world with respect to certain facts, that is if the actual world is among those in the modal base. In all the examples we have considered the modal base is realistic. An ordering source is realistic if worlds are ordered according to how closely they approximate a set of certain actual facts. [49a] is an example where a realistic ordering source is involved. An ordering source is trivial if any two worlds are related by the partial ordering relation. This situation arises when the relevant conversational background is empty. [49b] is an example where the ordering source is trivial, assuming that in all worlds the same physical entity cannot be in two different locations at the same time.

[49]   a. These days if a building is designed by an avant-garde architect, it has a spiral-shaped dome.
       b. A monument on Naxos is not in Athens.

As with modals, certain generic operators may be conventionally associated with and therefore select particular modal bases and ordering sources. For example, overt generic operators like *typically* and *normally* select only stereotypical ordering sources. This is why generic sentences with these operators, such as those in [50], express descriptive generalizations, rather than normative ones.

[50]   a. A country with rich natural resources typically shares them with its neighbors.
       b. # A monument on Naxos is normally not in Athens.

[50a] and [50b] have only the descriptive generalization reading. [50b] in fact is odd since it implies that there might be monuments on Naxos which are (also) in Athens.

Conventional association with particular modal bases and ordering sources may also account for the seemingly differential force or even opposite truth values of otherwise identical generic sentences containing operators with the same quantificational force. For example, [50b] expresses a weaker generalization than [49b].

The interpretation of the generic operator as a human necessity operator is weak enough and flexible enough, thanks to its relativization to the two context-dependent parameters, but it is still not without some problems. There are cases where it is plainly too strong. This problem is discussed by Krifka et al. (1995) and Asher & Morreau (1991, 1995). Consider [51a].

[51]   a. A turtle lives to be very old.
       b. A turtle normally lives to be very old.

[51a] is intuitively true but the semantics of the generic operator would make it false if we assume that maximally normal worlds with respect to the characteristics of turtlehood have to be worlds where the same biological facts hold as in the actual world. The semantics of the generic operator in this case is too strong as it requires of all individuals that are turtles to live until very old in all maximally normal worlds. But since such maximally normal worlds are also worlds with the same ecological pressures as the actual world it cannot be true that all turtles survive, even in those maximally normal worlds. The fact that this problem shows up with the singular indefinite indicates that one cannot resort to a kind reading, which involves no quantification, in order to avoid the problem. Although there is no apparent way to fix this problem within this approach by using only one operator, it is not clear that this type of modal analysis is entirely on the wrong track since the problem is contained. Note that [51b] is intuitively false, which is what we would expect if we start with a circumstantial modal base and a stereotypical ordering source.[63] See the appendix for an alternative interpretation for [51a].

4.4 Conclusion

The indefiniteness analysis assimilates the bifurcation in the readings of bare plurals to that of other indefinite NP's. It predicts that, all else being equal, the range of interpretations for a bare plural are the same as those of any other indefinite NP. Furthermore, in all phenomena that depend on indefiniteness bare plurals should behave like indefinites. For instance, bare plurals should participate in all phenomena involving the interaction of indefiniteness, quantification and anaphora, such as donkey-anaphora (see Diesing (1988), Wilkinson (1991)). Unlike Carlson's analysis, which crucially distinguishes between generic sentences with adverbs of quantification (the former involving quantification, the latter not), the indefiniteness analysis unifies the two cases.

The indefiniteness analysis is also more explicit on how context affects the type of generic statement involved (e.g., normative vs. descriptive regularities): the contextual effects are manifested in the choice of modal base and ordering source.

The indefiniteness analysis and the kind analysis differ on the predictions they make about the clustering of readings for a given NP in a given language. Since it does not distinguish between I-genericity and D-genericity, the kind analysis predicts that if an NP has a kind reading, then it can have an existential reading as well since existential quantification is introduced by the predicate. Definite generic and kind-denoting NP's such as *this kind of N* present problems for this prediction. Given the way it captures the variable quantificational force of indefinites, the indefiniteness analysis predicts that an NP can have an existential reading iff it can have an I-generic reading.[64]

A prediction that both analyses share is that a bare plural will have universal force only in generic sentences. The functional reading of bare plurals, which is the topic of the next chapter, presents a problem for this prediction.

APPENDIX

An alternative strategy for deriving the interpretation of [52] is outlined below.

[52] A turtle lives to be very old.

Let us assume that the interpretation of [52] involves two operators: in addition to the standard generic operator there is a monadic operator $\odot$ taking scope over the nuclear scope. The logical form of [52] then is as in [53].

[53] $G_x(turtle(x), \odot\, live\text{-}long(x))$

The operator G has a stereotypical modal base determined on the basis of facts having to do with biological laws and inherent properties of turtles and a trivial ordering source.

The operator $\odot$ has the same stereotypical modal base as G and an ordering source which depends on the restriction of G: for each individual verifying the restriction of G there is an ordering source which orders worlds according to how close they come to being optimal for the survival of that individual.

[54]   a. $[[53]]^g_{M,c,w} = 1$, where c determines a modal base R_w and an ordering source $\leq_w$ iff for every $g' \stackrel{x}{\approx} g$ and for every $w_1 \in R_w$ such that $[turtle(x)]^{g'}_{M,c,w_1} = 1$, $[\odot\, live\text{-}long(x)]^{g'}_{M,c,w_1} = 1$.

   b. $[\odot\, live\text{-}long(x)]^{g'}_{M,c,w_1} = 1$ iff there is a c' that determines a modal base R_{w_1} and an ordering source $\leq_{w_1,g'}$ such that for every $w_2 \in R_{w_1}$ there is $w_3 \in R_{w_1}$ such that $w_3 \leq_{w_1,g'} w_2$ and for every w_4 such that $w_4 \leq_{w_1,g'} w_3$, $[live\text{-}long(x)]^{g'}_{M,c',w_4} = 1$.

The interpretation of $\odot$ is non-standard in one respect. In Kaplan's (1989) terms, the operator $\odot$ is a *monster*, since the formula in its scope is interpreted relative to a different context than the formula headed by $\odot$.

NOTES

1. This already presupposes that generic sentences can be true or false like any other declarative sentence. Of course, the *evidence* for their truth might be of a different type than that of non-generic sentences.

2. Other theorists, however, may place a stronger condition on the semantics of generics, requiring that it interact with an appropriate notion of defeasible consequence so as to account for the kinds of reasoning supported by generics. Such a view is clearly articulated and developed by Asher & Morreau (1991, 1995).

3. See Dahl (1975), who makes the point very persuasively.

4. As is common practice, I will use the term 'quasi-universal' in order to indicate the tolerance for exceptions.

5. See also Carlson (1987, 1988, 1989). For a more comprehensive and critical review of Carlson's analysis and analyses in its steps see Schubert & Pelletier (1987).

6. See also Carlson (1989) for discussion on this point.

7. Gabbay & Moravcsik and Carlson differ, however, on how they execute the idea formally. Gabbay & Moravcsik explicitly construe individuals as functions from points of evaluation to basic elements in their ontology, corresponding to the temporal stages of individuals. Carlson, as we will see, assumes that both the intensional individuals and their extensional manifestations are basic elements of the ontology.

8. For a similar position see also Nunberg & Pan (1975).

9. The model-theoretic construal of kinds and stages need not be as in Carlson. For instance, Chierchia (1982) proposes that kinds be construed as nominalized properties, Ojeda (1991) takes kinds to be the mereological sum element of subsets of the universe of discourse, while Hinrichs (1985) construes stages as spatio-temporal locations. To a large extent, these reconstructions are compatible with Carlson's overall analysis of genericity although they differ from it in certain significant ways. For example, Ojeda's proposal has the consequence that the use of a definite generic carries with it the presupposition of existence of actual instantiations, something that is not true of Carlson's analysis.

10. Superscripts on variables indicate the restriction on the sort of entity the variables can take as their value: k stands for kinds, o for objects and s for stages. $\imath$ is the definite descriptor.

11. In what follows I limit attention to bare plurals in subject position.

12. Although Carlson does not consider episodic kind-level predicates, they can be easily accommodated in his analysis as long as kind-level episodic predicates do not introduce quantification over stages. This accommodation is possible because the analysis does not dispense with times as parameters of evaluation in favor of stages, a choice that can otherwise be criticized as introducing a lot of redundancy (for such criticism see Schubert & Pelletier (1987)).

13. For purposes of this discussion I will ignore the contribution of *be* and will treat the whole predicate as stage-level or individual-level.

14. Whether such predicates disallow the universal reading for the bare plural and lack a characteristic property reading can be contested (see Diesing 1988, 1990). If we admit the characteristic

property reading, they would not constitute a separate category and would be treated on a par with those in category [5c].

15. Thus, 'Unskilled thieves left a visible trace,' involving an unmediated derived predication, entails the existence of a visible trace in the actual world, while 'Unskilled thieves leave a visible trace,' involving a mediated derived predication, does not.

16. Technically, Carlson follows Montague's (1974) PTQ system in having NP denotations apply to VP denotations.

17. Predications involving stage-level predicates applying to stage-denoting NP's do not exist since there are no stage-denoting NP's.

18. When applied to an object-denoting NP, we get a habitual reading, as in 'John walks in the woods.'

19. This is simplifying in that the translation of the bare plural involves a constant; the complete translation is that given earlier in [4]. For the purposes at hand this is an innocuous simplification.

20. Notice that truth of a sentence involving a kind-level predication does not imply necessity. That dinosaurs are extinct is true in the actual world but nothing in the analysis forces it to be necessarily true. Diesing (1988), in effect, criticizes Carlson's analysis for treating all generic sentences as non-accidental generalizations when in fact it treats all generic sentences as accidental generalizations, in the sense that in order to determine whether a sentence is true in a given world we need not look at any other world. See the discussion below and in section 3.3.

21. An inferred generalization approach to generics, while not having any quantification in the semantics, might encode the connection between predicating something of a kind and inferring something of its instantiations by putting further constraints on models in the form of meaning postulates. Carlson posits no such further constraints (the quasi-meaning postulates in Carlson (1979) have no formal status). Heyer (1985), aiming to characterize different types of kind predications in terms of the inferences about particular instantiations they give rise to, does precisely that. He has direct predications over kinds but places constraints on models such that if a certain predicate is true of a kind then it is true of all its realizations (or all its typical realizations) in each world.

22. I take it that at least normative generalizations, if not dispositional ones as well, are irreducibly modal, that is, their truth depends on the denotation of the relevant predicate across a subdomain of worlds.

23. Also, one could have a uniform analysis of genericity (at least the kind of genericity which does not involve proper kind predication) without assuming that all generic NP's are kind-denoting. Farkas (1985) and Schubert & Pelletier (1988, 1989) argue that generic singular indefinites are object-denoting indefinite NP's while bare plurals are kind-denoting NP's.

24. It must be noted that a kind-denoting NP with a basically kind-level episodic predicate is possible, as in 'Dinosaurs ate kelp but at some point they resorted to grass.' However, this sentence means that the kind changed its eating habits and not that all dinosaurs resorted to eating grass on a particular occasion.

25. See Carlson (1989) for the significance of such cases.

26. Even if one were to claim that *in this part of the Pacific* is a locative subject in [12b] and hence provides a kind-level entity, this would not help us account for one of the readings of [12a] since there the subject is uncontroversially the bare plural *typhoons*.

27. In the characterization of the two readings, I am following the terminology of Evans (1977). Some authors use the two terms interchangeably.

28. Since I am concentrating here on cases where the pronoun is outside the scope of its antecedent I will ignore bound variable readings.

29. I am disregarding plurality.

30. For an E-type pronoun existence and uniqueness are part of the meaning of the pronoun itself—they are part either of its truth-conditional content, if we follow the Russellian line, or of its presuppositional content, if we follow the line of the presuppositional analyses. For a pronoun of laziness, on the other hand, existence and uniqueness are a by-product of the interpretation of free variables and of the general requirement that the context should provide a unique value for each free variable.

31. This presupposes that the stages of an individual-level entity denoted by an individual-denoting NP do not become salient as a matter of course. They only become salient when they are implicated in the truth-conditions of the sentence containing the individual-denoting NP.

32. If we require that the context should entail the existence of some unique individual-level entity that is fragrant (thereby making the existence and uniqueness part of the presuppositional content of the pronoun), we must distinguish between existence entailed by the previous discourse on the basis of the truth conditions of the sentences comprising it and existence pragmatically inferred.

The former is the case in [14c], where the meaning of the first sentence involves existential quantification over stages, the latter in [14g], where no existential quantification over stages or objects is involved. Nevertheless, if the first sentence of [14g] is true, then it can be inferred (but not guaranteed by the semantics) that some object realizations of the kind strawberries are fragrant. In order to exclude the reading for the pronoun in [14g] that is equivalent to the definite description *the strawberries that are fragrant*, we must, therefore, require that existence should be entailed by the previous context in the strict sense.

33. This holds if the bare plural and the pronoun are not in the background of a focus structure. For instance, in contrast to [16], I find (i), and therefore the pronoun of laziness interpretation, acceptable:

   (i) John ate prickly pears$_i$ [yesterday]$_F$, while Mary ate them$_i$ [today]$_F$.

I will not address this problem.

34. [16] is non-deviant if the predicate is given a habitual interpretation; in that case the pronoun would be a pronoun of laziness.

35. This appears to be true for the factors discussed here. Uniform episodic interpretation of the two predicates, as in [16], excludes it:

   (i) # John ate no apples$_i$. Mary, on the other hand, ate them$_i$ a lot.

Uniform habitual interpretation of the two predicates or a particular focus structure make it available:

   (ii) John used to eat no apples$_i$. Mary, on the other hand, used to eat them$_i$.
   (iii) John ate most apples [yesterday]$_F$, while Mary ate them$_i$ [today]$_F$.

36. A further argument for distinguishing proper kind anaphora and anaphora involving a pronoun of laziness interpretation comes from cross-linguistic considerations. In Modern Greek, only *pro* can have a a pronoun of laziness interpretation; overt pronouns, clitic and non-clitic alike, exclude this kind of interpretation but they can, nevertheless, be anaphoric on kind-denoting NP's.

37. This reading of a kind-denoting NP could be subsumed under what Krifka (1987) and Krifka et al. (1990) have termed *representative object interpetation*.

38. We can also use this kind of evidence to argue against analyzing *this kind of N* as synonymous with *an N of this kind*, as proposed in Wilkinson (1988b, 1991). *An N of this kind* is a true indefinite and, therefore, gets an existential interpretation and gives rise to E-type anaphora. McNally (1992) uses evidence from anaphora and scopal interaction with adverbs of quantification to contrast *that kind of N* and *an N of that kind*, claiming that the former does not involve existential quantification over instantiations of the kind. The strongest piece of evidence in favor of analyzing *this kind of N* as a disguised indefinite comes from its acceptability in *there*-insertion sentences. However, McNally (1992) has proposed an account of this fact that is compatible with taking the NP to be definite and kind-referring.

39. Carlson (1987) draws the distinction between non-verifying instances and exceptions.

40. One could try to account for this by introducing meaning postulate, as does Heyer (1985), or by adding a non-monotonic logical apparatus to the kind analysis in order to determine the inferences we get.

41. Wilkinson (1991) points out that Carlson's analysis itself has problems with [23b] since the truth conditions it gives it amount to there being many objects that are Texans and tall (see Carlson (1977:207)). The problem is that Carlson gives [23b] a first-order translation involving unrestricted quantification and conjunction of the two arguments of the quantifier.

42. Carlson's examples are: 'John doesn't like wombats' and 'Jill believes professors are insane'.

43. As L. Horn (p.c.) points out, the weaker reading, corresponding to wide scope negation, is most natural as a direct denial. Obligation-type modals show similar behavior: 'he shouldn't go' in isolation has only the narrow scope negation reading, as opposed to 'he shouldn't go' in response to 'he should go,' in which case it can have either the wide or the narrow scope negation reading. Krifka (1987) and Krifka (1988) also contain discussion of the relative scope of negation and the generic operator. Krifka (1988) claims that the readings corresponding to both scopes are available.

44. Possibility modals favor narrow scope with respect to negation, which again results in a stronger statement. See Horn (1972, 1989).

45. The absence of the narrow scope reading might not be a restriction on scope *per se* but a consequence of the interpretation of negated generics. (I have in mind Stalnaker's (1968) proposed in-

terpretation for negated conditionals which results in the following equivalence: $\neg(\phi \rightarrow \psi)$ iff $\phi \rightarrow \neg\psi$.)

46. See Farkas & Sugioka (1983), Stump (1985), Diesing (1988), Wilkinson (1991) for arguments against treating adverbs of quantification as VP operators. My criticism is independent of whether adverbs of quantification are treated as monadic VP operators or as dyadic sentential operators.

47. Heim (1982) applied this idea to the singular indefinite generic.

48. We might need to further subdivide D-genericity; see, for instance, Heyer's (1985) distinction between absolute generic reference and personal generic reference.

49. This is a bit of a simplification since it excludes cases of existential quantification in the restriction. For the time being I am concentrating on the generic reading of indefinites and hence on the cases where they are directly bound by the generic operator.

50. The plurality of the NP might, of course, impose further restrictions on its predicate, such as that it include plural entities in its denotation. See Hinrichs (1985), Schubert & Pelletier (1987) and Wilkinson (1991) on this issue.

51. The notation $g' \stackrel{x}{\approx} g$ means that g' is exactly like g except possibly with respect to the value it assigns to x.

52. Rooth sets aside the distinction between stages and objects.

53. Chierchia (1992) takes the generic reading of indefinites, which he uniformly analyzes as dynamic existential quantifiers, to arise when the indefinite is selected as topic and is subject to existential disclosure, an operation that results in the creation of a free variable and the binding of the indefinite by the adverb of quantification.

54. These correspond to Carlson's [7bii], [7cii], [7ciii], [7dii], as discussed in section 3.

55. This issue is also related to Lawler's (1972), Dahl's (1975) and Kleiber's (1985) discussion of existential generics. See also de Swart (1987).

56. Carlson does not actually consider stage-level predicates with adverbs of quantification or other generic operators but it is reasonable to assume that this is how he would analyze such cases.

57. Carlson would, of course, take the predicate of [39c] to be derived from a stage-level predicate via the operator Gn; Kratzer would take it to be an underived individual-level predicate.

58. Some proposals have opted for claiming vagueness of the operator with respect to the number of assignments it takes for

the sentence to be true rather than intensionality (Farkas (1985), Wilkinson (1991)). Vagueness alone without intensionality, however, does not suffice; Carlson's arguments against an extensional account carry over. Schubert & Pelletier (1989), although they take the generic quantifier to be intensional, do not construe it as universal since it allows for exceptions.

59. There seems also to be an implication for actual instantiations with [43a].

60. See also Wertheimer (1972).

61. The notation $g' \stackrel{A}{\approx} g$ means that g' is exactly like g except possibly with respect to the values it assigns to the elements of A.

62. Of course, [48c] may contain a dependent definite, as in 'The members of this club never drink whisky.'

63. An analysis like Asher & Morreau's (1991, 1995) accounts for the truth of [51a] but not for the falsity of [51b]. In other words, the argument from the turtle problem cuts both ways.

64. Potential problems arise with *des*-NP's in French, which can have an existential but no generic reading (de Swart 1992, 1996), and with definites in languages such as Romanian (Farkas 1985), Greek (Condoravdi 1992), and French (de Swart 1996), which can have an I-generic reading but do not have an existential reading. The latter problem with regard to Greek is addressed in Condoravdi (1992) along the lines of the proposals made in chapter 4.

3
Functional Reading of Bare Plurals

1. INTRODUCTION

Indefinite descriptions have played a central role in natural language semantics. Their properties relating to their intuitive quantificational force inside and outside the scope of various operators and their potential for serving as antecedents to pronouns have had pervasive consequences on the overall design of semantic theories.

Starting with Russell (1919), indefinite descriptions have traditionally been analyzed as inherently existentially quantified. More complex facts, having to do with their variable quantificational force when in the restriction of operators, originally noted by Lewis (1975), and their ability to serve as antecedents to pronouns outside their syntactic scope, as in intersentential and donkey anaphora, have led to an analysis of indefinites as non-quantificational expressions. In such theories, the intuitive quantificational force of indefinites arises as a result of either construal rules, such as operator indexing and existential closure (Heim 1982), or of principles of interpretation, such as the definition of truth and the satisfaction conditions of dyadic operators (Kamp 1981, Heim 1982).

Standard theories of indefinite NP's, including both those that analyze them as inherently existentially quantified and those that analyze them as non-quantificational, variable-contributing elements, predict that indefinites always have existential force if outside the scope of any operator, that they assert rather than presuppose existence, and that they are never anaphoric. Those theories, moreover, in which indefinites can inherit the force of the operator whose scope they are under (Kamp 1981, Heim 1982, Chierchia 1992) predict that an indefinite will have non-existential force only in the restriction of an operator. Finally, indefinites are not considered as essentially context-sensitive, although it is acknowledged that their interpretation may be supplemented by implicit contextual restrictions.

In this chapter, I show that there are indefinites which, in one of their readings, do not have existential force even in the absence of any operator, presuppose rather than assert existence and are crucially context-sensitive. Bare plural indefinite descriptions in English are of this type.

In the previous chapter I discussed two influential analyses of the bare plural that have sought a unified treatment for its existential and generic readings. One treats bare plurals as kind-denoting terms (Carlson 1977b). The other treats bare plurals as indefinite NP's, relying on the analysis of indefinites developed by Kamp (1981) and Heim (1982) as inherently non-quantificational NPs contributing a free variable and conditions on that variable (Gerstner & Krifka 1987, Krifka 1987, Krifka et al. 1995, Wilkinson 1988a, 1991). It distinguishes between two types of genericity and analyzes one type as involving a sentential dyadic modal operator binding free variables in its restriction.

Both analyses are designed to account for the following two generalizations: (i) if the bare plural has universal force, then the reading for the whole sentence is generic; (ii) if the reading for the whole sentence is episodic, then the bare plural has existential force.[1] In this chapter I show that English bare plurals exhibit a universal reading which arises both with individual-level predicates in non-generic sentences, violating (i), and with stage-level predicates in episodic sentences, violating (ii). I refer to this reading as the *functional reading* since, as will be shown in the next chapter, a contextually salient function is implicated in its analysis.

I first present the reading and its associated properties (section 2) and then explore the ways it can be analyzed within a framework of standard assumptions about genericity and indefiniteness (section 3). For purposes of this discussion I will assume the DRT-Heimian quantifier-free treatment of indefinites. However, the argument does not depend *crucially* on these assumptions and can be reconstructed within the framework of more recent proposals, whereby indefinites are analyzed in terms of first or higher order dynamic existential quantifiers (e.g., Groenendijk & Stokhof 1991b, Chierchia 1992).

2. THE FUNCTIONAL READING OF BARE PLURALS

2.1 Initial Observations

A prediction of the standard indefiniteness analysis of bare plurals is that the universal reading of a bare plural, as of any indefinite, will arise only in quantificational contexts. As outlined in the previous chapter, such contexts require the presence of an overt adverb of quantification, a modal, or implicit genericity.

A universal reading, however, arises in a wider range of contexts which cannot be straightforwardly assumed to be quantificational. Consider [55a] and three possible continuations, [55b]–[55d].

[55] a. In 1985 there was a ghost haunting the campus.
 b. Students were aware of this fact/the danger.
 c. The students were aware of this fact/the danger.
 d. There were students who were aware of this fact/the danger.

Intuitively, [55b] appears synonymous with [55c]. Unlike [55d], [55b] does not make an existential assertion but, like [55c], it is an assertion about the totality of the contextually relevant students, whose existence in the actual world seems to be presupposed by both [55c] and [55b]. Although the bare plural receives a universal reading, [55b] is not generic in any obvious way; it does not express a non-accidental generalization about students in general, nor a regularity about the occurrence of awareness in other situations in which a ghost was haunting the campus. The individual-level predicate is not understood as expressing a characteristic property.[2]

That the bare plural in [55b] lacks an existential reading is not surprising given that the predicate *be aware* is individual-level. The question is whether genericity is involved in [55b]. If implicit genericity is involved, how does this square with our intuitions about the meaning of [55b]? If not, what does the universal reading amount to in the absence of genericity?

Although this use[3] of the bare plural in English is quite pervasive, as even a casual look at actual texts makes clear, it has gone virtually unnoticed in the literature. The only works I am aware of that acknowledge it are Lahiri (1991) and Prince (1992). Lahiri observes parenthetically that certain bare plurals take a universal reading with stage-level predicates and assumes that bare plurals may have a definite reading. Prince notes that there appear indefinites in episodic contexts with an unexpected universal reading in the text under scrutiny in her article.[4] Interestingly, these indefinites are categorized as 'inferrable' within the typology of information-status she proposes.[5] However, inferrable indefinites with a universal reading are inconsistent with the generalizations she advances about the formal marking of an NP, its information-status and its interpretation. According to these generalizations, only inferrable definites can have a universal reading. Prince ultimately assumes that such uses of indefinites are deviant and that the text would have been more natural with definites in their place.

I will show that the appearance of such indefinites, far from being deviant or a marginal phenomenon, stems from a hitherto unrecognized semantic property of some indefinites, including bare plurals in English. This property gives rise to a universal reading with both individual-level and stage-level predicates in the absence of genericity or any operator.

In the remainder of section 2, I discuss the properties associated with such indefinites and show that the synonymy with the definite, the presence of contextual restrictions, the lack of genericity and the presupposition of existence constitute a real and pervasive phenomenon and are not incidental to example [55]. Throughout section 2 my interest is in ascertaining the properties of the functional reading, and therefore the discussion is cast in such a way as to be neutral with respect to the question of whether this reading is due to the presence of an implicit operator. Section 3 spells out a possible analysis in terms of an implicit operator. I will eventually reject it on the grounds that it fails to provide a unified account of the phenomena described. I will present an alternative analysis in the next chapter.

2.2 Functional Reading with Individual-Level Predicates

A crucial step in the argument that the functional reading constitutes a distinct interpretation is to establish that it is not a special case of the generic interpretation. If the functional reading were a special case of the generic interpretation, then it would arise in one of the following three ways: (a) as an entailment of the generic reading, (b) as an implicature of the generic reading, or (c) because of the presence of an extensionalized generic operator. I consider and reject the first possibility in section 2.2.1, where I provide evidence that can tease apart the functional from the truly generic reading. I consider and reject the second possibility in section 2.5. I consider and reject the third possibility in section 3, where I develop an account in terms of an extensionalized generic operator, taking into consideration the full range of facts presented in section 2.

A generalization that will emerge is that contextual restrictions are consistently associated with the functional reading and that they constitute an integral part of that interpretation (sections 2.2.1, 2.2.2). However, not any contextual restriction is possible, as I show in section 2.2.2, where I discuss the limitations on what can constitute a contextual restriction.

2.2.1 Genericity and the Functional Reading

As we saw in the previous chapter, both the kind analysis and the indefiniteness analysis of bare plurals take for granted that the universal reading for the bare plural depends on a generic reading for the whole sentence. In [55b], however, the two do not coincide. [55b] expresses a generalization restricted to the actual students on campus on a particular occasion. As discussed in the previous chapter, actual generalizations are not equivalent to generic generalizations since a generic generalization can be true even when the actual generalization is not, and vice versa.

The issue is whether the functional reading, which can be described as a contextually restricted actual generalization reading, is in fact the interpretation of [55b], or whether it is a consequence of the generic interpretation under certain circumstances. Now, in order for [55b] to be true, the actual students on campus in 1985 have to have been aware of the danger or of the fact that a ghost appeared. In other words, if [55b] is true, then so is [55c]. But this by itself is not necessarily inconsistent with [55b]'s having a generic interpretation. For instance, the functional reading could be an entailment of a descriptive generic generalization when the generic operator is construed with a realistic modal base and trivial ordering source. If we are to definitively distinguish the functional reading from the truly generic reading, we must show not only that the generalization expressed by [55b] is true in the actual world but also that whether it is true or not depends on *nothing but* the actual world. If the latter is true, then the bare plural is not in the scope of a modal operator.

I present three arguments to distinguish between the generic interpretation and the functional interpretation. The first argument is based on the contextually restricted nature of the generalization expressed by the functional reading. The second argument is based on the implication of existence in the actual world associated with the functional reading. The third argument is based on the scopal interaction between the bare plural and quantificational adverbs and modals. The presence of contextual restrictions and the implication of existence show some fairly straightforward dissimilarities between the generic and the functional reading. The implication of existence and the scopal facts show that the bare plural has wide scope with respect to overt generic operators and modals, hence its interpretation is not dependent on a modal operator.

a. Implicit Contextual Restrictions

Contextual restrictions, supplied by the previous discourse, are present with the functional reading of the bare plural in [55b], as they are with the definite in [55c]: [55b] is no more general than [56b], where the restrictions are part of the descriptive content of the NP, and similarly for [55c] and [56c].

[56] a. In 1985 there was a ghost haunting the campus.
b. Students on the campus at that time were aware of this fact.
c. The students on the campus at that time were aware of this fact.

Moreover, if no students other than the ones on campus at that time were aware of the ghost's appearance, [55b] would still be true. In other words, individuals satisfying the descriptive content of the bare plural NP but not the contextual restrictions are irrelevant in ascertaining the truth of [55b].

While the context of utterance affects the descriptive content of a bare plural NP with the functional reading, this does not happen with generic indefinite NP's. Generic statements do not accept *implicit* contextual restrictions. This is a general way of stating the observation made by Dahl (1975), Croft (1986) and Krifka (1987), on the basis of examples like [57] and [58], that nominal quantifiers are easily amenable to contextual restrictions while adverbial quantifiers and the implicit generic operator are not, at least with respect to individuals. Specifically, [57b] and [57d] have a reading equivalent to that of [57c] but neither [58a] nor [58c] or [58e] have a reading equivalent to that of [58b] or [58d].

[57] a. (Out of the blue:) Every lion has a mane.
(non-restricted)
b. There are lions and tigers in the cage. Every lion has a mane.

(restricted or non-restricted)
c. There are lions and tigers in the cage. Every lion in this cage has a mane.
d. (Context: we are near a cage with lions and tigers) Every lion has a mane.
(restricted or non-restricted)

[58] a. There are lions and tigers in the cage. A lion always has a mane.
(non-restricted only)
b. There are lions and tigers in the cage. A lion in this cage always has a mane.
c. There are lions and tigers in the cage. A lion/Lions has/have a mane.
(non-restricted only)
d. There are lions and tigers in the cage. A lion/Lions in this cage has/have a mane.
e. (Context: we are near a cage with lions and tigers) A lion/Lions has/have a mane.
(non-restricted only)

The crucial point here is the difference between overt restrictions, which are part of the linguistic descriptive content of an NP, and implicit restrictions, which are provided by the context of utterance. The context of utterance in [57] and [58] provides information on the basis of previous linguistic discourse ([57b], [58a], [58c]), or some salient facts established by the extralinguistic context ([57d], [58e]).

The assumption that the functional reading is an entailment of the generic reading which is present when the generic operator is construed with a realistic modal base and ordering source does not by itself explain why the bare plural appears to be contextually restricted. If contextual restrictions are not part of the generic interpretation, then they cannot come for free in the functional reading. We might be able to supplement the entailment assumption with some pragmatic story to the effect that the contextual restrictions are present to guarantee coherence with the previous discourse but I will not pursue this direction any further since there is overwhelming evidence against it.

b. Implication of Existence

Unlike generic statements, [55b], repeated here as [59b], implies the existence of students on campus in 1985 in the actual world.[6] That this is a non-trivial implication can be perhaps better appreciated if we consider bare plurals with additional descriptive content, as in [59c].

[59] a. In 1985 there was a ghost haunting the campus.
b. Students were aware of the danger.
c. Students with police connections were aware of the danger.
d. (But) there were no students (with police connections) on the campus in 1985.

Although the existence of individuals satisfying the descriptive content of the bare plural in [59c] cannot be taken for granted, [59c] certainly implies that there were actually students with police connections on the campus in 1985. Continuing the discourse comprised of [59a] and [59b] or [59c] with [59d] leads to a contradiction. If the generic interpretation were the only interpretation for [59b] and [59c], no implication of existence would be guaranteed since [59b] and [59c] could be true, and even entail the equivalent actual generalization, even if no students with police connections actually existed on campus in 1985.

Intersentential anaphora provides an additional piece of evidence for this implication. In order for intersentential anaphora with an indefinite antecedent in a modal/generic environment to be possible, the indefinite must be asserting existence in the actual world. This generalization was already made by Karttunen (1976) and most theories capture it by assuming that the indefinite takes wide scope with respect to the modal/generic operator.[7] For example, within the framework of Kamp (1981), in order for this kind of intersentential anaphora to be possible, the discourse referent introduced by the bare plural must be at the top-level DRS and therefore accessible to the discourse referent of a pronoun outside the scope of the modal or generic operator. Within the framework of Heim (1982, Ch. II), the indefinite must have wider scope than any other operator, in which case it will be captured by text-level existential closure and will bind the pronoun.[8] Of course, the problem with respect to both frameworks is how the indefinite can have widest scope, on the one hand, and not be interpreted existentially, on the other. This is something I will address in detail later, as it is the focus of the revised theory of indefiniteness that I will propose. At this point, I want to establish that the evidence from anaphora places precisely the constraint for entailment of existence and therefore the requirement for wide scope.

The bare plural of [55b] and [59b] can be the antecedent of a pronoun in intersentential anaphora: each of these sentences can be felicitously continued by either [60a], which contains an individual-level predicate, or [60b], which contains a stage-level predicate. The contextual restrictions are present in the anaphora as well: *they* picks out the students (with police connections) on campus at the time of the ghosts's appearance, not just the students (with police connections) in the actual world at large. Therefore, [55b] and [59b] must entail existence in the actual world in order for anaphora to be possible.

[60] a. They were well-informed.
b. They had been informed by the police.

Since modal subordination and an interpretation for the pronoun as a pronoun of laziness are alternative options which are consistent with the bare plural antecedent's being within the scope of a generic operator, we must make sure that the right type of anaphora is involved. We must, therefore, exclude the possibility of modal subordination and the pronoun of laziness interpretation for [60a] and [60b].

If we assumed that there was modal subordination in [60a] with the pronoun being a pronoun of laziness, this assumption would be open to the same problems as assuming genericity for [55b] or [59b]. Of course, no modal subordination is involved in [60b] since it is an episodic sentence. The pronoun *they* is not a pronoun of laziness: being aware of the danger and being well-informed are understood to be attributed to the same individuals.[9] If *they* were a pronoun of laziness, then in the episodic context of [60b] it would have an existential reading, equivalent to that of *some students (with police connections) had been informed by the police*, a reading that is absent. Moreover, in chapter 2 we saw that if the bare plural antecedent is construed with an individual-level predicate while the pronoun anaphoric on it is in an episodic context, the result is rather deviant (examples [14g] and [15a]). [60b], on the other hand, is perfectly acceptable.

There is one remaining option that we must consider. If we take the functional reading to be an entailment of the generic reading relative to a realistic modal base and ordering source, we might still be able to account for the possibility of anaphora by treating the pronoun as an implicit definite description and by assuming accommodation of the information that the actual world did indeed have the relevant individuals at that time. This kind of anaphora is presumably involved in [61], where *they* is construed as *the pomegranates in actual existence right now* in [61b] and as *the pirate ships in actual existence right now* in [61d].

[61] a. Pomegranates do not have a crowned end.
b. ?? They had it/them chopped off.
c. Pirate ships fly a black flag.
d. ?? They (all) bought it/them from the same shop.

We can assume, along the lines of Heim (1990) and Chierchia (1992), that these pronouns correspond to free functor variables which in these cases take as value a function from worlds and times to the individuals satisfying the descriptive content of the NP at the relevant world and time. The additional contextual restrictions involved in the anaphora in [60] can be accounted for by taking the functor variable to have as value a function from worlds, times and individuals to the individuals satisfying the descriptive content of the NP, i.e., a function from worlds, times and campuses to the students associated with each campus at the relevant world and time . However, there is a clear difference in acceptability between the anaphora in [61] and the anaphora in [60]; in fact, some speakers find the anaphora in [61] totally unacceptable. The difference in acceptability can be linked to the readiness with which the information about the existence of the relevant individuals can be accommodated. Of course, if [55b] and [59b] themselves entail the existence of the relevant individuals, then no accommodation is necessary and the anaphora should be perfectly acceptable, as it in fact is.

c. Wide Scope

That [55b] is not generic can also be seen by providing the sentence with an adverb of quantification or an overt generic operator. If the truth of the actual, contextually restricted generalization, which is associated with the functional reading in [55b], were an entailment of the generic reading, we would expect that in the presence of an overt operator the bare plural would be in its scope and we would get the familiar descriptive generic generalization reading, with the entailment about the actual world depending on the force of the operator. But this is not what we find.

The universal reading of the bare plural persists even when an overt adverb of quantification with non-universal force is present, which shows that no direct binding by the adverb of quantification is involved. Consider [62]: in [62b], as in [62c], there is an assertion about the totality of the contextually relevant students, with the adverb of quantification taking on a temporal reading. In fact, because the adverb of quantification has a temporal reading, the sense of *be aware* shifts to *be consciously aware* in [62b] and [62c], so that the predicate can be temporally relativizable.

[62] a. In 1985 there was a ghost haunting the campus.
b. Students were usually aware of this fact.
c. The students were usually aware of this fact.
d. Most students were aware of this fact.

Since their interpretation does not depend on the adverb of quantification, the bare plural of [62b] and the definite of [62c] must outscope it. If the bare plural were within the scope of the adverb of quantification, it would be bound by it, and if we took the adverb of quantification to have a modal dimension with a realistic modal base and ordering source, [62b] would at most entail [62d], and not something about the totality of the contextually relevant students.[10] In other words, if the functional reading were simply an entailment of the generic reading, the intuitive reading of [62b] would appear to be [62d] rather than [62c].

In the previous chapter, I claimed that adverbs like *normally* or *typically* are generic operators with particular requirements on the nature of their modal base and ordering source. At this point, they can be used as diagnostics for a true generic reading because they cannot be stripped of their modal force. When these adverbs are added to examples like [55], they lead to infelicity, as in [63].

[63] a. In 1985 there was a ghost haunting the campus.
b. (#)Normally/Typically students were aware of this fact.
c. (#)Normally/Typically the students were aware of this fact.
d. (#)Normally/Typically there were students who were aware of this fact.
e. The normal/typical students on campus were aware of this fact.

The bare plural still patterns with the definite in picking out the totality of the contextually relevant students in the actual world. [63b]–[63d] are infelicitous to the extent that quantification is vacuous, which is a consequence of the fact that the bare plural is not within the scope of the operator in this case. In order to preserve coherence with [63a], a contextually restricted reading is sought for the bare plural which, however, results in the bare plural's outscoping the operator. Crucially, the reading that is missing is one where the operator has been stripped of its modal force and the domain of quantification consists of the contextually relevant students with the adverbs contributing an extra restriction on that domain. In other words, [63b] does not share a reading with [63e].[11]

[63b] and [63d] may, of course, have an interpretation in which the adverbs are interpreted as modal operators and the bare plural is within the scope of the adverb but on that interpretation the bare plural is not contextually restricted, no claim is being made about the actual students associated with campus during that time and the sentences are not natural continuations for [63a]. The operators in [63b], [63c] and [63d] can also be interpreted as quantifying over temporally individuated situations. In that case, the bare plural in [63b] outscopes the operator and exhibits the functional reading, a situation parallel to that of [62b].[12]

Thus, we have seen that the bare plural can outscope both an adverb of quantification and an overt generic operator. The wide scope of the bare plural with respect to a quantificational adverbial affects the interpretation of the adverbial in terms of what provides its domain of quantification and results in the functional reading for the bare plural.

The functional reading surfaces with modals as well, with the bare plural taking wide scope with respect to the modal. [64b], like [64c], has a reading in which the students are taken to be the actual students. That the modal base of the deontic operator is not realistic is illustrated by [64d], which is a perfectly felicitous continuation for [64b] and [64c].

[64]   a. A ghost is haunting the campus.
       b. Students should be aware of the danger.
       c. The students should be aware of the danger.
       d. Unfortunately, they are not.

Note that anaphora in [64d] is possible (without the need for modal subordination) precisely because [64b] and [64c] entail the existence of students in the actual world.

If the bare plural indeed takes wide scope with respect to generic and modal operators, then the truth of sentences like [55b], [59b], [62b] and [64b] depends on nothing but the actual world, and therefore the functional reading is not an entailment of the generic reading.

2.2.2 Contextual Restrictions

In the previous section it was shown that bare plurals with the functional reading can be contextually restricted, in contrast to bare plurals within the scope of adverbs of quantification and generic operators. In this section I will show that bare plurals *must* be contextually restricted on their functional reading. I will call this effect the *positive contextual sensitivity* of the functional reading. However, the functional reading is systematically blocked if the context providing the contextual restrictions has certain properties. I will call this effect the *negative contextual sensitivity* of the functional reading.

NP's are often dependent on the context of utterance to supply information that determines their interpretation either by restricting their domain of quantification or by providing additional conditions for their descriptive content. The information supplied by the context may be based either on information provided directly by the previous linguistic discourse, or on the shared beliefs between speaker and hearer and the speaker intentions recoverable by the hearer. The role that the context plays in restricting the interpretation of NP's may be viewed either as a purely pragmatic phenomenon, or as the result of an interplay between semantics and pragmatics: the semantics makes available a certain parameter whose value is determined by pragmatic factors, such as saliency, discourse coherence, etc. In any case, whether an NP in a given context of utterance is interpreted as contextually restricted or not, or which contextual restrictions are chosen, depends solely on pragmatic factors. Bare plurals with the functional reading are different in this respect; I will argue that the positive contextual sensitivity and the negative contextual sensitivity of the functional reading depend on semantic properties of the bare plural.

a. Positive Contextual Sensitivity

The bare plural in [55b], [59b], [62b], or [64b] must be contextually restricted. The implicit contextual restrictions on the bare plural seem to be part of its meaning as they not cancellable. The discourse in [65] is contradictory.

[65] a. In 1985 a ghost was haunting the campus.
b. Students were aware of the danger.
c. However, none of the students associated with the campus was aware of the danger.

If the bare plural is construed as having a generic reading, no contradiction arises, as in [66].

[66] a. A ghost is haunting the campus.
      b. In general, students are aware of this kind of danger.
      c. However, none of the students associated with the campus is aware of this kind of danger.

For indefinites, in general, there is a preference for a contextually restricted reading, which, however, can always be overridden if, for instance, it leads to contradiction. Therefore, the discourse in [67] is perfectly coherent.

[67] a. In 1985 a ghost was haunting the campus.
      b. Some students were aware of the danger.
      c. None of the students associated with the campus was aware of the danger.

Although the indefinite in [67b] can, in principle, be interpreted as contextually restricted with the contextual restrictions contributed by [67a], the presence of [67c] rules out this kind of interpretation. How we take the context of utterance to affect the interpretation of the indefinite in [67b] is irrelevant to the argument. We can attribute the presence of contextual restrictions purely to pragmatics, in which case [67b] would be true depending on the existence of *any* students having the relevant property. Or we can allow the context of utterance to provide an additional condition to the descriptive content of the indefinite. In the former case, the hearer would draw the inference that some students *on campus* have the relevant property, so as to make [67b] both more informative and more relevant to the current discourse. In the latter case, the previous discourse could provide the relevant restriction while the continuation with [67c] would indicate to the hearer that he was wrong in assuming the context provided a restriction and should reconsider. The crucial point is that the meaning of the indefinite in [67b] is such that it is compatible with any number of contextual restrictions, or none at all, while that of the bare plural requires a specific kind of contextual restriction.

Not only should the bare plural be contextually restricted but the contextual restrictions must be provided by the discourse prior to the utterance of the bare plural. Consider the difference between the discourses in [68] and [69].[13]

[68] a. A burglar was roaming Santa Clara county.
      b. Deputy sheriffs were aware of the danger.

c. #They had been sent from LA county to investigate.
[69] a. A burglar was roaming Santa Clara county.
   b. Several deputy sheriffs were aware of the danger.
   c. They had been sent from LA county to investigate.

The same point is also made by cases in which the sentence containing a bare plural is first in a discourse, with the NP that can provide the contextual restrictions in the following sentence, as in [70].

[70] a. Students were roaming the streets.
   b. A school nearby had ended classes early.

In that case, the bare plural has only an existential reading although the next sentence can, and in fact does, provide additional restrictions for it.

b. Negative Contextual Sensitivity

Necessary as the contextual restrictions may be for the functional reading to arise, not any contextual restriction is possible. There are contexts which provide extra information that can in principle constitute a further restriction for the bare plural but which in fact does not. [71c] still expresses the same generalization as [55b] in the context of [71a] and [71b], not the more contextually restricted one corresponding to *every student in this dormitory*. The contextually restricted reading is easily available for the definite in [71d] and the quantificational NP in [71e].

[71] a. There is a ghost haunting the campus.
   b. There are 500 students in this dormitory.
   c. Students are aware of the danger.
   d. The students are aware of the danger.
   e. Every student is aware of the danger.

Admittedly, a discourse comprised of [71a], [71b] and [71c] sounds incohesive. Rather than being at odds with the point being made here, this can be taken as further support for it, since the more contextually restricted reading is absent even when discourse cohesiveness would require it. Such a discourse would in any case improve if it were followed by something that would justify the shift from one group of students to the other, like e.g. 'The students of the dormitory have, moreover, taken strict precautions.'

Similarly, in a deictic context, like that of [72], the bare plural receives the same reading as [55b], not the more contextually restricted one picking out the perceptually salient students.

[72] (Context: We know that there is a ghost haunting the campus. We are standing in front of the library and we can both see several students.)
Students are afraid to enter the library.

While the perceptually salient students can be taken as providing the *evidence* for the generalization, the generalization is not restricted to them as far as the meaning of [72] is concerned.

As descriptions and nominal quantifiers in general readily accept contextual restrictions constrained only by pragmatic considerations, the selectivity of the bare plural is highly surprising and unprecedented. The following question arises at this point: is what matters the contextually supplied information, or the kind of context that supplies it? In [71], as in [55] and in all the examples we have looked at so far except for [72], the context supplying the information and hence the relevant restrictions is the previous linguistic discourse. In [72] the context is extralinguistic. However, the fact that the bare plural in [72] *can* have a contextually restricted reading that encompasses all the students on campus shows that the extralinguistic context can supply the relevant information. We are driven, therefore, to viewing the kind of information that is contextually supplied as being responsible for what is an acceptable and what is an unacceptable contextual restriction. Later I will argue that this is not a limitation on contextual restrictions *per se* but a consequence of the fact that the bare plural cannot be anaphoric in some technical sense. A theory that would allow us to account for this limitation in these terms is preferable to one that would identify the phenomenon as direct limitation on the contextual restrictions. Contextual factors affect the common ground, that is the information state in which speaker and addressee presume themselves to be and against which new linguistic utterances are evaluated.

2.3 *Functional Reading with Stage-Level Predicates*

If the functional reading were an entailment of the generic reading, we would expect it to be limited to bare plurals construed with individual-level predicates or with stage-level predicates within a quantificational context. In this section, I demonstrate that the universal reading of bare plurals shows up with stage-level predicates in purely episodic contexts.

Consider [73], where the bare plurals *opponents* and *proponents* appear in an episodic context.

[73] Although the odds still seem to favor Senate approval of Thomas, *opponents* redoubled their effort and tried to delay a floor vote on confirmation ... *Proponents*, in contrast, demanded a vote next week.
(*San Francisco Chronicle*, Sept. 28, 1991)

[73] can be understood either as an existential statement about some opponents and proponents of the approval, or as a statement involving the totality of the opponents and proponents of the approval. The former reading is the expected reading for a bare plural in an episodic context but the latter is rather surprising. Moreover, the totality effect associated with the second reading is independent of the kind of predication involved. Both readings allow for a distributive or a collective predication, that is both readings are compatible with there having been either individual attempts for delay and demands for a vote, or a single collective attempt and a single collective demand.

Similarly, the examples in [74] are ambiguous: on one reading, they are synonymous with the corresponding ones in [75], and on the other, they are understood as involving the totality of the entities specified by the NP. On the latter reading, for example, [74a] is a statement about all (relevant) linguistic theories, [74b] implies that the total number of victims rescued by rescue teams is 28,950,[14] [74c] is a promise about all (relevant) details and [74d] an announcement about all (relevant) prices. In none of these cases do we have a generalization over episodes.

[74] a. Linguistic theories have posited abstract representations.
      b. Rescue teams have rescued 28,950 victims.
      c. Details will be presented tomorrow.
      d. Prices went up today.

[75] a. There are linguistic theories that have posited abstract representations.
      b. There are rescue teams that have rescued 28,950 victims.
      c. There are details that will be presented tomorrow.
      d. There are prices that went up today.

Let us look a bit more closely at the kinds of contexts that give rise to the functional reading with stage-level predicates and the kinds of contextual restrictions present. In [73] what is explicitly uttered provides the contextual restrictions: the approval of a nomination is at issue and the bare plurals *opponents* and *proponents* are understood as elliptical descriptions whose full form would be *opponents of the approval* and *proponents of the approval*, respectively. I have not provided any explicit context for [74]; however, for [74b] and [74c] a situation is easily conjured up that could provide the contextual restrictions: in [74b] a natural disaster, in [74c] a presentation. [74a] and [74d] are somewhat different in that they can be uttered without any explicit context. Rather, the existence of the relevant entities relies on some general background facts that seem to constitute general background knowledge and taken for granted by a given linguistic community, for example, an economy such that goods have prices, or one with intellectual disciplines that have theories. The generalization emerging from these cases is that the existence of the entities satisfying the description of the bare plural is stereotypically tied to some other entity or to some world where some typical facts hold and which we take the actual world to be. These observations relate to Prince's observations about 'inferrable indefinites' with a universal reading.

The fact that a bare plural *can* have a universal reading with a stage-level predicate in an episodic context contradicts the generalization stated in the previous chapter that a bare plural with a universal reading does not combine with an episodic predicate. It also provides rather striking evidence that the functional reading is not generic. Adding a generic operator results in complete ill-formedness, as in [76], where the possibility of a regular generic reading is absent because the verb corresponds to an episodic predicate.[15]

[76] a. #Normally/Typically rescue teams rescued 28,950 victims yesterday.
b. #Normally/Typically details will be presented tomorrow.
c. #Normally/Typically prices went up today.

A correlate of the ambiguity exhibited by the bare plural with stage-level predicates in episodic contexts is that a pronoun outside the c-command domain of the bare plural has a totality reading in addition to an E-type interpretation. The E-type interpretation correlates with the existential reading for the bare plural, the totality reading with the universal reading for the bare plural. Consider [77] and [78].

[77] a. Prices went up today.
b. They were expected to go up.

[78]   a. There are prices that went up today.
       b. They were expected to go up.

If [77a] is interpreted as synonymous with [78a], the pronoun in [77b], as in [78b], is interpreted as equivalent to *the prices that went up today*. In that case [77b] and [78b] would be true in a situation in which only some prices were expected to go up and those were the prices that actually did go up. If, on the other hand, the bare plural in [77a] has the functional reading, then the pronoun in [77b] is interpreted as equivalent to *all prices*.

The functional reading also arises in quantified contexts, where, as with individual-level predicates, the indefinite outscopes a modal or an adverb of quantification, the latter having a temporal reading.

[79]   a. Prices must come down (for the good of the people).
       b. Unfortunately, they will not.

[80]   a. There were several alerts today.
       b. Rescue teams usually reacted promptly.

One could claim that the wide scope reading, and, more generally, the functional reading of bare plurals with stage-level predicates, is really a specific existential reading. I argue against this possibility in section 2.5.

2.4   Other Indefinites

The functional reading does not arise with other indefinites. [81b] shows that the singular indefinite, in exactly the same context as that of [55b], has only an existential reading. Similarly for the plural indefinite with the determiner *some* in [81c].

[81]   a. In 1985 there was a ghost haunting the campus.
       b. A student was aware of the danger.
       c. Some students were aware of the danger.

Given that the bare plural lacks an existential reading and the singular and plural indefinites the universal reading, [81b] and [81c] have no reading in common with [55b].[16] No such discrepancy between the singular indefinite and the bare plural occurs in standard cases of generic quantification. For instance, in the context of [82a] both [82b] and [82c] have a generic interpretation.

[82]   a. A single bad grade ruins a student's reputation forever.
       b. Students are (always) aware of this danger.
       c. A student is (always) aware of this danger.

In parallel fashion, indefinites other than the bare plural construed with a stage-level predicate show no ambiguity between an existential and a universal reading.

[83]   a. A linguistic theory has posited abstract representations.
       b. A detail will be presented tomorrow.
       c. An opponent redoubled his effort.
       d. Some details will be presented tomorrow.
       e. Some food prices went up today.

This is another piece of evidence that the usual notion of genericity is not involved in the contextually restricted universal reading.

2.5   Excluding a Purely Pragmatic Account

Before continuing, I want to establish that the functional reading of a bare plural cannot be given a purely pragmatic account, thereby supporting the claim that it constitutes an interpretation distinct from either the generic or the existential. A pragmatic account might seem *prima facie* desirable, at least on methodological grounds, since it would avoid multiplying ambiguities. In this section, I will outline the general character of a pragmatic account and identify the inadequacies of failing to recognize the functional reading as the actual interpretation of the bare plural in the cases considered so far. Further facts associated with the functional reading that will be presented in later sections exclude a purely pragmatic account altogether. However, a pragmatic analysis is untenable even for the facts discussed so far and I believe it is interesting to see why.

A purely pragmatic account would claim that the facts of the functional reading are not facts about the *meaning* or *interpretation* of bare plurals but solely facts about their *use*. An account in which pragmatics plays a role by fixing some aspect of the interpretation, such as the analysis based on degenerate genericity presented in section 3 of this chapter, is not a purely pragmatic account by this criterion. In a purely pragmatic account, the role of context consists in generating implicatures and not in satisfying preconditions for interpretation. Such an account would capitalize on the Gricean distinction between sentence meaning and speaker meaning and would attribute the effects of the functional reading to speaker meaning. In Grice's seminal distinction, sentence meaning is that given by the semantic interpretation, and, relative to the specifications a given context of utterance provides for the context-sensitive expressions in the sentence, it determines *what is said*. Speaker meaning, or *what is meant*, is what the speaker intends to communicate relative to a given occasion of utterance and is determined in part by general principles underlying rational communication.

According to a pragmatic account, therefore, bare plurals with stage-level predicates in episodic sentences have just the usual existential reading and bare plurals with individual-level predicates have just the usual generic reading, and that is all the semantics should be responsible for. The functional reading arises when, due to certain contextual factors, what is meant is distinct from what is said.

There are two ways I can see of working this out. One is to analyze the functional reading as an implicature that can be associated with both the generic reading and the existential reading. I will call it the *implicature approach*. The other is to assimilate the functional reading to the referential or specific uses of indefinite descriptions. I will call it the *referentiality approach*. In what follows I will spell out these two approaches in more detail and examine them in turn. For the sake of concreteness, let us assume that what is said and what is meant are (possibly distinct) propositions and let us follow common practice (e.g., Ludlow & Neale (1991)) in referring to the former proposition as the *proposition expressed* and to the latter as the *proposition meant*.

2.5.1 The Implicature Approach

The implicature approach would aim to derive the actual, contextually restricted generalization reading as an implicature from the generic reading, in the case of individual-level predicates, and from the existential reading, in the case of stage-level predicates. Thus, for an example like [55b], where the predicate is individual-level, the proposition expressed corresponds to a generic generalization, while the proposition meant corresponds to an actual, contextually restricted generalization. For an example like [73], where the predicate is stage-level, the proposition expressed is existential, while the proposition meant is the (stronger) actual, contextually restricted generalization. The question then is what contextual factors give rise to the difference between the proposition expressed and the proposition meant.[17]

The functional reading with individual-level predicates could arise if the generic generalization is patently false and this fact is obvious to both speaker and hearer. Under the assumption that the speaker would not try to communicate something for which he has insufficient evidence or something that is mutually believed to be false, the hearer would draw the inference that the speaker actually intends to communicate something weaker but true, namely an actual and contextually restricted generalization.

The functional reading with stage-level predicates could arise if the speaker has every reason to believe that the individuals of whom the existential statement is true are exactly all the individuals of whom the statement is true and intends to communicate that to the hearer, while the hearer is aware of the speaker's relevant beliefs and intentions.

If the functional reading is attributed to speaker meaning, the presence of contextual restrictions and the implication of existence could be accounted for.[18] The speaker would intend to communicate the proposition corresponding to the functional reading when his or her beliefs are formed on the basis of some actual individuals in a particular context. Such a take on the issue, while having these advantages over the entailment alternative—which in any case could not account for the existence of the functional reading with stage-level prediactes—faces some serious problems as well.

First, the implicature approach gives two disparate explanations for the functional reading in episodic sentences and in generic sentences. The explanations are, in general, distinct because the mechanisms responsible for getting from what is said to what is meant are not the same. In the reading with stage-level predicates what is meant is stronger than what is said (universal vs. existential), while in the reading with individual-level predicates what is meant is weaker than what is said (accidental vs. generic generalization). To illustrate let us consider a variation of [73], in which one of the NP's is construed with an individual-level predicate and the other with a stage-level predicate.

[84] The odds still seem to favor approval of the nominee but proponents believe it will be a close vote. Opponents, for their part, tried to delay the vote yesterday, hoping time is on their side.

According to the implicature analysis, the first sentence is false and the second sentence is true while the speaker, by uttering them, intends to communicate with both something about the entire set of proponents or opponents of the nomination.

More seriously, an indefinite NP does not aquire a universal reading just because the equivalent universal statement also happens to be true. In general, there is no intuition of a universal reading, in the same way that there is one in the case of the functional reading, in contexts in which both speaker and addressee have evidence supporting the truth of the universal statement. For instance, suppose I utter [85] while looking outside the window, having every reason to believe that the dogs I can see are all the dogs of the neighborhood and all of them are tearing up my backyard, and intending to communicate that belief, while the hearer is aware of that fact as well as of my intention.

[85] Dogs are tearing up my back yard.

[85] does not acquire the functional reading in such a context. Although what I intend to communicate could well be something about all the dogs in my neighborhood, this does not affect the reading of the indefinite NP, whose force remains existential, even when the hearer draws the appropriate inference.

If generic sentences could be used in order to indirectly communicate information about actual entities in the way outlined above, then, on the one hand, all else being equal the type of the NP should make no difference, and on the other, a wider range of false generic statements should be subject to this charitable reinterpretation. Neither of these implications is true. Utterances of generic sentences are not appropriate for such a task and fail to communicate a contextually restricted actual generalization. As shown in section 2.4, the functional reading is restricted to bare plurals. The fact that an actual generalization is manifestly true does not affect the interpretation of the corresponding generic generalization so as to make it true, nor does it give rise to the functional reading. False generic statements remain false and do not give rise to the functional reading even when the context of utterance is such that it would support the truth of the contextually restricted actual generalization.

False generic statements, as in [86] (from Carlson (1977b:37)), where the equivalent non-generic, contextually restricted, universal statements are true, are a case in point.

[86] a. Books have between 100 and 150 pages.
      b. Sleds are black.
      c. Dogs are collies.

Carlson uses these examples to show that the existential reading is absent with individual-level predicates since they are judged as false; if the existential interpretation were available, all the sentences in [86] would be true on that reading since there exist books that have 100 to 150 pages, sleds that are black, and dogs that are collies. We can also use these cases to show that the functional reading does not arise even when the context of utterance supports its truth.

On the implicature account, the proposition expressed by each one of [86] is false but the proposition meant, which is one embodying an actual and restrictive generalization, is true.[19] Not only do the sentences in [86] remain false, no functional reading for the bare plural is detected, even if they are uttered in a context where all the contextually relevant books do indeed have between 100 and 150 pages, or all the contextually relevant sleds are indeed black, or all the contextually relevant dogs are collies. On the other hand, the functional reading arises regardless of what we believe about the truth of the corresponding generic statement, i.e., a sentence could be true both on the generic and the functional reading of the bare plural, as illustrated by [87].

[87] a. A ghost is haunting the campus.
      b. Students are aware of dangers of this kind.
      c. Unfortunately, the students on this campus are not.

Finally, the implicature account both overgenerates and undergenerates functional readings. Negative contextual sensitivity and false generic sentences lacking the functional reading exemplify overgeneration and infelicity or contradiction due to the functional reading of the bare plural exemplify undergeneration. Negative contextual sensitivity cannot be accounted for since there is nothing that would exclude the relevant speaker's meaning in the presence of a previous NP with identical descriptive content. Previous discourse in general helps provide contextual restrictions for NP's and there is no way it can be excluded here on any principled grounds.

As for undergeneration, if the actual generalization reading is simply an implicature, why is the implicature not cancelled, or to put it somewhat differently, why does the implicature arise in the first place in cases where it is strongly disfavored? For example, the presence of *normally* or *typically* in [63] leads to infelicity rather than cancellation of the implicature, and in the discourses of [59] and [65], [59c] and [65c] lead to contradiction rather than cancellation of the implicature. The functional reading of the bare plural has a direct influence on the interpretation of the quantificational elements and consequently on sentence meaning.

2.5.2 The Referentiality Approach

The referentiality approach would claim that the functional reading is the manifestation of specificity or referentiality with bare plural indefinite descriptions. For the sake of concreteness, let us frame the issue in terms of the conception of referentiality and specificity of Ludlow & Neale (1991). Ludlow & Neale's primary aim is to argue against an ambiguity for indefinites, and in the course of their argument they develop a typology of uses of indefinite NP's that is useful for our purposes.

Ludlow & Neale's aim is to defend the Russellian account of indefinites as uniformly quantificational elements against the evidence arguing for an ambiguity between a quantificational and a referential interpretation. According to Russell's account, a sentence containing an indefinite expresses a *general* proposition: it makes an existential statement and therefore its truth or falsity depends on there being an object, any object, that satisfies the relevant conditions. A sentence containing a referring expression, on the other hand, expresses a *singular* proposition:[20] it is a statement about the object referred to by the referring expression so its truth depends on whether that object satisfies the relevant conditions.[21]

As part of their argument, Ludlow & Neale develop a taxonomy of the distinct uses of indefinites and characterize the utterance contexts that give rise to them. They make a three-way distinction between the proposition expressed by a given utterance, the proposition meant, and *speaker's grounds*, the proposition which is the object of the speaker's belief providing the grounds of an utterance. For an utterance containing an indefinite, the proposition expressed is *always* a general proposition with existential import. But on different contexts of use the speaker's grounds and the proposition meant could well be singular. An indefinite has a *referential use* if the speaker grounds and the proposition meant constitute a singular proposition. An indefinite has a *specific use* if the speaker grounds constitute a singular proposition and the proposition meant a general proposition.

As a matter of course, bare plurals have both referential and specific uses, at least when interpreted existentially. An example of referential use is [85]. An example of specific use is an utterance of [88] where the speaker knows directly the individuals providing the information about the president and intends to communicate that she knows.

[88] Sources close to the president told us that he is ready to resign.

However, referential or specific use is neither necessary nor sufficient for the functional reading to arise.

Deictic contexts are prime candidates for supporting the referential use of descriptions. Let that be the context for [89]: suppose I utter it while my addressee and I are looking outside the window, intending to communicate the belief that the particular dogs that are perceptually salient will tear up my back yard, while my addressee is aware of my intention to communicate something about those dogs.

[89] Dogs will tear up my back yard.

[85], however, does not acquire the functional reading in such a context. The context is optimal for the referential use of the bare plural *dogs* (in fact, the bare plural *is* used referentially) and yet the functional reading does not arise.

A context in which I have some particular individuals in mind and assert something of them while expecting my addressees to recognize that I am intending to communicate something about those particular individuals (although they may not know who the individuals are) is a good candidate for the specific use. Let that be the context for [90]: suppose I know exactly *which* raccoons ate my flowers—say because they have made multiple appearances in my garden, so I have a way of identifying them uniquely, and I saw them at work the night before—and that my addressees also know that I have some particular raccoons in mind.

[90] Raccoons with a ferocious appetite ate my flowers last night.

Again, however, [90] does not acquire the functional reading in such a context. The context is optimal for the specific use of the bare plural *raccoons with a ferocious appetite* (in fact, the bare plural *is* used specifically) but the bare plural has only existential force. So specific and referential uses of a bare plural are not sufficient conditions for the functional reading to manifest itself.

Conversely, the presence of the functional reading does not imply that the bare plural indefinite is used referentially or specifically. I may utter [84] without having the slightest idea who the opponents and proponents of the nomination are, nor do I indicate by such an utterance that I do in fact know.

The arguments against the referentiality approach carry over to the analysis of the functional reading as a semantic phenomenon involving specificity/referentiality. The position that indefinites, such as the singular indefinite, can be ambiguous between a referential and a non-referential interpretation is defended, among others, by Chastain (1975), Fodor & Sag (1982) and most recently by de Hoop (1992) with respect to indefinites and the individual/stage-level contrast. De Hoop claims that individual-level predicates require a strong reading whereas stage-level predicates simply allow it, where the strong reading comprises a family of interpretations including the referential interpretation.

Under such a view, the existence of the functional reading would be seen as evidence for semantic ambiguity.[22] The proposition meant would be taken to be identical with the proposition expressed and they would both be singular propositions because the bare plural would be given a directly referential interpretation. This account would have the advantage of giving a unified explanation for the functional reading both with individual-level and stage-level predicates (since in both cases the reading would come about because of the semantic ambiguity of the indefinite), and of explaining the wide scope of the bare plural with respect to adverbs of quantification and generic operators. But if referential or specific use is not sufficient for the referential or specific interpretation to arise, and if the referential or specific interpretation does not require referential or specific use, how can the bare plural be directly referential but not context-sensitive? As I understand it, the proponents of a referential interpretation for indefinites must be committed to both theses: direct reference and context-sensitivity Although direct reference by itself does not presuppose context-sensitivity, the case for the referential interpretation of descriptions is made precisely by instances when the context of utterance provides a referent satisfying the descriptive content of the description. Unless the context of utterance provides a referent, the interpretation of such descriptions cannot be fixed.

More importantly, the functional reading does not always correlate with widest scope possible for the indefinite, as we will see in the next section. This, of course, more than anything else undermines any pragmatic account, as well as the semantically referential approach.

2.6 Functional Reading in Quantified Contexts

In section 2.2.1 I established that the interpretation of the bare plural on its functional reading does not depend on an adverb of quantification, a generic operator, or a modal. A crucial piece of evidence is that in the presence of an overt operator of this kind the bare plural can take wide scope. But is wide scope a necessary characteristic of the functional reading? After all, if the functional reading precluded anything but widest scope possible for the bare plural, then this would give credence to the directly referential interpretation analysis outlined in the previous section. If, however, the functional reading is a distinct interpretation and not reducible to direct reference, it should in principle be independent of the scopal interactions of the bare plural with respect to various operators. In this section I show that this is indeed the case.

2.6.1 Dependent Functional Reading

The functional reading can arise when the bare plural is within the scope of an adverb of quantification and in that case it affects the way the elements in the domain of quantification are individuated. The bare plural is dependent on some other variable which is directly bound by the operator (a situation variable) and the contextual restrictions are sensitive to that variable as well.

Consider [91], and take [91b]–[91d] to be possible continuations for [91a]. The adverb of quantification *usually* is given a non-modal interpretation and its domain of quantification is determined, at least in part, by the occasions of a ghost's appearance.

[91]   a. Ghosts have occasionally haunted this campus.
        b. Students were usually aware of the danger.
        c. The students were usually aware of the danger.
        d. A student was usually aware of the danger.

To begin with, there is a difference between [91b] and [91c] on the one hand, and [91d] on the other. When the bare plural and the definite are within the scope of the adverb of quantification, they affect the restriction of the operator. The singular indefinite, on the other hand, is not part of the restriction; an indefinite cannot in general constitute the restriction by itself when the adverb of quantification is non-modal.[23] [91d] has only the reading in which the indefinite has wide scope relative to the adverb of quantification or a nuclear scope existential reading.[24]

The bare plural and the definite can scope freely with respect to the adverb of quantification. They take wide scope in [91] if it is assumed that the students on campus have remained the same throughout the time during which occasional appearances of ghosts took place. They take narrow scope if it is assumed that the choice of students depends on the choice of occasion in which a ghost appeared on campus. In either case the bare plural exhibits the functional reading. For [91b] as well as for [91c] to be true, it must be the case that for most ghost appearances the totality of the students on campus at the time were aware of the danger. In other words, the force of the bare plural does not directly depend on the adverb of quantification.

Let us consider more closely how that interpretation of [91b] could come about. [92] contains two possible logical form representations for [91b]. In [92a] quantification is symmetric over situations of a ghost's appearance and students. In [92b] quantification is asymmetric over student-containing situations of a ghost's appearance.

[92]   a. $Usually_{s,x}(s: \exists_y(ghost(y)\ \&\ be\text{-}on\text{-}campus(y,s))\ \&$
       $student(x)\ \&\ be\text{-}on\text{-}campus(x,s),$
       $be\text{-}aware\text{-}of\text{-}the\text{-}danger(x))$
   b. $Usually_s(s: \exists_{y,x}(ghost(y)\ \&\ be\text{-}on\text{-}campus(y,s)\ \&$
       $student(x)\ \&\ be\text{-}on\text{-}campus(x,s)),$
       $be\text{-}aware\text{-}of\text{-}the\text{-}danger(x))$

The bare plural has universal force regardless of whether we take quantification to be symmetric or asymmetric. Both representations in [92], if unsupplemented by any further conditions on the individuation of the elements in the domain of quantification, give us the wrong reading for [91b]. For [92a] to be true it must be the case that for most ghost appearances most students on campus at the time were aware of the danger. For [92b] to be true it must be the case that for most ghost appearances in which there were students on campus those students were aware of the danger associated with that appearance. Now whether this gives us the right reading or not depends on how we individuate the situations in the domain of quantification.[25] For each situation we must select the maximal collection of students on campus during the occasion of a ghost's appearance. This is necessary, or otherwise we would run into the proportion problem. For example, assume there have been four appearances of a ghost, and during one of them the number of students happened to exceed the number of students of the other three occasions taken together. If in the former case the students were aware of the danger while in all the others they were not, then, unless we allow for maximality, [91b] should be true, whereas intuitively [91b] is judged to be false. Imposing maximality on the student variable in [92a] will also give us the right reading for [91b]. Thus, if we analyze the bare plural in [91b] as bound by the adverb of quantification, then the corresponding variable must pick out the maximal collection of students in each case. Alternatively, if we quantify asymmetrically over situations, the situations must be individuated in such a way as to contain the maximal collection of students in each case.

Interaction with nominal quantifiers, which always quantify asymmetrically, shows that the problem is not simply in needing asymmetric quantification (and therefore not quantifying directly over students) but that the whole restriction is affected by the maximality effect of the functional reading, as in [93]. Of course, this is also shown by the fact that [92b] is not an adequate logical form representation for [91b] even though it involves asymmetric quantification.

[93] Most of the ghosts that students liked were good-spirited.

In order for [93] to be true most of the ghosts that were liked by the totality of the students must have been good-spirited.

The cases of the proportion problem that are familiar from the literature arise when a quantificational sentence is analyzed as involving symmetric quantification over (at least) two variables when in fact it should be analyzed as involving asymmetric quantification over one variable with the second variable being dependent on it. In the case described here, the maximality forced by the functional reading of the bare plural constrains the individuation of the entities in the domain of quantification; if it is not taken into account the proportion problem arises. What is common to both cases is that the individuation of the entities in the domain of quantification is the wrong one; what determines the right individuation is, however, different in each case. A complex array of factors is responsible in choosing between symmetric and asymmetric quantification, as various authors[26] have argued. For the case involving the functional reading, as I will argue in the next section, the reason is simple: individuation is determined by a presupposition of existence associated with the functional reading. In that respect, the behavior of bare plurals with the functional reading under quantification parallels that of definites under quantification.

In particular, the maximality effect of the bare plural on the domain of quantification parallels cases in which the presence of a donkey pronoun analyzed as a definite description affects the individuation of situations/eventualities in the domain of quantification of a given adverb of quantification, as argued by Kadmon (1987, 1990) and Heim (1990). In those analyses, definite descriptions are associated with existence and uniqueness/maximality presuppositions.

Similar effects to those in [91] can be seen in cases where the restriction of the adverb of quantification is provided directly by a conditional clause rather than by previous discourse and the indefinite or definite NP is in the main clause, as in [94], or in cases in which the restriction is provided partly by previous discourse and partly by an overt conditional clause which contains the indefinite or definite NP, as in [95].

[94]   a. Usually, when a ghost haunted this campus, students were aware of the danger.
       b. Usually, when a ghost haunted this campus, the students were aware of the danger.
       c. Usually, when a ghost haunted this campus, several students were aware of the danger.

[95]   a. A ghost has occasionally haunted this campus.
       b. Usually, when students were aware of the danger, the ghost was satisfied.
       c. Usually, when the students were aware of the danger, the ghost was satisfied.
       d. Usually, when a student was aware of the danger, the ghost was satisfied.

The indefinite *several students* in [94c] and the bare plural *students* in [94a] differ in force, and even in the effect they have on the domain of quantification. *Several students* has a nuclear scope existential reading and it does not affect in any way the individuation of the elements in the domain of quantification, which consists of the temporally maximal occasions of a ghost's haunting the campus. The bare plural has the dependent functional reading and it does affect the domain of quantification, which consists of those occasions of a ghost's haunting the campus in which there are students present on campus and such that they are distinct if the student body changes. The definite has a dependent reading and affects the domain of quantification in the same way. For example, assume a situation in which there have been 7 distinct occasions of a ghost's haunting the campus; during 4 of them no student was in attendance while during the other 3 students were in attendance and during 2 of those latter all students were aware of the danger. Now in such a situation [94c] can be judged false whereas [94a] and [94b] are judged true, the reason being that the irrelevant occasions in which no student was in attendance are part of the occasions in the domain of quantification for [94c] but not for [94a] or [94b].[27] This is not to deny that [94c] may be interpreted with respect to a more contextually restricted domain of quantification, one which excludes the irrelevant occasions. The point is that the occasions in which there are no students in attendance simply do not count for [94a] and [94b] but they may count for [94c].[28]

In [95b] and [95c] quantification is taken to be over situations and maximal collections of students. In [95d] quantification is either symmetric over situations and students or asymmetric over situations in which at least one student was aware of the danger.

With stage-level predicates, where the bare plural is ambiguous between the existential and the functional reading, the maximality effect arises only when the bare plural is not interpreted existentially, as seen in [96] and [97]. Therefore, the maximality effect is not due to the plurality of the bare plural.

[96] a. Ghosts have occasionally haunted this campus.
      b. Students usually protested in the main square.

[97] a. This proposal has been made many times in the last 100 years.
      b. Proponents usually tried to defend it on the basis of... while opponents usually tried to attack it from within.

The functional reading within a quantified context preserves the crucial properties of the functional reading in an unembedded context. The presence of contextual restrictions is necessary: whether students other than those associated with the relevant campus are aware of the danger or not is irrelevant to the truth of [91b], [93], [94a], [95b] and [96b]. Moreover, all of these sentences have an implication of existence of individuals satisfying the descriptive content of the bare plural relative to the bound situation variable. Again, this point can be made more convincingly with a bare plural with additional descriptive content, as in [98b].

[98] a. Ghosts have occasionally haunted this campus.
      b. Students with police connections were usually aware of the danger.

[98b] implies that there were students with police connections during all the occasions of a ghost's appearance. It must be said that there is a certain variability of judgment with respect to this implication: rather than a universal implication, the sentence may have a (weaker) existential implication, namely that in some such situations there were students with police connections.[29] I will come back to this issue in the next section.

2.6.2 Quantificational and Modal Subordination

In the examples we considered in section 2.6.1, the choice of students varied with respect to the choice of situation but the element associated with the NP providing the contextual restrictions did not. Now, if the NP providing the contextual restrictions for the bare plural is itself within a quantified environment, the bare plural requires quantificational subordination. Consider [99].

[99] a. Every campus I visited had a ghost.
b. Students were aware of the danger.
Students loved the ghost.
c. The students were aware of the danger.
The students loved the ghost.
d. Some students were aware of the danger.

The bare plural in [99b], like the definite in [99c], has to be relativized to the choice of campus.[30] The indefinite in [99d], on the other hand, does not need to be subordinated *even when it is contextually restricted*. Therefore, it is not the contextual restrictions alone that trigger the subordination. The need for quantificational subordination must be related to the *requirement* of the bare plural for contextual restrictions.

If the NP providing the contextual restrictions for the bare plural is in a modal environment, modal subordination is necessary for the functional reading to arise. Consider first [100] and take the indefinite *a campus* to have narrow scope with respect to the epistemic possibility modal *may*.

[100] a. A ghost may be haunting a campus.
b. Students must be careful.
c. Students are careful.

The modal base of the modal in [100b] is relativized to those worlds in which a ghost is haunting a campus and the students are taken to be those associated with *that* campus. [100c], where there is no modal subordination, is taken to be a descriptive generalization about students in general.

Consider next [101] and [102], where the NP providing the contextual restrictions for the bare plural is within the scope of (and bound by) a deontic necessity operator.

[101] a. A campus should have its own ghost.
b. Students must be careful (in that case).
c. The students must be careful (in that case).
d. Students are careful (in that case).
e. The students are careful (in that case).
f. Some students are careful/Some students are careful in that case.

[102] a. It is required that the discussion about a proposal of this kind finish within a day.
b. Proponents usually/must make a case for it quickly.

[101b], [101c], [101d] and [101e] are interpreted as if they had an implicit antecedent of the form *if a campus has a ghost*. [101b] and [101c] contain on overt modal which is interpreted deontically with a modal base determined by the [101a]. [101d] and [101e] must be interpreted as descriptive generic generalizations,[31] where the worlds in the modal base are those in which what is commanded in [101a] holds and the choice of students is relativized to the choice of campus with a ghost. Similarly [102b] is interpreted as if it had an implicit antecedent of the form *if a proposal of this kind is under discussion*. Moreover, the choice of students is relativized to the choice of campus ([101b], [101d]), the choice of proponents to the choice of proposal ([102b]). We can say that in those cases we have both quantificational and modal subordination. Interestingly, [101f] can be making a claim about actual students.

Apart from underscoring the necessity for contextual restrictions, the modal subordination facts are also significant in that they show that any attempt to explain away the functional reading as a by-product of a generic generalization involving a realistic modal base and trivial ordering source is bound to fail.

The generalization from the quantificational and modal subordination facts is that if the licensing NP is under the scope of an operator, the bare plural too must be under the scope of that operator or an operator subordinated to the former. In other words, the bare plural does not scope independently of its licensing NP. This requirement is similar to that of anaphoric definites with indefinite antecedents in the scope of an operator, as originally observed by Lakoff (1972) and Karttunen (1976). Quantificational and modal subordination have become prominent in recent discussions of anaphora. Their more general characteristic, of which anaphora is a special case, is that quantificational and modal structures provide a context which serves as the context for subsequent sentences in the discourse. The problem of discourse subordination, in its most general form, is characterized as follows by Roberts (1989:717): "in each case, the second sentence in a discourse is interpreted as involving an operator (explicit or implicit) whose force is relativized so that it ranges only over the type of situation given in part by the first sentence." There are at least three different sources for discourse subordination:[32] (a) domain selection, (b) presupposition triggering elements, (c) elements interpreted as bound variables.[33] At first sight, we might be inclined to add necessary contextual restrictions to the list but as I will argue later this can be subsumed under (b). Therefore, (b) is involved in inducing quantificational subordination in [99]; (a) and (b) in inducing modal subordination in [101], [102].[34]

To sum up section 2.6, the bare plural on its functional reading exhibits scopal interactions which have an effect on the individuation of the domain of quantification parallelling that of definite descriptions. The need for contextual restrictions induces quantificational and modal subordination. Subordination should be taken here to be a descriptive term and need not imply subordination at some level of representation. The real issue is that the interpretation of some expression is relativized to elements in the previous discourse not in the usual way; for instance, it may be relativized to elements whose scope it is ostensibly not under.

2.7 The Presupposition of Existence

When not in the scope of a modal operator, a bare plural on its functional reading entails existence in the actual world, without, however, having existential force or asserting existence.[35] When the bare plural is in the scope of a modal operator, what is entailed depends on the previous discourse. For example, [100b] on its own does not entail that there are students but in the context of [100a] it implies a conditional statement of existence: if there is a campus that is haunted by a ghost, then that campus has students. Where does the information about existence come from? And why is it sensitive to the discourse preceding the sentence containing the bare plural?

In this section I will argue that the functional reading presupposes existence. To say that the bare plural presupposes existence means that entities satisfying the descriptive content of the NP plus the additional contextual restrictions are presupposed to exist (in the actual world, when in the outermost context). In section 2.7.1 I argue that simple sentences of the sort we have been looking at possess this presupposition. In sections 2.7.2 and 2.7.3 I concentrate on more indirect effects that the presence of the presupposition has. One effect is that the presupposition exhibits the usual presupposition projection effects (section 2.7.2). If an adverb of quantification is present, its domain of quantification is restricted as a result of the projection of this presupposition. If the bare plural is in the antecedent of a conditional then the previous context must entail the existence of the entities satisfying its descriptive content. A different and more striking effect is that bare plurals can co-occur with a special class of quantificational adverbials, which I call contextually restricted proportional adverbs of quantification. I will argue that these adverbials presuppose the existence of the group forming the basis of the proportion and quantify over the atomic parts of this group (section 2.7.3).

In the discussion below I take presupposition failure to result in a truth-value gap and infelicity. This implies both a semantic and a pragmatic notion of presupposition. How these two notions can be unified will be discussed in chapter 4.

2.7.1 Simple Cases

That students with police connections exist is a precondition for a felicitous utterance of [103b] and of the negated [103c] and must be taken for granted by the discourse participants.[36]

[103]   a. In 1985 there was a ghost haunting the campus.
       b. Students with police connections were aware of the danger.
       c. Students with police connections were not aware of the danger.

Moreover, the contextual restrictions are part of what is presupposed. What must be taken for granted for a felicitous utterance of [103b] or [103c] is not simply the existence of students with police connections at large, nor the existence of such students on some campus or other, but the existence of students on the campus that makes [103a] true.

The fact that the implicit contextual restrictions are part of the presuppositional content of the bare plural explains why the information contributed by them is not cancellable, as shown by [65] and [68], and why they are only provided by prior discourse, as shown by [68] and [70].

That a presupposition is present can be established most convincingly by cases in which it is known by the discourse participants that the relevant entities do not exist, as in [104]. Both [104b] and [104c] are infelicitous and cannot be assigned a truth-value since it is the case that Yale has no fraternities and therefore there are no fraternity members associated with it.

[104]   a. A ghost was haunting Yale last year.
        b. # Fraternity members were aware of the danger.
        c. # Fraternity members were not aware of the danger.

If [104b] were false, then [104c] would be true, contrary to intuitions.[37]

An interesting contrast arises when the bare plural is construed with a stage-level predicate, which allows for either the existential reading or the functional reading. If the bare plural in [105] is interpreted existentially, the existence of opponents of the proposal is asserted and certainly it need not be taken for granted for a felicitous utterance of [105]. If, on the other hand, the bare plural receives the functional reading, the existence of opponents of the proposal must be taken for granted for a felicitous utterance of [105].

[105] The proposal will be voted on tomorrow. Opponents demanded that the vote be shifted to next week.

A more indirect effect of the presence of the existential presupposition arises with *if any* elliptical clauses. Bare plurals pattern with definites and contrast with other indefinites in supporting the hedge of an *if any* elliptical clause, as seen in [106].

[106]   a. There is a ghost haunting the campus.
        b. The students with police connections, if there are any, must be aware of the danger.
        c. Students with police connections, if there are any, must be aware of the danger.
        d. #Some students with police connections, if there are any, must be aware of the danger.

If any elliptical clauses, in my view, do not simply cancel a conversational implicature; if they did, the existential implication associated with definite descriptions would simply be a conversational implicature. Rather, they make the assertion of the sentence they are associated with conditional. In fact, they might signal that the speaker takes himself to be in two conversational backgrounds, one in which the existence of the relevant individuals is taken for granted and one in which it is not. *If any* elliptical clauses then can be seen as relativizing the assertion to the former conversational background; elements presupposing existence would be felicitous with respect to such a conversational background, whereas elements asserting existence would not.

2.7.2 Projection of the Existential Presupposition

If an existential presupposition is present, then, given the way presuppositions are inherited by complex constructions containing the presupposition-triggering element, it should surface, in a modified form, when the bare plural is within the scope of an operator. Indeed, the existential presupposition associated with the functional reading has the following consequences. (a) It affects the domain of quantification of a given operator, (b) it shows the usual presupposition projection effects in one-case (epistemic) conditionals, (c) it shows presupposition projection effects and affects the domain of quantification in multi-case conditionals.

In section 2.6 I discussed how the functional reading of the bare plural restricts the domain of quantification and affects the individuation of the elements in it. We also saw there that a sentence like [98b], repeated here as [107b], implies that for each occasion there were students with police connections, or that for some occasions there were students with police connections.

[107] a. Ghosts have occasionally haunted this campus.
       b. Students with police connections were usually aware of the danger.

In fact, it is the existential presupposition associated with the bare plural inherited by the whole sentence that is responsible for these effects. The instability in the judgements of what the actual presupposition is is manifested in all cases where a presupposition-triggering element is within the scope of an operator.

Let me give some background on the standard views on the effects of presuppositions on domain selection and on presupposition projection in conditionals. It is an interesting and unsettled issue what the presuppositions of sentences with various operators are, or in other words, what the filtering effects of various operators are.[38] It is an unsettled issue because intuitions oscillate between a strong (universal) version and a weak (existential) version and because existing theories are equipped to handle one but need special provisions to handle the other one.[39]

Let us consider the problem with respect to nominal quantifiers and the existential presupposition associated with a definite description. What the filtered presupposition is depends, among other things, on whether the presupposition-triggering element is in the restriction or the nuclear scope of the quantificational structure and on what the force of the quantifier is. In [108a] and [110a] the presupposition-triggering element is in the nuclear scope; in [109a] it is in the restriction. The universal presupposition of [108a], [109a] and [110a] is the proposition expressed by [108b], [109b] and [110b], respectively; the existential presupposition is the proposition expressed by [108c], [109c] and [110c], respectively.

[108] a. Every nation cherishes its king.
b. Every nation has a king.
c. Some nations have a king.

[109] a. Every nation that cherishes its king will be rewarded.
b. Every nation has a king.
c. Some nations have a king.

[110] a. No nation cherishes its king.
b. Every nation has a king.
c. Some nations have a king.

The theory of Heim (1983) without provisions for local accommodation predicts universal presuppositions for [108a], [109a] and [110a]. Universal presuppositions can be gotten by global accommodation, existential presuppositions by local accommodation. Cooper (1983) predicts universal presuppositions too. Beaver (1992) opts for the weakest presuppositions possible with the caveat that anything stronger could be built on top. For universal quantifiers he basically builds the presupposition as domain restriction (see the inference table on p. 12).[40] Similarly, in van der Sandt's (1992) analysis presuppositions end up as domain restrictions, as a consequence of intermediate accommodation.

Intuitions are indeed unstable. However, the degree of variability and the factors affecting the choice in particular instances do not vary with respect to the existential presupposition of definite descriptions and the existential presupposition of bare plurals with the functional reading. For example, some speakers find that in cases of restricted quantification where the proposition corresponding to the universal presupposition is definitely not within the common ground (because, for instance, it is presupposed to be false) a definite description in the nuclear scope is deviant, as in [111a]. Those speakers also find that a bare plural in a similar environment cannot have the functional reading, as in [111b].

[111]   a. Every European Community country adores its royal family.
        b. Always, if a ghost is present on an Ivy league campus, fraternity members are aware of the danger.

The inheritance properties of presuppositions in conditionals work out in the following way: the presuppositions of the antecedent are inherited by the whole conditional, the presuppositions of the consequent are filtered through in the form of a conditional whose antecedent consists of the content of the antecedent of the main conditional and whose consequent consists of the presuppositions of the consequent of the main conditional. Another way of formulating the inherited presuppositions of the consequent is the following: those presuppositions that are not entailed by the antecedent are inherited by the whole conditional, those that are entailed are filtered through in the form of the conditional mentioned above. The presupposition (in their terms, conventional implicature) that Karttunen & Peters (1979) associate with 'if ϕ then ψ' is ϕ^i & $(\phi^e \rightarrow \psi^i)$.[41] Subsequent works have accepted these as the presuppositions that ought to be associated with conditionals although they have tried to derive the projection properties on the basis of the interpretation of conditionals.

Let us then see that the existential presupposition associated with the bare plural on its special reading is projected in the usual fashion in conditional sentences. Indeed, [112a] and [112b] as a whole presuppose that there are students with connections in the police department.

[112]   a. If students with connections in the police department are aware of the danger, they will inform the rest.
        b. If a ghost is present on the campus, students with police connections are aware of the danger.

The conditionals in [112] are meant to be one-case conditionals, so the implicit necessity operator (assumed to be present in all conditionals) is to be taken as having an epistemic modal base. Also in [112b] the presupposition is inherited by the whole conditional under the assumption that the presence of a ghost makes no difference one way or another with respect to the existence of students with police connections on the campus. More accurately, we might say, following Karttunen & Peters (1979), that the actual presupposition is 'If a ghost is present on the campus, there are students with police connections' and that we get the stronger 'there are students with police connections' by pragmatic strengthening.

In the consequent of a conditional, the singular indefinite may have an existential reading, as in [113b].[42] In the same position, the bare plural in [113a] has only the universal reading. Moreover, [113a], but not [113b], seems to presuppose that there are students with connections in the police department in all campuses in the domain of quantification. This must be because of the existential presupposition associated with the bare plural.

[113] a. Usually, if a ghost is present on a campus, students with police connections are aware of the danger.
       b. Usually, if a ghost is present on a campus, a student with police connections is aware of the danger.

Assuming the account of presupposition projection proposed by Karttunen (1974) and Heim (1983), the existential presupposition associated with the bare plural in the consequent of [113a] affects the domain of quantification as follows. Given that the presuppositions of the consequent must be entailed by the previous context augmented by the local context provided by the antecedent, the existence of students with connections in the police department must be entailed for each choice of campus and occasion of a ghost's presence on a campus. Therefore, we assume either (*i*) that there aren't any campuses without students with police connections (universal presupposition and global accommodation), or (*ii*) if such campuses exist, that they are not in the domain of quantification (existential presupposition and local accommodation resulting in domain restriction).

2.7.3 Functional Reading with Adverbs of Quantity

Bare plurals on their functional reading can co-occur with a class of adverbs which are sensitive to certain properties of the NP's they co-occur with. The bare plural in [114b], like the plural definite in [114c] and in contrast to the singular indefinite in [114d] or the plural indefinite in [114e], is compatible with such adverbs. The only possible reading for [114d] and [114e] is one in which *mostly/for the most part* are predicate modifiers, arguably within the AdjP headed by *aware*, specifying the degree of awareness.[43] Such a

reading is excluded in [114f] because of the syntactic position of
the adverb, hence [114f] is unconditionally unacceptable. [114g],
on the other hand, is acceptable, indicating that the quantificational reading for the adverb arises with the bare plural as well as
with the plural definite.

[114] a. There is a ghost haunting the campus.
       b. Students are mostly/for the most part aware of the
          danger.
       c. The students are mostly/for the most part aware of the
          danger.
       d. (#) A student is mostly/for the most part aware of the
          danger.
       e. (#) Some students are mostly/for the most part aware
          of the danger.
       f. # A student/Some students for the most part is/are
          aware of the danger.
       g. The students/Students for the most part are aware of
          the danger.

The pattern in [114] shows that the distribution of *mostly/for the
most part* is not just a matter of the plurality of the accompanying
NP, nor a matter of definiteness alone.

The ambiguity of the bare plural with a stage-level predicate
disappears once such an adverb is added to the sentence. The bare
plural in the variation of [73] given in [115] has only the functional
reading.

[115] Although the odds still seem to favor Senate approval of
      Thomas, opponents, for the most part, redoubled their
      effort and tried to delay a floor vote on confirmation.

This is telling evidence that what the adverbs are sensitive to is
the interpretation of the NP they co-occur with rather than some
superficial co-occurrence restrictions. Let us call this the *selective
affinity* of bare plurals for such adverbs.

Similarly, in contexts mirroring those of [71], [72] and [58]
where contextual restrictions for the bare plural are impossible,
the functional reading does not arise and the adverbs of quantity are not interepreted as contextually restricted. Consider [116],
where only the non-contextually restricted reading is possible for
the bare plural—giving rise to falsity, in fact—while the contextually restricted reading is present for the definite NP.

[116] a. There are lions and tigers in this cage.

b. The lions are mostly/for the most part old.
c. Lions are mostly/for the most part old.
(no contextually restricted reading)

Once again, the constraints on the selection of appropriate contextual restrictions are not determined entirely by the quantifier but depend crucially on the indefinite NP.

That bare plurals can co-occur with such adverbs is an observation that was independently made by Lahiri (1991), who named the adverbs 'adverbs of quantity.' In fact, it was in this connection that he noted that bare plurals may have a universal reading with stage-level predicates. He also noted that the existential reading for the bare plural excludes an adverb of quantity. The examples he offered are given in [117].[44]

[117]   a. Experts, for the most part, are blaming government policies for the recession.
b. ?Men, for the most part, are playing in the garden right now.

Lahiri attributed the co-occurrence of bare plurals with adverbs of quantity to their denoting kinds, relying on Carlson's analysis of bare plurals as kind-denoting terms, and as such having part structures.[45] He attributed the selective affinity of bare plurals for such adverbs to the stage-level predicate's introducing existential quantification which binds the variable corresponding to the bare plural and thus leaving no variable for the adverb to bind. As will become clear below, I will adopt one of the central insights of Lahiri's analysis of adverbs of quantity but will provide an alternative account of what determines the class of NP's these adverbials can co-occur with, an account which does not rely on an analysis of bare plurals as kind-denoting.

First let us see that these adverbs are special in certain respects. Within the Lewis-Kamp-Heim tradition, the paradigm case of quantificational adverbials are adverbs of quantification like *always, usually, never*, which are analyzed as quantifying over the parameters of evaluations, i.e., worlds and assignment functions. Adverbs of quantification bind variables corresponding to indefinites and when they have a modal dimension they give rise to the generic reading of indefinites. However, there is evidence coming form different sources that the class of quantificational adverbials is not homogeneous. Evidence from indirect questions, free relatives and correlatives indicates that the class is split between the standard adverbs of quantification and another class into which adverbs of quantity fall (see Berman (1990), Srivastav (1991), Lahiri (1991), Ginzburg (1992)). On the basis of different considerations, Löbner (1985, 1987) drew the distinction between *referential* and *generic* quantification. Standard adverbs of quantification participate in generic quantification. Adverbs of quantity participate in referential quantification. According to Löbner, referential quantification, as in [118a], requires a specified, contextually restricted domain of quantification, which is provided by a definite NP. Generic quantification, as in [118b], operates with an open set as the domain of quantification.

[118] a. The apples were for the most part sour.
       b. Apples are usually sour.

Kroch (1979) observed that adverbs of quantity can quantify over times (or occasions), that they can always co-occur with a definite NP on the relevant reading, and that they cannot co-occur with a quantificational NP on the relevant reading. For instance, he observed that [119a] is ambiguous between the reading of [119c] and the reading of [119d], while [119b] only has the reading of [119c].

[119] a. My friends are generally/mostly/by and large honest.
       b. All of my friends are generally/mostly/by and large honest.
       c. All my friends are honest on most occasions.
       d. Most of my friends are honest.

The various discussions in the literature in which the contextually restricted proportional adverbs of quantification have figured share the concern with the following two issues. One of the issues is whether they are monadic VP operators or dyadic sentential adverbs of quantification. The other issue is the proper characterization of the NP's they co-occur with.

Kroch (1979), whose interest was to distinguish plural definites from universally quantified plurals, assumed that adverbs of quantity quantify over elements of the set denoted by the plural subject NP and claimed that they cannot co-occur with universally quantified NP's because there can be no double quantification over the same variable.

Dowty & Brody (1984) focused on floated quantifiers like *all, each, both* but one can extend their proposal to the adverbs under discussion. They analyzed floated quantifiers as monadic VP operators which, given their semantics, must be hosted by NP's that denote principal filters. That is, the host NP's must denote families of sets having a non-empty intersection. This includes both definites and quantificational NP's with a universal determiner.[46]

De Swart (1991) takes the quantifying adverbials of referential quantification to be floating quantifiers, and following Dowty & Brodie (1984), analyzes them as relations between sets of individuals: the set that is the generator of the definite NP and the set that is the set of individuals denoted by the VP.

If we follow the Dowty & Brody/de Swart line of analysis, we would have to analyze the bare plural exactly like a definite in order to account for its co-occurrence with these adverbials. In other words, we would have to assume that a bare plural is ambiguous between an indefinite and a definite interpretation. I take the negative contextual sensitivity facts to argue strongly against this ambiguity analysis. A bare plural is never anaphoric even on its functional reading. Somehow the analysis of the functional reading should not give up the assumption that the bare plural is indefinite.

Lahiri (1991) proposed that adverbs of quantity involve amount quantification and analyzed them as denoting a function from ordered pairs of individuals to truth values. The individuals that are the arguments of such a quantifier are the maximal elements of which a given predicate is true and the quantifier compares their extent, that is it compares the number of their atomic subparts. Lahiri suggested that bare plurals are compatible with adverbs of quantity because they are kind-denoting and kinds have a part structure. Now if this is the reason why bare plurals can co-occur with these adverbs this cannot explain their co-occurrence with bare plurals on the functional reading. As I have been assuming so far, the kind interpretation is not responsible for the functional reading.

But even assuming that bare plurals are kind-denoting (and disregarding the functional reading for the moment), it is not obvious why stage-level predicates disallow the co-occurrence of bare plurals with adverbs of quantity. For example, why aren't the arguments of the quantifier *for the most part* in [120a] construed as in [120b]?

[120] a. #Boys, for the most part, are playing.
       b. *Most($\sigma x[boys(x)]$, $\sigma x[boys(x)$ & $\exists y(R(y, boys))(play(y))]$

According to the interpretation that [120b] receives, the number of boys that have stage-level realizations that are playing is greater than the number of boys that do not. Moreover, whatever the means by which that interpretation is excluded they should be such that they do not exclude it for pronouns anaphoric on a bare plural. As can be seen in [121], such a pronoun can co-occur with an adverb of quantity. [121b] is interpreted according to [121c].

[121] a. Boys are hiding in the garden.
 b. For the most part, they are playing.
 c. $Most(\sigma x[boys(x)\ \&\ \exists y(R(y, boys))(hide\text{-}in\text{-}the\text{-}garden(y)], \sigma x[boys(x)\ \&\ \exists y(R(y, boys))(play(y))]$

Therefore, as far as I can see, Lahiri's proposal cannot account for the co-occurrence of bare plurals with adverbs of quantity only if they do not have an existential reading (which of course includes the functional reading).

I will follow Lahiri (1991) and Ginzburg (1992) in assuming that these adverbials quantify over atomic elements. I will, moreover, assume that they presuppose the existence of the element whose atomic parts they quantify over. It is exactly the presupposition of existence that makes both definites and bare plurals on their functional reading acceptable with these adverbials. Adverbs of quantity seem to be the adverbial equivalent of partitives.

2.8 Overview

Contrary to what any current theory of indefinites would lead us to expect, bare plurals exhibit a reading which is closer to the interpretation of definite NP's. This is most immediately obvious with stage-level predicates in episodic sentences, where the force of the bare plural is universal rather than the expected existential. But it is also the case with individual-level predicates, although in that case one has to provide subtler arguments and more extensive evidence to distinguish the functional from the generic reading.

A successful analysis of the functional reading would have to account for the following facts:

- the universal force of the bare plural
- the non-generic interpretation of the bare plural
- its occurrence with both individual-level and stage-level predicates
- the scope dependence of the bare plural on its licensing NP
- its apparent synonymy with the definite in certain contexts
- its positive and negative contextual sensitivity
- its implication of existence

- its sole association with bare plurals rather than all indefinites
- its effect on the domain of quantification of adverbs of quantification
- the existential presupposition
- its acceptability with adverbs of quantity

An obvious possibility is to say that the bare plural is ambiguous between an indefinite and a definite interpretation. After all, it appears to be in free variation with the corresponding definite in certain contexts, such as in [55], [62] and [63], and the quantificational contexts of [91], [94], [95]; it co-occurs with an adverb of quantity on a non-generic reading, as in [114]; and it has an existential presupposition, the hallmark of definiteness. Moreover, unlike an indefinite, it is context-sensitive in that it must be contextually restricted in a particular way. But ultimately, we do not want the bare plural to be a disguised definite description of the usual sort. [71d], [72], [58c], [58d], [58e], [86] and [116c] constitute evidence against such an approach. On the disguised definite description analysis the question is what kinds of antecedents are acceptable for the bare plural on its definite interpretation. The generalization emerging from the facts considered is that the bare plural never has an anaphoric reading, that is a definite reading where an explicit antecedent is available. In other words, putting together the evidence from the presupposition facts and the negative contextual sensitivity facts, we arrive at the following generalization: a bare plural on its functional reading is associated with an existential presupposition but it is *never* anaphoric. In fact, it is in free variation with the corresponding definite only when the definite is neither anaphoric nor deictic. At this point, I use 'anaphoric' and 'deictic' as descriptive terms. The DRT and Heimian analysis of definiteness makes all definites anaphoric semantically, even those that one would not characterize this way on descriptive grounds. The descriptive term for those definites that appear to have something in common with bare plurals on their functional reading is 'associative' (see Hawkins (1978), to whom the term is due, and Heim (1982), who discusses how associative definites can be assimilated to anaphoric definites).[47] I will come back to this issue in the next chapter.

The real challenge, therefore, is to account for the properties of the functional reading while maintaining that the bare plural is an indefinite NP. The question then is in what way the theory of indefiniteness should be revised in order to accommodate the functional reading. Let us take the facts listed below to be the central facts of the functional reading; already in my presentation of the full array of facts connected to the functional reading I have indicated how they all revolve around these three basic facts and how once we have an account of these three the rest would follow.

- the universal force
- the positive and negative contextual sensitivity
- the existential presupposition

In what follows I will explore two alternatives: one, in keeping with standard assumptions about indefiniteness, attributes the functional reading to an operator; the other, in a more radical move, attributes the functional reading to the fact that a certain felicity condition of familiarity is associated with bare plurals. In the next section I propose an operator analysis, which starts from the universal force of the bare plural and accounts for the other properties by certain additional assumptions. In the next chapter I will propose an account that rests on a more fine-grained conception of novelty and gives a formulation of it that will allow for the functional reading and for a characterization of the difference among indefinites.

3. AN OPERATOR ANALYSIS

Is the functional reading of the bare plural due to the presence of an implicit operator? Are there cases in which apparent non-generic quantification is a trivial case of generic quantification? In this section I will consider how these two questions can be answered affirmatively. I will develop an operator analysis, which starts with the assumption that nothing special needs to be said about the bare plural and no revision in the analysis of indefiniteness is required. The bare plural is not ambiguous and its range of readings depends on whether it is under the scope of an operator or not, and, if it is, on the type of operator it is under. Rather, it is our analysis of genericity and of adverbial operators that needs some revision.

An operator analysis of the functional reading will assimilate it to the universal reading of indefinites arising in quantificational contexts. This is of course the most obvious way of accounting for the functional reading as it would stay in line with all other assumptions about indefinites. According to this view, what appears to be an unbound indefinite is in fact bound by an operator with the caveat that this operator has somewhat different properties from those standardly associated with adverbial operators. However, as I show, the operator analysis fails to provide a unified account of the functional reading, and it leaves unanswered the central question how the positive and negative context sensitivity and the presence of a presupposition of existence relate to each other and to the reading. In the process of developing the operator analysis, I also relate the functional reading to other proposals about indefinites that have been made recently within the overall program of analyzing indefinites as non-quantificational, and show that none of them is sufficiently equipped to account for the functional reading either.

In what follows, I will adopt the theory of indefinites presented in Heim (1982, ch. II), with which I will assume basic familiarity. The analysis of indefinites will have to be supplemented with additional assumptions, as will become clear, but not in ways that require a major departure from the central assumptions of that theory.

3.1 Degenerate Genericity

We have established that the functional reading cannot be explained away simply as an entailment or as an implicature of a realistic generic generalization reading. Instead it must be recognized as the actual interpretation of the bare plural. We can reconcile this fact with the standard view that connects the universal force of a bare plural with genericity if we assume that the functional reading is a special case of the generic reading when we have *degenerate genericity*.

Degenerate genericity is the case when a generic generalization reduces to an actual generalization. It will arise from an extensionalized generic operator, that is a generic operator with a trivial modal dimension. In that case, quantification is vacuous with respect to worlds and the generic operator ends up quantifying only over individuals. Once we have a degenerate generic generalization, the corresponding actual generalization is not just entailed by the generic generalization but it concides with it. Degenerate genericity should thus be an option allowed by the semantics, with the pragmatics determining when it arises.

Degenerate genericity parallels the case in which conditionals, which are essentially modal,[48] reduce to material implication. This happens when the implicit necessity operator is associated with a totally realistic modal base and trivial ordering source (see Kratzer

(1981) and Heim (1982)). A totally realistic modal base is one which contains only the actual world, i.e., for all w_1, $w_1 \in R_w$ iff $w_1 = w$. A trivial ordering source is such that $w_1 \leq w$ for any w_1 and w. As the modal dimension of a generic operator is context-dependent, the apparent ambiguity of the bare plural is due to the choice of modal dimension for the implicit generic operator: the generic reading results when the operator has a non-trivial modal dimension, the functional reading results when the operator has a trivial modal dimension.

On that analysis then, our initial example [55b] involves the familiar quantificational structure in [122a] and ends up expressing an actual generalization because the modal base is determined by the context to be totally realistic and the ordering source is determined to be trivial. In addition to a trivial modal dimension, we must assume that restrictions supplied by the context of utterance further limit the domain of quantification to the relevant entities. For example, for [55b] the context restricts the domain of quantification to the set of students on the campus in 1985 during the ghost's appearance.

[122] a. $G'_x(student(x) \& CR(x), be\text{-}aware(x,\phi))$

b. In order for the text of which [122a] is part to be felicitous relative to some context c, c must provide a modal base and an ordering source for the operator G'.

c. Relative to a totally realistic modal base and a trivial ordering source, $\langle g, w \rangle$ satisfies [122a] iff for every $\langle g', w \rangle$, where $g' \stackrel{x}{\approx} g$, if $\langle g', w \rangle$ satisfies $student(x)$ & $CR(x)$, then it also satisfies $be\text{-}aware(x, \phi)$.

In the representation [122a], G' stands for the extensionalized generic operator. CR is a cover designation for the additional contextual restrictions, such as being on campus in 1985. We can follow Cooper (1979) and assume that it is a property-denoting metavariable containing only variables and parentheses. In this case, it can be instantiated as $P(y)(x)$ (ignoring the temporal restriction), where P is given the value *be-on* by the context and y is the variable corresponding to the NP *the campus* in [55a].[49] For the sake of concreteness, I have given the predicate *be aware* a formula as its second argument. I am assuming that *be aware of* is a propositional attitude predicate even when subcategorizing for an NP but I will not be concerned here with how the content of ϕ is construed.[50] The interpretation of [122a] as given in [122c] coincides with that of a sentnce with an extensional universal quantifier.

On this approach then, nothing special needs to be said about the operator itself or the bare plural. Any special properties the operator might have ought to follow from the modal dimension it is associated with and therefore, ultimately, from certain facts about the context of utterance which determines this kind of modal dimension. In what follows, I will consider to what extent this can be maintained and at what cost.

Since, as argued in section 2.4, in exactly the same contexts that give rise to the functional reading of a bare plural, a singular indefinite has only an existential reading, the generic operator with a trivial modal dimension must somehow be prohibited from binding a variable contributed by a singular indefinite. The kind of explanation forced upon us is to say that the singular indefinite does not have the functional reading because it is incompatible with an extensionalized generic operator. We can assume that the singular indefinite selects for the kinds of modal bases and ordering sources that the operator can be construed with in such a way that it excludes the combination of a totally realistic modal base and a trivial ordering source.

An analysis capitalizing on the context dependency of the modal dimension of the implicit generic operator raises the question of whether we can in general use the implicit generic operator with a totally realistic modal base and trivial ordering source to make non-generic universal statements. For instance, why isn't the modal dimension determined to be trivial in cases like [58], [61], or [86]? We have to spell out the conditions under which a trivial modal dimension is selected and their connection to contextual restrictions.

Does the trivial modal dimension correlate with the interpretation of the predicate? One could claim that the modal dimension of the generic operator is trivial because of the particularity of the propositional argument of the predicate, which has the result that the predicate is not interpreted like a characteristic property. How likely would it be that students in general, actual and potential, would be aware of this *particular* fact or the actual danger? However, the particularity in the nature of the predicate is, in general, neither a sufficient nor a necessary condition for the functional reading to arise.

That it is not sufficient is shown by examples with an overt generic operator, such as the one associated with *used to*. In [123b] and [124b], as opposed to [123a], the argument of the predicate is a particular fact. However, the operator is not restricted so as to pick out only the actual students on campus or a contextually restricted set of financial wizards, hence the oddness of [123b] and [124b]. In [124c], on the other hand, where the bare plural exhibits the functional reading, and, according to the proposal under discussion, there must be an implicit operator involved, the operator is construed with a trivial modal dimension and quantifies over a contextually restricted set of financial wizards.

[123] a. Students used to be aware of that kind of danger.
       b. ??Students used to be aware of the danger.

[124] a. Yesterday's fundraising event solved the university's fiscal problems.
       b. ??Financial wizards used to be aware that yesterday's fundraising event would bring in millions of dollars.
       c. Financial wizards were aware that yesterday's fundraising event would bring in millions of dollars.

The conclusion from this contrast is that not all generic operators can be construed with a trivial modal dimension, even when the interpretation of the predicate requires it.

That the particularity of the predicate is not necessary is shown by examples where the predicate is given an argument which does not constitute a particular fact. In that case the functional reading of the bare plural is still present, although the modal dimension need not be trivial. For example, [125a] is ambiguous between a truly generic and a functional reading (in the right context), and the bare plural in [125b] has the same reading as in [55b].

[125] a. Students are aware of dangers of this kind.
       b. Students were aware of dangers of this kind.

This shows that the functional reading is compatible with an interpretation of the predicate as a characteristic property,[51] and that therefore a generic operator is not determined to be degenerate simply on the basis of the interpretation of the predicate, when no other construal of genericity would do.[52] Therefore, it remains an open question exactly under what conditions the modal dimension is determined to be trivial.

3.2 Degenerate Genericity and the Functional Reading

Since I identify the functional reading with degenerate genericity, I must reexamine the properties distinguishing between the functional and generic readings discussed in section 2.2.1, namely: the presence of contextual restrictions, the implication of existence, and the scopal interaction between the bare plural and overt operators. The presence of contextual restrictions must be connected to the nature of the modal dimension. The implication of existence is easily seen to be compatible with the view of the functional reading as a case of degenerate genericity. Scopal interaction poses some more challenging problems for the operator analysis, which lie not with the fact that genericity is degenerate but rather with the presence of an operator. These three points will be taken up in order.

3.2.1 Implicit Contextual Restrictions

Why are implicit contextual restrictions associated with the functional reading if generic operators do not accept implicit contextual restrictions? Can we relate the presence of contextual restrictions to the triviality of the modal dimension? In order to understand why degenerate generic generalizations can be contextually restricted, we must first understand why regular generic generalizations cannot be contextually restricted.

I will suggest an account of the impossibility of contextual restrictions with generic operators in this section. This account relates the possibility of contextual restrictions in the case of the functional reading with the triviality of the modal dimension of the operator. However, it is independent of the analysis of the functional reading as involving an operator, so it can stand even if the degenerate genericity account of the functional reading is ultimately to be dismissed.

There are two alternative ways of construing contextual restrictions that I will concentrate on here. Up to now, I have construed them as additional conditions on the descriptive content of the NP, as exemplified in [122a]. But we can also relativize the interpretation of the NP to a contextually given set of entities, following proposals by Westerståhl (1984), van Deemter (1991, 1992) and Enç (1991), among others. The first alternative is consistent with the usual assumption, shared by the Kamp–Heim analysis of NP's, that the range of variable assignments is the entire set of individuals in the model (the entire universe of discourse). What is given contextually is a salient property and the value of the variable associated with an NP must satisfy the condition given by that property. The second alternative relativizes the interpretation of an NP to a contextually given set of entities, which amounts to "interpreting conditions relative to shifting domains," as van Deemter puts it. What is given contextually is a set of elements that the value of the variable must be in.[53] This contextually given set of entities is the value of a *restricting set variable* and the interpretation of an NP is relativized to such a restricting set.[54]

Let us examine the second alternative more closely. Van Deemter, working within a DRT framework, proposes that restricting set variables be treated as discourse referents and that conditions corresponding to NP's be relativized to any accessible set-denoting discourse referent; he thus brings in DRT's apparatus for anaphoric relations to account for how restricting set variables get their values.[55] Enç (1991) makes a similar proposal except that she takes relativization to a restricting set to be a presuppositional requirement of certain indefinite NP's. In what follows, I will focus on relativized conditions corresponding to non-quantificational NP's.

A non-quantificational NP may bear a pair of referential indices, $NP_{\langle i,j \rangle}$. Its corresponding condition, symbolized as $CN^{x_j}(x_i)$, is interpreted according to [126] (assuming CN to comprise a simple predicate; $[\ ]$ is the basic interpretation function relative to a model assigning to each n-place predicate a function from possible worlds to D^n).[56]

[126] $\langle f, w \rangle$ satisfies $CN^{x_j}(x_i)$ iff
$f(x_i) \in [CN]_w \cap f(x_j)$ if x_i is individual-denoting and
$f(x_i) \subseteq [CN]_w \cap f(x_j)$ if x_i is set-denoting.

The restricting set variable x_j of any condition $CN^{x_j}(x_i)$ must satisfy the condition in [127].[57]

[127] If some operator binds x_j, then there must be some condition $\alpha(x_j)$ to the left of $CN^{x_j}(x_i)$ bound by that operator.

Given [127], x_j is either anaphorically related to some NP or it is a free variable given a value by the context of utterance. This generalizes the traditional conception of restricting sets as determined by the context of utterance (see, e.g., Westerståhl (1984), Neale (1990) and references therein).

Van Deemter and Enç motivate their account of indefinites relativized to a restricting set by noting that indefinites may have a partially anaphoric interpretation. This is illustrated by [128], where *a boy* in [128b] can be understood as designating an element within the set of children that came in. In other words, [128b] in the context of [128a] may have an interpretation equivalent to that of [128c].

[128] a. Some children came in.
b. A boy destroyed the piano.
c. A boy among the children that came in destroyed the piano.

According to van Deemter and Enç, this reading arises when the indefinite NP *a boy* is relativized to the discourse referent associated with the NP *some children*, as in [129]. According to [126], the value of the discourse referent x_i corresponding to the relativized indefinite *a boy* must be such that it is a boy and one of the children that came in.

[129] $\exists_{x_j, x_i}(children(x_j)$ & $came\text{-}in(x_j)$ & $boy^{x_j}(x_i)$ & $destroyed\text{-}the\text{-}piano(x_i))$

In order for [129a] to be true in a world relative to some context, there must exist in that world a set of children that came in and a boy amongst them that destroyed the piano. Note that the discourse referents x_i and x_j are at the same level of the logical form's structure, the top-level, and as a consequence they are both bound by the same operator, text-level existential closure. So a relativized indefinite NP bound by text-level existential closure asserts the existence of an individual within a set of individuals, already established by the discourse or contextually salient, such that the individual satisfies the descriptive content of the NP. By the time we evaluate $boy^{x_j}(x_i)$, any pair $\langle f, w \rangle$ that satisfies it is one whose f has a fixed assignment for x_j and which satisfies any conditions associated with x_j that have been encountered so far.

This way of construing contextual restrictions can help us make sense of the absence of contextual restrictions in generic sentences. The problem reduces to why we cannot have generic quantification over a domain determined by a fixed restricting set. Ideally, we should not have to stipulate that indefinites within the scope of an adverbial operator cannot be relativized to a restricting set because we want a bare plural in the scope of a degenerate generic operator to be so relativized. Rather, the answer must lie in the properties of relativized conditions within a modal operator.

A relativized NP bound by a generic operator is within the scope of a modal operator but its restricting set need not be. Let us then consider what happens when a modal operator intervenes between the discourse referent that functions as a restricting set and its corresponding conditions, on the one hand, and the relativized NP, on the other.[58] [130] exemplifies such a case for an indefinite within the scope of an epistemic modal.

[130]   a. Some schoolboys wanted a moped.
        b. A smart boy may/could have rented one.
        c. It may/could be the case that there was a smart boy among the schoolboys who wanted a moped that rented one.

Since [130b] has an interpretation equivalent to that of [130c], the indefinite *a smart boy* in [130b] can have narrow scope relative to the modal and it can, at the same time, be understood as relativized to the set of schoolboys verifying [130a]. [131] gives the logical form representation corresponding to the discourse of [130a] and [130b], on this reading.

[131] $\exists_{x_j}(schoolboys(x_j)$ & $want\text{-}moped(x_j)$ &
      $May\ (\exists_{x_i}(smart\text{-}boy^{x_j}(x_i)$ & $rent\text{-}moped(x_i))))$

[131] is true in a world w relative to context c iff there is a set of schoolboys that wanted a moped and there is an epistemically accessible world w' from w such that there is a smart boy among the set of smart boys who rented one. As can be seen, the NP providing the restricting set and the indefinite NP relativized to that set have corresponding conditions at different levels of the logical form's structure. However, since an epistemically accessible world is among the worlds determined by the common ground, it is also a world in which there is a set of schoolchildren that wanted a moped. In other words, all conditions placed on x_j prior to its appearance inside the scope of the modal operator are satisfied by any $\langle f, w \rangle$ satisfying the formula inside the scope of *May*.

When this situation obtains, the value of the discourse referent corresponding to the restricting set (e.g., the discourse referent x_j in [131]) will be preserved for those occurrences of it within the scope of the modal since assignments to top-level discourse referents are preserved throughout the discourse. The question is whether the information associated with that discourse referent—for instance, the properties the discourse has established for it up to that point—should be preserved in the alternative worlds we are considering. This is not logically necessary but it is reasonable to assume that language imposes the requirement that such information should be preserved. In other words, if an indefinite within a modal operator is to be understood as relativized to a discourse referent outside the modal operator, the modal dimension of the operator should be such that it preserves the facts associated with that discourse referent that have been established up to that point in the discourse. The condition in [132] achieves this effect.

[132] *Consistency Condition for Restricting Sets:*
If $\langle f, w \rangle$ satisfies $\text{CN}^{x_j}(x_i)$ and $\alpha(x_j)$ is some condition having $\text{CN}^{x_j}(x_i)$ in its scope, then $\langle f, w \rangle$ must also satisfy $\alpha(x_j)$; if x_j is a free variable, then $f(x_j)$ (the referent of x_j) must have in w any properties under which it is salient in the context of utterance.

What is the status of the Consistency Condition? According to [126], in order for $\langle f, w \rangle$ to satisfy $\text{CN}^{x_j}(x_i)$ it does not have to satisfy any of the relevant conditions $\alpha(x_j)$. The properties of the restricting set are not part of the assertive content of an NP relativized to that set, nor should they be part of the presuppositional content of the NP. The Consistency Condition is a necessary requirement for truth: in order for ϕ to be true/false in w relative to context c, the consistency condition must be obeyed for every occurrence of a relativized condition within ϕ. The Consistency Condition is thus neither a necessary condition for satisfaction of a relativized condition nor a condition regulating the values supplied by the context for the modal dimension of a modal operator. If it were, then it would not help account for the inability of generic sentences to accept contextual restrictions. For instance, in the case of a generic operator with a circumstantial modal base and an indefinite in its restriction relativized to a restricting set variable bound by text-level existential closure, generic quantification would end up being over worlds that are both epistemically and circumstantially accessible, and therefore a contextually restricted interpretation for the indefinite would be acceptable.

It is easy to see that in extensional contexts, such as that of [129a], the Consistency Condition will always be satisfied. However, in cases where x_j and $\alpha(x_j)$ are at the top-level but $\text{CN}^{x_j}(x)$ is within the scope of some modal operator, as is the case with [131], whether the Consistency Condition is satisfied depends on the modal base of the operator. The Consistency Condition is satisfied for [131] because epistemic modal bases preserve all the facts that have been established up to that point in the discourse.[59]

The cases discussed in the literature in which contextual restrictions are prohibited are exactly those where the modal dimension of the generic operator is not such that satisfaction of the

Consistency Condition is guaranteed. For example, [133a], as discussed in section 2.2.1, lacks a reading equivalent to that of [133b].

[133] a. There are lions in the cage. Lions (always) have a mane.
       b. There are lions in the cage. Lions in this cage (always) have a mane.

The contrast between [133a] and [133b] shows that the domain of individuals an adverbial operator quantifies over cannot be implicitly restricted so as to pick out only lions that are in the cage.

The two alternatives of construing contextual restrictions outlined above can be clearly contrasted in this case. [134a] gives the logical form for [133a] under the assumption that implicit contextual restrictions are additional conditions on the descriptive content of the NP. P is a free property denoting variable which in this context can be instantiated as *be-in-the-cage*.

[134] a. $\exists_{x_j}(lions(x_j)\ \&\ in\text{-}the\text{-}cage(x_j)\ \&\ G_{x_i}(lion(x_i)\ \&\ P(x_i), has\text{-}mane(x_i)))$
       b. If something is a lion and it is in the cage, then it has a mane.

The interpretation of the formula headed by G in [134a] can be intuitively stated as in [134b], and it is indeed unclear why that interpretation is excluded for the second sentence in [133a], since the property of being in the cage is a contextually salient property and could thus be assigned as the value of the property variable P.

[135a] gives the logical form for [133a] under the assumption that implicit contextual restrictions are due to the relativization of the NP to a contextually given set of entities.

[135] a. $\exists_{x_j}(lions(x_j)\ \&\ be\text{-}in\text{-}the\text{-}cage(x_j)\ \&\ G_{x_i}(lion^{x_j}(x_i), has\text{-}mane(x_i)))$.
       b. If something is a lion and it is one of the lions that are actually now in the cage, then it has a mane.

The interpretation of the formula headed by G in [135a] can be intuitively stated as in [135b] and it is now clear that this interpretation is excluded on the basis of the the Consistency Condition since nothing guarantees that if some $\langle f, w \rangle$ satisfies $lion^{x_j}(x_i)$ it would also satisfy $be\text{-}in\text{-}the\text{-}cage(x_j)$. The modal base consists of worlds in which facts having to do with inherent properties of lions hold. It is certainly not a such fact about lions that the group of lions actually in the cage is in the cage. But if w' is a world which agrees with the actual world w with respect to inherent characteristics of lions, then it is not a world where it is guaranteed to hold that the individual $f(x_j)$ has the property of being in the cage in w'.

This kind of approach implies that the impossibility of relativizing an indefinite in the scope of an adverbial operator is not across-the-board. Specifically, relativization of such an indefinite to a restricting set and, therefore, the presence of implicit contextual restrictions are predicted to be possible in the following two cases.

The first case is that of an indefinite in a conditional with a realistic modal base determined by the common ground. The prediction is borne out, as can be seen in [136], where [136b] in the context of [136a] can have an interpretation equivalent to that of [136c].

[136] a. There are lions and tigers in the cage.
b. If a lion roars, I immediately feed it/I know it is intelligent.
c. If a lion among the lions in the cage roars, I immediately feed it/I know it is intelligent.

Note that indefinites in conditionals appear do not in general accept contextual restrictions: [137b] in the context of [137a] has an interpretation equivalent to that of [137c] or [137d] only if the modal base is determined by the common ground.

[137] a. There are lions and tigers in the cage.
b. If a lion roars a lot, it is intelligent.
c. If a lion in the cage roars a lot, it is intelligent.
d. If a lion among the lions in the cage roars a lot, it is intelligent.

The modal base of generic operators is not determined by the common ground, whereas that of conditionals may be determined by the common ground.

The second case involves modal subordination: if the restricting set variable is itself within the scope of a generic operator and its value can therefore vary with the choice of world, generic statements with implicit contextual restrictions should be possible. This prediction is also borne out. For instance, in the context of [138a], [138b] should have a reading equivalent to that of [138c]. ([138a]–[138c] can be either descriptive or normative generalizations.)

[138] a. People in this university dress formally.
b. Professors wear a tie.

c. Professors in this university wear a tie.

Indeed, *professors* can be relativized to the set of individuals associated with this university and therefore [138b] can be interpreted as implicitly contextually restricted.[60]

Finally, once the modal dimension of the generic operator becomes trivial, the Consistency Condition is satisfied, as always in extensional contexts, and therefore the domain of the degenerate generic operator can be relativized to a contextually given set of entities.

For an example like [55b], we can take the contextually given set of entities to be the set of individuals associated with the campus in 1985. So we would have to revise [122] to [139].

[139] $G'_{x_i}(student^{x_j}(x_i), be\text{-}aware(x_i, \phi))$

Since the value of x_j is the set of individuals associated with the campus, [55b] is contextually restricted to the set of students on campus. How do accessible antecedents of this kind become available in cases where they do not correspond to any material that is overtly uttered? x_j was accommodated on the basis [55a] and of general background information that connects campuses to a set of individuals associated with them.

While this might be a plausible explanation for why there *can* be contextual restrictions, it does not answer the question of why there *must* be contextual restrictions. We cannot derive the fact that there are contextual restrictions from the fact that we have a totally realistic modal base since the generalization expressed could have been about *all* actual students, not just those on campus in 1985. At most, the relativization to the set of individuals on campus is predicted to be only one of possible readings. I will return to the question of the positive contextual sensitivity in section 3.4.

3.2.2 Implication of Existence

A bare plural bound by an operator with a trivial modal dimension implies existence in the actual world. The implication of existence associated with the functional reading can thus be seen as arising in the same way as the implication of existence associated with (extensional) nominal quantifiers. (Let us disregard for the moment whether this is a conversational implicature, an entailment, a presupposition, or a conventional implicature.) Minimally, both [140b] and [140c] imply existence because otherwise [140b] and [140c] would be trivially true.

[140] a. In 1985 there was a ghost haunting the campus.
b. Every student with police connections was aware of the danger.
c. Students with police connections were aware of the danger.

Intersentential anaphora is possible for the same reason except that since an operator is present we cannot say that the indefinite (or the operator binding the indefinite) binds the pronoun directly. Rather the case is the same as anaphora to a group with (distributive) quantificational NP's. Various theories have different means of accounting for the anaphora in this case either as E-type anaphora (Chierchia 1992), as involving direct binding with abstraction giving rise to the antecedent (Kamp & Reyle 1993), or as involving direct binding given the semantics of operators (Poesio 1991) or the semantics of NP's in general (van Deemter 1992).

3.2.3 Scopal Interaction

In section 2.2.1 we saw that the bare plural is interpreted independently of various overt operators since it neither inherits their force nor does it need to be in their scope in order to have universal force. To account for the facts that led to this conclusion we must assume that the implicit extensionalized operator that is responsible for the functional reading is not a default type of operator and that therefore it is present along with an overt operator, the two scoping freely with respect to each other. Moreover, the implicit extensionalized operator is the only extensionalized adverbial operator that can directly bind indefinites, hence in the examples of section 2.2.1 involving adverbial operators the functional reading is the only possible reading for the bare plural.

I noted in sections 2.2.1 and 2.6.1 that, quite apart from the functional reading, an indefinite by itself cannot be interpreted as being in the restriction of an adverb of quantification quantifying over a contextually given set of situations.[61] For example, [62b], where the adverb of quantification *usually* is construed with a trivial modal dimension, does not have a reading equivalent to that of [62d]. Similarly, [91d] and [91b] lack the reading in which the singular indefinite or the bare plural is in the restriction of the adverb of quantification *usually*. This can be seen as the result of the following two conditions: extensionalized adverbs of quantification bind directly only situations, and restrictive indefinites[62] cannot be in the existentially closed subordinated domain in the restriction of an adverb of quantification.[63] These two conditions conspire to exclude restrictive indefinites from the restriction of an extensionalized adverb of quantification. Regardless of whether there is a deeper (and less stipulative) explanation for what is going on, the end result is that we must exclude one way or another the case in which an indefinite is bound by an extensionalized adverb of quantification.

Given that the bare plural in [62b] cannot be in the restriction of the overt adverb of quantification, if the implicit operator were not available, [62b] would be uninterpretable. The reading that [62b] gets requires that the implicit operator have wide scope relative to the overt adverb of quantification. The corresponding logical form representation is given in [141]. The domain of quantification of the adverb of quantification *usually* is supplied contextually.

[141] $G'_x(student^Y(x),$ Usually$_s(s: \exists_y(ghost(y)$ & $be\text{-}on\text{-}campus(y,s))), be\text{-}aware(x,\phi))$

Note that the logical form for [62b] in [141] can be derived only if we allow the bare plural NP to move out of its S-Structure [Spec, IP] position and adjoin to IP at LF. The assumption that indefinite NP's bound by an operator remain in [Spec, IP] at LF is explicitly made in Diesing (1992b). If upheld, it would exclude the functional reading in this case since it predicts that in case of stacked operators, the operator that the indefinite subject NP is bound by correlates strictly with the relative scope of the operators, namely, it can only be bound by the operator with the narrowest scope.[64] So this in turn predicts that the functional reading arises only when the G' operator is the lowest operator, i.e., the one having narrower scope (which of course includes its being the sole operator).

Like adverbs of quantification, overt generic operators such as *typically* or *normally* cannot be stripped of their modal dimension unless they bind situations,[65] and for that reason they cannot be reduced to degenerate generic operators binding the bare plural. Therefore, [63b] is infelicitous because it involves vacuous quantification; the implicit operator takes wide scope but then there is no variable for the overt operators to bind. Generic operators, unlike modals, cannot simply quantify over worlds. [63b] becomes felicitous if the overt operators are taken to quantify over situations, parallelling the case with overt adverbs of quantification.

The implicit generic operator is thus special in that, unlike overt adverbs of quantification and generic operators, it *can* directly bind variables corresponding to indefinite NP's when stripped of its modal dimension. I must emphasize that the assumptions about extensionalized adverbs of quantification and overt generic operators are independent of the functional reading and we need to make them in any case since the relevant readings must be excluded. Of course, if it were not for the possibility of the functional reading, sentences like [62b] would be uninterpretable.

With modals things turn out to be more complicated. Given that in the functional reading we need to quantify over actual students, it would seem that the implicit operator takes wide scope relative to the modal. However, the distributivity of the operator and its relative scope with the modal lead to problems. Consider [142], with an epistemic reading for the modal.[66]

[142] a. A ghost is haunting the campus.
       b. Students may/could be aware of the danger.

The reading of [142b] can be stated as '(as far as we know) there is the possibility that each actual student (on campus) is aware of the danger.' [143] contains two possible logical forms for [142b], each corresponding to the relative scope of the two operators.[67] I make no reference to contextual restrictions at this point but see below.

[143] a. $G'_x(student(x), May\ (be\text{-}aware(x,\phi)))$
       b. $May\ (G'_x(student(x), be\text{-}aware(x,\phi)))$

Neither of the two representations captures the reading stated above, nor does [142b] have the readings corresponding to the logical forms in [143].

The reading corresponding to the logical form in [143a], where the extensionalized generic operator has wide scope, can be informally stated as follows: 'for each actual student there is the possibility that he or she is aware of the danger.' In slightly more technical terms, wide scope for the operator associated with the bare plural results in the choice of possible world being dependent on the choice of student. According to this interpretation, the discourse comprised of [142a] and [142b] would be true even if there is no epistemically accessible possible world in which all the students (on campus) are aware of the danger as long as for each student there is an epistemically accessible possible world in which that student is aware of the danger.

The reading corresponding to the logical form in [143b], where the extensionalized generic operator has narrow scope, under standard assumptions about the interpretation of NP's in the scope of modals, can be informally stated as follows: 'there is the possibility that each student (relative to that possibility) is aware of the danger.' In slightly more technical terms, wide scope for the modal results in not having quantification over actual students. According to this interpretation, [142b] would be true if there is an epistemically accessible possible world in which every student in that world is aware of the danger.

The reading of [142b] requires that we have wide scope for the modal while ensuring that we end up with a generalization over actual students. The bare plural must be within the scope of the operator G' so as to inherit its force but the condition associated with the nominal description must be evaluated relative to the actual world and not the active world of evaluation, which is determined by the modal *may*. In fact, as we will see later, this is only part of the whole story. More generally, the evaluation of the bare plural must be relative to the world with respect to which the licensing NP for the bare plural is evaluated, as for example, in the case when the licensing NP itself is within the scope of a modal operator such as the cases of modal subordination discussed in section 2.6.2. The active world of evaluation is determined by the modal because of the trivial modal dimension of G': a trivial modal dimension for an operator within the scope of another modal operator amounts to preserving the world of evaluation currently active under the previous operator.

Under standard assumptions about the interpretation of NP's in intensional contexts, the descriptive content of the NP is evaluated relative to the parameters (e.g., world and time) supplied by that context. But as a growing body of work shows (Enç (1986), Cresswell (1990), Farkas (1993)),[68] the descriptive content of an NP can be evaluated relative to parameters that are independent of those determined by the intensional context. For example, according to standard assumptions, [144a] should have two readings depending on the relative scope of the NP and the modal. If the NP has scope over the modal, the choice of possible world depends on the choice of candidate and, therefore, that reading does not require the existence of a possible world in which all candidates win. If the NP has narrow scope with respect to the modal, then there must be a possible world such that every candidate in that world wins.

[144]   a. Every candidate may win.
        b. It is possible/might be the case that every candidate wins.

But, as the works cited above argue, [144a] has a third reading according to which there is a possibility that every actual candidate wins. The modal takes scope over the distributive *every* but the descriptive content of the NP is evaluated relative to the actual world. Moreover, as Farkas (1993) argues, while a quantificational NP and a modal can scope freely with respect to each other if and only if they are clausemates, the evaluation of the descriptive content of such an NP can always be relative to the actual world. So [144b], in which the NP can only have narrow scope with respect to the modal, shares two readings with [144a].

Farkas (1993) proposes that NP's are optionally indexed with a *modal address*, that is a world or a set of worlds relative to which the descriptive content of the NP is evaluated. [145] gives the interpretation for a condition with a modal address. Conditions without a modal address are interpreted in the usual way, that is an NP would be evaluated relative to the parameters provided by its context.

[145] a. $\langle f, w \rangle$ satisfies $CN(x)_{w_0}$, where w_0 is a possible world, iff $f(x) \in [CN]_{w_0}$.
b. $\langle f, w \rangle$ satisfies $CN(x)_{W_0}$, where W_0 is a set of possible worlds, iff for all $w_0 \in W_0$, $\langle f, w_0 \rangle$ satisfies $CN(x)$.

According to this proposal, the third interpretation of [144a] can be had by indexing the NP to the actual world, as in [146a].

[146] a. *May (every$_x$ (candidate$(x)_{w_0}$, win(x)))*
b. $\langle f, w \rangle$ satisfies [146a] iff there is some w' epistemically accessible to w such that $\langle f, w' \rangle$ satisfies *every (candidate$(x)_{w_0}$, come(x))*, i.e., iff for every $\langle f', w' \rangle$ such that $f \leq f'_x$ and $f'(x) \in [candidate]_{w_0}$ it is also the case that $f'(x) \in [win]_{w'}$.

We can then exploit this proposal to account for the interpretation of [142b], by giving the bare plural a separate modal address, that is indexing it to the actual world.

[147] a. *May (G'_x(student$^Y(x)_{w_0}$, be-aware(x,ϕ)))*
b. [147a] is true with respect to w and g and relative to an epistemic modal base R_w iff there is $w' \in R_w$ such that for every $g'=g_x$ *student(x) & $x \in Y$* is true with respect to w and g' *be-aware(x,ϕ)* is true with respect to w' and g'.

The reading of [142b] comes about with the modal taking wide scope. G', having a trivial modal dimension, preserves the world of evaluation currently active under the previous operator but indexing to the actual world of the condition corresponding to the bare plural results in the description's being evaluated at the actual world.

However, allowing an NP bound by G' to have its own modal address distinguishes the G' operator from other adverbial operators, including the regular implicit generic operator. Generic statements have the requirement that the domain of individuals the generic operator quantifies over should not be fixed independently of the choice of worlds.[69] We can state this more formally in the form of the felicity condition in [148].

[148] For any selection index x, G_x (ϕ,ψ), where ϕ contains a condition of the form $CN(x)$, is felicitous only if for all f and w: if $\langle f, w \rangle$ satisfies ϕ, then $f(x) \in [\![CN]\!]_w$.

[148] is of course commonplace under standard assumptions about the interpretation of NP's in intensional contexts. Once, however, we have the option of indexing an NP to a separate modal address, [148] does some real work by ensuring that this does not happen in the case of generic quantification. For example, we cannot have regular (non-degenerate) generic quantification over just a set of actual entities: [149a] does not have a reading equivalent to [149b].[70]

[149] a. Pomegranates have a crowned end.
b. If something is actually a pomegranate, then it has a crowned end.

[149a] is stronger than [149b] in that it does not suffice that in the alternative worlds we are considering anything that happens to be a pomegranate in the actual world has a crowned end in some maximally ideal (with respect to certain stereotypical facts about pomegranates) alternative world. Rather [149a] requires that for each alternative worlds we are considering everything that is a pomegranate in that world has a crowned end in some maximally ideal world.[71]

Although we have been able to account for the reading that [142b] has, we have not excluded the readings that [142b] lacks, namely those represented by [143a] and [143b]. An adverbial operator may even have scope over a modal if it c-commands it at surface structure, as in [150b].

[150] a. John may have always cheated on his exams.
b. John always may have cheated on his exam(s).

This will remain an open problem for the operator analysis. We must keep in mind, however, that wide scope for the bare plural relative to the modal is a problem only if an operator, such as G', is associated with it.

3.3 Stage-Level Predicates

The empirical generalization that has formed the basis of all exisiting accounts of bare plurals, namely that a bare plural with a stage-level predicate has only an existential reading, was based on data that precluded degenerate genericity. The approach pursued here entails that degenerate genericity will also be present with stage-level predicates and will result in a universal reading for the bare plural but no generalization over episodes.

However, this analysis has an unwelcome consequence: it predicts that a bare plural on its functional reading with a stage-level predicate should give rise only to distributive predications. The existential reading of the bare plural and the functional reading are predicted to differ crucially in this respect: whereas the former is compatible with either a collective or distributive predication, the latter is predicted to be compatible only with a distributive predication. However, both [73] and [151], which contains a purely collective predicate, can be interpreted as involving a single group and a single eventuality.[72]

[151] Proponents met to discuss their strategy.

The problem might be more general since there are sentences with a distributive nominal quantifier and a group-level predicate, such as [152].

[152] Most students met to discuss their fears.

Whatever mechanism we might invoke for accounting for [152][73] the problem for distributive quantificational NP's is more general while the same problems do not arise for the bare plural. For instance, when the G' operator takes wide scope relative to an adverb of quantification and the main predicate is a group-denoting predicate, as in [153], then we run into trouble because of the distributivity of the operator.

[153]   a. Students usually met to discuss their fears.
        b. The students usually met to discuss their fears.
        c. ??Most students usually met to discuss their fears.

The operator analysis also leads to problems for particular theories that try to account for the correlation between the possibility of an existential reading for the bare plural and the type of predicate involved, such as that of Kratzer (1995) and Diesing (1990, 1992a). I have chosen this theory for two reasons. One is that it is the most articulated theory at present, apart from Carlson's, on the interaction between indefiniteness and the individual/stage-level contrast. The other reason is that, as far as I can see, degenerate genericity is the only resource such a theory would have for the functional reading. The relevant assumptions of that theory are as follows: (*i*) if a predicate is stage-level, it contains a Davidsonian variable, (*ii*) the presence of a Davidsonian variable affects the D-Structure position of the subject NP,[74] (*iii*) VP's are existentially closed. These assumptions interact to give us the following consequences: (a) in order for an indefinite not to receive an existential reading it would have to move out of the VP, which is the domain of existential closure, (b) subject NP's of stage-level predicates originate within the VP and move to [Spec,IP] at S-Structure.[75]

The difference in interpretation of indefinite subjects of stage-level predicates depends on whether the NP is reconstructed into its original position ([154a]) or is interpreted in situ in its [Spec, IP] position ([154b]).

More concretely, [154a] is the logical form representation for [73] corresponding to the structure in which the indefinite subject has remained within the domain of existential closure. [154b] is the logical form representations corresponding to the structure in which the indefinite subject has moved outside the domain of existential closure.[76]

[154]   a. *before-now(l)* & $\exists_X(proponents(X)$ & *demand-vote(X,l))*
(distributive and collective reading)
b. $(G'_x\colon proponent(x)$ & *before-now(l))* $\exists_{l'}(l' \leq l$ & *demand-vote(x,l'))*
(distributive reading)

In [154a] the indefinite is caught by existential closure hence the existential interpretation of the bare plural. Depending on the predicate, we can have a distributive or a collective reading. An indefinite outside the domain of existential closure must be bound by an operator; otherwise, the sentence would be uninterpretable since indefinites cannot be given a value by the context of use. Therefore, once an operator is present, there is quantification over the atomic individuals comprising the group and a collective interpretation for the predicate is excluded, contrary to fact.[77]

3.4 Positive Contextual Sensitivity

A bare plural on its functional reading is crucially context-sensitive and, contrary to other indefinites, the contextual restrictions are picked rigidly. As shown in section 2.7, the implicit contextual restrictions are non-cancellable and are presupposed. Therefore, the context-sensitivity of the bare plural on its functional reading cannot be a matter of pragmatics alone.

In general, the context-sensitivity of NP's can be taken to be either a pragmatic phenomenon or a combination of a semantic and a pragmatic phenomenon. The purely pragmatic approach capitalizes on the distinction between sentence meaning and speaker meaning; the implicit contextual restrictions are incorporated only into speaker meaning. The semantic approaches all have in common that they supplement the interpretation of the description in some way but differ on how this is done. The semantics makes available some parameter which the role of pragmatics is to help fix.

In section 3.2.1 I considered two such alternatives as applied to indefinite NP's: one alternative supplements the description with some property variable whose value is supplied by the context of use, the other relativizes the interpretation to a context set. I also argued that there are good reasons, independently of the functional reading, for building the context-sensitivity into the interpretation. This way we can, among other things, make sense of the possibility or impossibility of implicit contextual restrictions in generic sentences. Having established that contextual restrictions must be given a semantic account in any case, let us now consider the question of why the functional reading *requires* contextual restrictions.

Recent theories of indefinites have emphasized the context-sensitivity of indefinites and have proposed ways to capture it. As discussed in section 3.2.1, according to some proposals, context-sensitivity can be construed as relativization to a restricting set, which is taken to be an accessible discourse referent. As Enç (1991:11) puts it, "it is reasonable to assume that *contextually relevant* means 'already in the domain of discourse,' since the contextually relevant individuals are those that have been previously established in the discourse." Relativization of an indefinite NP to an accessible discourse referent implies that the NP presupposes the existence of a discourse referent to which its own discourse referent is related and results in the NP having a 'subsectional anaphoric interpretation' or a relational interpretation. Enç argues, moreover, that partial anaphoricity is a basic dimension along which indefinites may vary and that certain indefinites may have the partially anaphoric interpretation obligatorily.[78]

Now the fact that indefinites may appear as partially anaphoric is not problematic for the standard theories of indefinites. In the analysis of indefinites as existentially quantified nothing prevents the entities in a model that verify, e.g., [128b] to be in the set of entities that verify [128a]. Similarly, the quantifier-free analysis of indefinites capitalizes on the fact that the mapping from discourse referents to entities in the model is not necessarily one to one or subject to a total disjointness requirement. Enç's argument derives its force from the fact that partial anaphoricity is not a free option for all indefinites and that it is the only available interpretation for others. She argues that Turkish has indefinites of these two kinds and, extrapolating from there, claims that English indefinites are ambiguous in this respect. On one interpretation they have the felicity condition requiring the presence of an accessible antecedent functioning as a restricting set, on the other interpretation they do not.

Enç (1991) moreover hypothesizes that all quantifiers are specific, meaning that all quantifiers require the existence of an accessible discourse referent which would, in conjunction with the restriction of the quantifier, determine the domain of quantification. Enç considers only nominal quantifiers but perhaps adverbial quantifiers are similar. So we can exploit this proposal in order to account for the necessary presence of contextual restrictions with the functional reading and we can use the apparatus of the restricting sets introduced in section 3.2.1 to account for this requirement.

Ideally then, the positive contextual sensitivity of the bare plural in its functional reading would not even have to be stipulated but would follow from the fact that it is in the scope of an (extensional) quantifier and that quantifiers require the relativization to a restricting set. Otherwise, we would have to stipulate that on its functional reading a bare plural is a specific indefinite. However, the analysis of specificity/non-specificity of indefinites is not without problems and the claim that quantifiers require the relativization to a restricting set is simply incorrect. Let us consider these two points in turn.

As formulated by Enç, the analysis makes non-specific indefinites have an interpretation that is not in complementary distribution with that of specific indefinites but rather one that *subsumes* the interpretation of specific indefinites. Let us see why. Specific indefinites translate as in [155a] and non-specific indefinites as in [155c]. Let us now assume that the two types of indefinites occur in precisely the same context, i.e., they occur in a logical form preceded by identical material, as in [155b] and [155d] ($\phi[Y]$ stands for some formula containing conditions on Y).

[155] a. specific indefinite: $\alpha^Y(x)$
b. $\exists_{Y,x}(\phi[Y]\ \&\ \alpha^Y(x))$
c. non-specific indefinite: $\alpha(x)$
d. $\exists_{Y,x}(\phi[Y]\ \&\ \alpha(x))$

Although a pair $\langle f, w \rangle$ satisfying $\alpha^Y(x)$ is such that $f(x) \in/\subseteq f(Y)$ (by definition), a pair $\langle f, w \rangle$ satisfying $\alpha(x)$ is *not* required to be such that $f(x) \notin/\not\subseteq f(Y)$. The discussion of particular Turkish examples in Enç (1991) implies that non-accusative marked indefinites have a strictly non-subsectional interpretation. The only way the strictly non-subsectional interpretation can be achieved is through a pragmatic implicature.

If the interpretation of non-specific indefinites subsumes that of specific indefinites, there is no reason to posit ambiguity in English. And if the facts of Turkish demand that non-specific indefinites be analyzed as requiring a strictly non-subsectional interpretation, then a more elaborate analysis is needed, where the discourse referent corresponding to such an indefinite is asserted to not be in, or not be a subset of, any other already introduced discourse referent.[79] Assuming the facts of Turkish turn out to be that way, is there a reason to believe that we must posit ambiguity in English that would mirror the ambiguity of Turkish? I think the answer is no. Consider the discourse in [156].

[156] a. Several boys danced on the piano.
b. A silly boy danced on the fireplace.
c. He was in fact one of the boys that danced on the piano.

If the indefinite *a silly boy* is interpreted as specific, then [156c] would be totally uninformative. If it is interpreted as non-specific, then [156c] would lead to a contradiction. Yet the intuition is that [156c] is neither contradictory nor uninformative. In general, language should give the option of introducing discourse referents for which one doesn't have information about their relation to other discourse referents.

Van Deemter, in contrast, does not claim ambiguity; he assumes that indefinites that do not appear to be contextually restricted are relativized to a restricting set whose value is the entire universe of discourse. In other words, all indefinites translate as [155a] and there is always some discourse referent corresponding to the entire universe of discourse. Between these two positions the ambiguity position seems prima facie preferable. To begin with what introduces a discourse referent with the entire universe of discourse as its value? Since indefinites can be uttered without any prior context, we would have to say that such a discourse referent is always available. More seriously, while this approach has the advantage of not introducing ambiguity, it has the disadvantage of not having any natural means of characterizing the difference between indefinites that must be relativized to a restricting set and those that must not be so relativized. Even if one were to assume that for those languages, no discourse referent is accommodated that takes the universe of discourse as its value, this can only work for languages in which *all* indefinites either require a restricting set or not. It cannot account for languages like Turkish, where only *some* indefinites are necessarily partially anaphoric or necessarily non-anaphoric.

We cannot say that adverbial quantifiers in general require the existence of an accessible discourse referent which would, in conjunction with the restriction of the quantifier, determine the domain of quantification. To begin with, adverbial quantifiers are, in general, modal and as we saw a lot of modal dimensions exclude relativization to an outside discourse referent because of condition [132]. Moreover, generic statements, such as [157a], can be uttered perfectly felicitously out of the blue. What the requirement for relativization to an accessible discourse referent demands is that in order for [157a] to be felicitous we must accommodate discourse referents such that they take as value the denotation of the CN.

[157] a. Pirate ships fly a black flag.
   b. $G_x\,(\textit{pirate-ship}^Y(x), \exists_y(\textit{black-flag}(y)\ \&\ \textit{flies}(x,y)))$

These considerations apply also to attempts to connect implicit partitive readings of indefinites to generic readings by attributing to both a restrictive clause such as in [157b] (Diesing (1990, 1992a). According to Diesing, the only difference between the implicit partitive reading and the generic reading of an indefinite is the operator involved; in the former case, there is an existential operator (associated with the indefinite) in the latter, an adverbial generic operator. In general, Diesing assumes that we always accommodate Y and its associated conditions since she dispenses with dynamic binding and assumes that indefinites not bound by existential closure are presuppositional. She assumes a syntactic version of accommodation, whereby accommodating involves copying pieces of LF structure into the restriction of an operator. Such a move commits one to saying that a discourse referent such as the Y in [157] is involved in the interpretation of all generic sentences. However, this essentially brings us full circle back to van Deemter's position of having a discourse referent with the universe of discourse as its value, and therefore predicting that partially anaphoric indefinites can be felicitous if uttered without any prior context since such a discourse referent can always be accommodated. This is not to deny that a lot of empirical factors point to the need for some unified analysis of the two, such as accusative case-marked object NP's in Turkish or VP-external subjects in Dutch; I am simply pointing out that the existing attempts, successful though they might seem do not really achieve this. Moreover, Diesing's assumptions have other problems. The general strategy of always accommodating presupposed material into the restriction of an operator will get into trouble in the general case. Accommodating presupposed material into the restriction is a good strategy only for presuppositions of the nuclear scope (recall the discussion in section 2.7). Also, we cannot have [132] (or an appropriately reformulated condition) anymore because, per assumption, we must accommodate both Y and $\alpha(Y)$. There is no sense that the restriction can be such that it *might* entail $\alpha(Y)$; given that the conditions $\alpha(Y)$ are built in as part of the restriction, the restrictor will always entail $\alpha(Y)$ (i.e., any assignment function-world pair that satisfies the restriction will also satisfy $\alpha(Y)$).

The claim is in any case incorrect for nominal quantifiers. The assumption that a quantifier like *every* is specific predicts that the anaphora in [158a] below should be OK as long as quantification is felicitous.[80]

[158] a. Every [man in this room]$_{i,j}$ thinks they$_j$ are obnoxious.
        b. Every [man in this room]$_{i,j}$ thinks he$_i$ is obnoxious.

In cases where nothing else has been mentioned about the men in the room quantification is felicitous, as witnessed by the acceptability of [158b], but the anaphora indicated in [158a] is not. Note that in this case we cannot appeal to failure of accommodation for pronouns given that the discourse referent has been accommodated in order to make the quantification felicitous.

Van Deemter (p.c.) suggests that this might be due to a requirement for surface agreement. However, the empirical evidence seems to suggest otherwise. Crucial cases are the sentences in [159].

[159] a. Each one of the men in the room thinks they are obnoxious.
  b. All men in the room think they are obnoxious.

The agreement story would predict that *they* in [159a] cannot be interpreted as the set of men in the room. A more semantic story would predict that this kind of anaphora is OK because there is an accessible antecedent for the pronoun, the very one that licenses the definite in the partitive *of*-phrase. Intuitions seem to agree with the predictions of the semantic story. The predictions would be the opposite for [159b]. On the agreement story this type of anaphora should be OK because the common noun of the antecedent is plural. On the semantic story it should not, assuming that *all men in the room* amounts semantically to the same as *every man in the room*. Again, intuitions side with the semantic story.

What all this amounts to is that quantified NP's in English, like standard indefinites, can but do not have to be relativized to a restricting set. The same is true for adverbial quantifiers, as we saw in section 3.2.1, although certain complicating factors, such as the fact that they are in addition modal operators and the effect of condition [132], obscure the presence of that possibility for most cases.

The situation is even worse in that we should not attach the requirement for relativization to a restricting set to the bare plural. If we did, this would predict that the bare plural is ambiguous and, as a result should manifest that interpretation, in cases where no operator is present. Specifically, we should expect the bare plural to have an existential, partially anaphoric reading. However, quite the reverse is the case. A bare plural can never have a partially anaphoric reading.

To sum up this section, in order to account for the positive contextual sensitivity of the functional reading, I incorporated to the analysis of the functional reading certain assumptions about the context-sensitivity of operators and of indefinites on a certain interpretation. I then showed, however, that these assumptions are problematic to begin with and in ways that do no ultimately ellucidate the requirement of the functional reading for contextual restrictions.

3.5 Summary

Let me summarize the main points of the operator analysis and how it accounts for the facts associated with the functional reading. The operator responsible for the functional reading must have a trivial modal dimension and it must admit of contextual restrictions. While it is generally assumed that G' is like the adverbs of quantification *always* or *usually*, we have seen that in certain instances it behaves like a contextually restricted adverbial that does not need to quantify over situations.

The universal force and the actual (non-modal) nature of the generalization expressed follow from assuming degenerate genericity. To account for the implicit contextual restrictions we introduced restricting sets and showed that under certain assumptions about the interaction of NP relativized to restricting sets and modal operators contextual restrictions can be present with a degenerate generic operator. The implication of existence follows from the trivial modal dimension of the operator. The absence of the functional reading for other indefinites follows from the assumption that they not accept an operator with a trivial modal dimension. The scopal interaction follows by assuming that the implicit operator is not a default kind of operator but is present along with other operators and scopes freely with them. All these facts then can be accounted for fairly straightforwardly by assuming degenerate genericity plus some additional assumptions about the contextual restrictions of NP's. One problem that remained open was the problem of distributivity which manifests itself with collective predications and with the interaction of the functional reading and overt modals.

For the other facts, degenerate genericity alone does not suffice and we must accept that the functional reading is something over and above a degenerate generic reading. To account for the positive contextual sensitivity we made the relativization to a restricting set obligatory, in other words we built it in as a felicity condition in the spirit of Enç. To account for the negative contextual sensitivity we would have to modify the felicity condition posited for the positive contextual sensitivity. Finally, we must associate the presupposition of existence with the operator and we combine it with the felicity condition needed for the positive and negative contextual sensitivity. All this amounts to positing an operator with properties all of its own and therefore we have not avoided positing ambiguity.

4. CONCLUSION

In section 2 I laid out the full range of facts associated with the functional reading and established that the functional reading is a distinct interpretation and that no genericity is involved. In section 3 I developed an analysis keeping the standard assumptions about indefiniteness in place. One conclusion I reached is that if we are to account for the functional reading under the usual assumptions about genericity and indefiniteness we need more resources than are currently available. But even if one were to provide the additional resources needed, the three central properties of the functional reading, namely the universal force of the indefinite, the particular kind of its contextual sensitivity, and the presupposition of existence it is associated with, are not given a unified analysis. This kind of analysis cannot but treat them as independent properties which accidentally converge on one type of NP. The analysis I will present in the next chapter, on the other hand, treats them as interdependent and derives them from a more basic property of the English bare plural.

NOTES

1. For Carlson (1977b) these two implications are equivalences.
2. The relevant argument of a propositional attitude verb affects whether the verb is given a characteristic property reading or not.
3. The word 'use' is to be understood as a theoretically neutral term; certainly, it is not to commit me to a pragmatic analysis of the facts to be described. In section 2.5 I will show that a pragmatic account is in fact untenable.
4. The article is devoted to a textual analysis of a fund raising letter against the backdrop of Prince's theory of the informational import of NP's.
5. Inferrable NP's are "NP's evoking entities which were not previously mentioned and which I as the reader had no prior knowledge of, but whose existence I could infer on the basis of some entity that was previously evoked and some belief I have about such entities" (p. 312).
6. Whether it also presupposes the existence of students in the actual world is something I will address in section 2.7.2.
7. Except if, as discussed by Karttunen (1976) and Roberts (1987, 1989), modal subordination is involved. See below.

8. Theories of anaphora employing dynamic binding are not the only ones that can capture this generalization. The crucial element of the generalization is that the sentence containing the indefinite antecedent must entail existence. The pronoun could then be construed as an E-type pronoun whose existential presupposition would thus be guaranteed.

9. Even if it were a pronoun of laziness, the implicit contextual restrictions would have to be incorporated in the recovery of the description.

10. I am ignoring the possibility of the bare plural's being bound by existential closure within the nuclear scope of the quantificational structure of the adverbial since that would result in an existential reading, which is disallowed with individual-level predicates.

11. On a colloquial use accepted by some speakers, the preposed adverbs can be interpreted as factive small clauses, i.e., something akin to *as is normal/typical*. That use requires intonational prominence on the adverb followed by a pause. On that interpretation, no infelicity arises for [63b]–[63d] since the adverbs are not interpreted as operators anymore, and the bare plural of [63b] retains its contextually restricted universal reading, as would be expected.

12. With other moods or other modals, *normally*, is also used to restrict the modal base of a counterfactual, as in 'Normally, I would be going to the movies tonight,' which is synonymous with 'if things were normal, I would be going to the movies tonight.' (Note also that in that case it is incompatible with an overt restriction supplied by a conditional clause: ?? 'If it weren't so hot, they would normally go to the beach.') A bare plural in this context retains its functional reading: 'Normally students/the students would have been aware of the danger' is interpreted as a counterfactual, something like 'if things had been normal the actual students would have been aware of the dangers.' Still there is no generic generalization over students. This might be related to the small clause reading, with the adverbs in this case providing the restriction of the counterfactual except that the reading persists even when the adverb is not preposed: 'The students/Students would have normally been aware of the danger.'

13. I owe these examples to Tony Davis.

14. The inference about the totality of victims is a by-product of the functional reading of the bare plural *rescue teams*. Compare with 'Some rescue teams have rescued 28,950 victims.'

15. The reading, irrelevant to our purposes, on which the adverbs are interpreted as factive small clauses, is implausible on pragmatic grounds in these cases.

16. The singular and plural indefinites can have an existential reading with an individual-level predicate while a bare plural cannot.

17. Note that context plays two distinct roles in the first case: it helps determine what is said by fixing the modal dimension of the generic operator, and what is meant by giving rise to the implicature of an actual, contextually restricted generalization. Context can be seen as playing a similarly dual role in the second case as well if we assume that the implicit contextual restrictions enter the interpretation of the existential statement and become part of what is said.

18. The pronouns in intersentential anaphora in [60] would be picking up speaker's reference.

19. Note that on this type of account both the proposition expressed and the proposition meant are general propositions.

20. The terms *general* and *singular* reflect a conception of propositions as structured objects but the distinction can be captured in a semantic framework that construes propositions as sets of possible worlds. See, e.g., Kaplan (1989), where the philosophical discussion is couched in terms of propositions as structured objects but in the formal analysis they are construed as functions from possible worlds into truth values.

21. In order to forestall a possible misunderstanding, let me make the following side remark. A non-quantificational analysis of indefinites does not necessarily take indefinites to be referring expressions. For example, in the non-quantificational analysis of indefinites proposed by Kamp (1981) and Heim (1982) indefinites are *not* referring expressions. As far as the semantics is concerned, variables corresponding to indefinite NP's are interpreted in such a way that there is existential quantification over them. 'A man is in the garden' is predicted to be true iff there is an individual who is a man and is in the garden and not if some particular individual is in the garden.

22. Although de Hoop claims that bare plurals cannot have a specific interpretation, these would be the cases arguing for a such a reading. Incidentally, the fact that bare plurals can have specific or referential *uses* (as in [88] and [85]) but cannot, according to de Hoop's claim, have a specific or referential *interpretation* undermines substantially any approach that takes specificity and

referentiality to be a semantic phenomenon. On what grounds can we distinguish referential use from referential interpretation in such cases?

23. Presumably, whatever excludes the readings in which the singular indefinite is mapped in the restriction of the operator in this context should also exclude the same readings for the bare plural. These are the plain bound variable readings and the reading in which the indefinite is within a subordinated existentially closed domain within the restriction, i.e., the readings represented by [92a] and [92b].

24. For some speakers a narrow scope (nuclear scope) existential reading is possible only if the adverb of quantification is preposed, as in 'Usually a student was aware of the danger.'

25. [91a] gives us an upper bound on the coarseness of individuation of the situations in the domain of quantification: there should be at least as many situations as there are ghost appearances. However, elements in subsequent sentences may impose further conditions, which would result in a finer individuation; needless to say, what these conditions are depends on interpretive properties of these elements. For example, the set of situations $\{s \mid \exists y, x(ghost(y)\ \&\ be\text{-}on\text{-}campus(y,s)\ \&\ student(x)\ \&\ be\text{-}on\text{-}campus(x,s))\}$ is not necessarily identical with the set of situations $\{s \mid \exists y(ghost(y)\ \&\ be\text{-}on\text{-}campus(y,s)\}$. The two sets would be distinct, for instance, if a ghost appeared during summer vacation when no students were in attendance, or if the student body changed during a single ghost's appearance.

26. Bäuerle & Egli (1985), Partee (1984), Berman (1987), Kadmon (1987, 1990), Kratzer (1995), Heim (1990), Chierchia (1992), Barker (1993), de Swart (1996) among others.

27. Perhaps a more transparent example is:

a. Since the Pleistocene, earthquakes have occurred frequently on Pitcairn Island.

b. Usually, when an earthquake hit, people were aware of it.

c. Usually, when an earthquake hit, several people were aware of it.

28. There are speakers who take all occasions of a ghost's haunting the campus to be in the domain of quantification both for [94c] and for [94a] and [94b]. In other words, such speakers do not automatically adjust the domain of quantification so as to satisfy the presuppositional requirements of the definite or the bare

plural. As a result, they find [94c] unequivocally false and have mixed judgements of falsity or infelicity for [94a] and [94b].

29. Those speakers who do not adjust the domain of quantification for [94a] and [94b] also get an unequivocally universal implication for [98b].

30. One could claim that summation is involved in [99b] and [99c]: a group of students is formed comprised of the students of every campus; but then we have the wrong reading because the students on campus 1 need not be aware of the danger on campus 2. Of course one could argue that the NP *the danger* might have a less straightforward interpretation that would allow the predication to be made of the whole big group. But this cannot be said about *loved the ghost* since there what each group of students loved was the ghost on *their* campus.

31. The implicit generic operator cannot be deontic in this case.

32. These are really cases involving conditional subordination. Farkas (1993) considers cases beyond conditional subordination, which have sources beyond what is outlined in (a), (b) and (c).

33. (c) can actually be reduced to (b), as Heim (1982) has essentially shown. I will come back to this issue in the next chapter.

34. (c) is also involved in the examples with the definite NP.

35. When the bare plural and its licensing NP are within the scope of a modal operator, as in [101] and [102], presumably existence is entailed for the worlds in the modal base.

36. Examples like 'Students with police connections were not aware of the danger because there were no such students' parallel exactly cases where the existential presupposition of a definite description is challenged, as in the famous 'The king of France is not bald because there is no king of France.'

37. Although one could judge an infelicitous utterance as false, this does not mean that the interpretation of the utterance should provide a truth value. This point also relates to the discussion in note 28.

38. This is the issue of *weakness* in Beaver (1992). See also the discussion in Cooper (1983, Ch. VI).

39. Whether it is the strong or the weak one that can be easily handled depends on the theory.

40. What is new to Beaver's proposal is that inheritance properties are a consequence of the semantics of the presuppositional operator so they can be expressed as inference patterns between formulas of the logical language he defines.

41. This ignores the conventional implicature about the epistemic possibility of the antecedent clause associated with the indicative mood of the conditional. ϕ^e stands for the truth-conditional content of ϕ, ϕ^i for its presuppositional content. → is taken to be material implication.

42. The singular indefinite can be mapped either in the restriction of the quantifier or in its nuclear scope, hence it can have either a generic or an existential reading.

43. The (#) notation is meant to indicate that the sentences are unacceptable on the quantificational reading for the adverbial and acceptable on the predicate modifier reading.

44. [117a] is his example (i) on p. 126, fn. 17 and [117b] is his example (232) on p. 125.

45. As we saw in the last chapter, Carlson does not assume a mereological structure for individuals and takes the realization relations to be primitive. Mereological reconstructions of Carlson's theory are given in Chierchia (1982), Hinrichs (1985) and Ojeda (1991). Lahiri is not explicit on the semantics for bare plurals he assumes, but given the semantics he proposes for the adverbials and what he assumes for plural definites, it seems that Ojeda's theory could be straightforwardly adopted for his purposes.

46. Dowty and Brody (1984) claim that such co-occurrence with quantificational NP's is possible and attribute the apparent deviance to pragmatic rather than semantic factors.

47. See also Clark (1977) and Clark & Haviland (1977).

48. See, for instance, Stalnaker (1968, 1976), Lewis (1973), Kratzer (1979, 1981).

49. This way, contextual restrictions are given an account that is the a mixture of Cooper's and Heim's approaches: P is a free variable but y is a discourse-bound variable.

50. The propositional interpretation of the nominal argument of a predicate like *be aware* have been attributed to ambiguity of the NP (e.g., Vendler 1967) or type-shifting from events to propositions effected by the verb meaning (Zucchi 1989). These works focus on morphologically derived nominals but we can conceivably extend their proposal to cover non-derived nominals as well.

51. Depending on how the content of the propositional argument of *be aware* is construed, a characteristic property reading for the predicate results either in a descriptive generalization or a dispositional generalization. The former is paraphrasable as 'if/whenever there is a danger of this kind, students are/would be

aware of it,' the latter as 'students are aware that dangers of this kind (can) come about.'

52. Whether we must assume that the examples in [125] involve two generic operators, a degenerate one binding the bare plural and a non-trivial one having scope over the predicate, depends on our assumptions about characteristic predicates and the effect of generic NP's as arguments of attitude predicates. I will not try to settle this here.

53. These two alternatives are particular cases of what Neale (1990) calls the *explicit* and the *implicit* approaches to dealing with the incompleteness of descriptions and quantificational NP's, in general. (These terms are a bit unfortunate since in both cases the element supplementing the interpretation is implicit.) Neale speculates that the two types of approaches might be notational variants of one another. However, as we will see below, the two alternatives discussed here turn out to be non-equivalent, at least for indefinite NP's within the scope of a modal operator.

54. Westerståhl and van Deemter refer to it as *context set*. I have changed their terminology because it coincides with the term that Stalnaker (1978) has coined for a different parameter of the context, as discussed in detail in the next chapter. These two authors also assume that the interpretation of NP's is always relativized to a restricting set; those instances of NP's that do not appear to be contextually restricted are the limiting case when the restricting set is identified with the whole universe of discourse.

55. Westerståhl (1984), working with a Generalized Quantifiers framework, posits restricted determiners; the following equivalence holds between a determiner restricted to context set Y and an unrestricted determiner: $D_M^Y AB \Leftrightarrow D_M A \cap YB$. A restricting set variable is a free variable that is given a value by the context of use.

56. This formulation is sufficient for the purposes of this discussion. See van Deemter (1992) for a formulation that covers a wider class of NP's.

57. [127] corresponds to van Deemter's requirement that conditions be relativized only to accessible reference markers and to Enç's requirement that the second variable associated with an NP be familiar.

58. Van Deemter's discussion is devoted exclusively to extensional cases. Enç considers cases in which an indefinite relativized to a restricting set (a 'specific indefinite' in her terms) has nar-

row scope with respect to a modal operator but simply states that narrow scope is possible.

59. The epistemic modal base involved in [131] is one determined by the common ground of the context. How update of the common ground as envisaged by Stalnaker (1978) comes about in a theory that can assign truth conditions only to complete texts rather than individual sentences is, however, an open question. Contextual update is discussed in the next chapter.

60. The discourse referent constituting the restricting set in this case would be formed by abstraction (see Kamp & Reyle (1993)) and would have to be mapped onto the set of people in this university in every world of the modal base.

61. Indefinites in conditional clauses are different in this respect. Consider, e.g., examples [94] and [95].

62. Heim (1982) uses the term 'restrictive indefinite' "to cover all cases where an indefinite exhaustively constitutes the restrictive term of an operator, visible or not." (p. 191)

63. In terms of Chierchia's (1992) theory we will have to say that existential disclosure must obligatorily take place. In terms of de Swart's (1996) theory we will have to say that for restrictive indefinites the individuation of situations must concide with the individuation of individuals. Since the domain of quantification of extensionalized adverbs of quantification is contextually determined on independent grounds nothing would guarantee that the two sets would coincide hence the absence of the relevant readings.

64. This is because of the following three assumptions: (*i*) adverbial operators adjoin to IP, (*ii*) non-quantificational NP's remain in [Spec, IP] at LF, (*iii*) operator indexing copies the index of an indefinite at [Spec, IP] onto the lowest c-commanding operator.

65. It is not clear to me whether these operators can be stripped of their modal force even when they bind situations. It depends on what we think about what 'Last month, John normally walked to school.' Does it mean that on all the actual occasions in which things were normal (with respect to walking to school) John walked to school? What if there were only 3 normal occasions out of a total of a hundred?

66. The same point can be made with a necessity modal but it is more transparent with a possibility modal.

67. In the logical forms in [143] I have included only the second argument of the modal *may* since its restriction is empty. The ordering source is trivial in this case.

68. Early work on the semantics of tense and indexicality, such as Kamp (1971), has provided similar insights for descriptions with indexical constituents.

69. This is one way of capturing the often stated intuition that generic operators quantify over an open set.

70. [149b] is as close as I can get to a sentence of English expressing the absent reading of [149a].

71. The same is true for adverbs of quantification and conditionals: while (a) might entail (b) (if the conditional is taken to have a realistic modal base), it does not have an interpretation equivalent to it.

 a. If a lion is intelligent, it always roars a lot.
 b. All actually intelligent lions roar a lot.

72. A similar argument can be made with respect to individual-level collective predicates.

73. This could end up meaning that there exists a set of students which includes most of the (contextually relevant) students and whose members met.

74. Kratzer and Diesing differ on how this comes about.

75. This is true for English, where the external argument must move to [Spec,IP] in order to receive case. Diesing (1990, 1992) argues that such movement is optional in German with a concomitant effect on the interpretation of the NP.

76. These representations reflect the assumptions outlined above. l is a variable over spatio-temporal locations and corresponds to the Davidsonian argument. Uppercase variables denote plural entities.

77. For cases with no iterative reading we would, in addition, have to ensure that the operator binds only the variable of the indefinite and not the Davidsonian variable. This is an additional problem for theories that rely on truly unselective binding (operator indexing in Kratzer's and Diesing's analysis does not depend on indefiniteness but structural position in logical form) to account for the range of readings exhibited by indefinite NP's and the Davidsonian argument.

78. Enç calls the indefinite NP's that are context-sensitive 'specific' and attempts to reduce all specificity phenomena that have been discussed in the literature to partial anaphoricity: the presupposition of specific indefinites (like that of definites) is a presupposition about the existence of a discourse referent. Therefore, specificity is analyzed as a semantic phenomenon, linked as it is to

the presence of a certain felicity condition. However, not all notions of specificity can be so reduced. The term 'specific' has been used in a variety of ways in the literature—such as specificity as asserting existence in the actual world, i.e., as having wide scope relative to intensional operators; specificity as referentiality (Fodor & Sag 1982); specificity as a pragmatic notion (Ludlow & Neale 1991)—and it is not the case that any one of them can be reconstructed in terms of some other. For example, the indefinite in (i) can be understood as specific in use—i.e., I might have a particular individual in mind and I might intend you to understand that I have that particular individual in mind—in contexts which do not entail the existence of a group of individuals of which that man is a part of.

(i) A man who I met yesterday/with connections in the administration will come to see me soon.

Specific indefinites in modal or attitudinal contexts require more detailed discussion but the same conclusion can be drawn: specificity arises in contexts which do not entail the existence of a group, necessary for partial anaphoricity. In general, we can have specific use without specific interpretation and specific interpretation without specific use. Also, an indefinite can have wide scope relative to an intensional operator without having a specific interpretation, and (as acknowledged by Enç) it can have a specific interpretation while having narrow scope relative to an intensional operator.

79. The framework of file change semantics, discussed in the next chapter, would be much more amenable for such an analysis.

80. Van Deemter (1992) has a similar problem because the semantics he gives to universally quantified NP's is such that *they* would find an accessible antecedent in the reference marker for the set of men in this room that is introduced at the top-level DRT.

4
Strong and Weak Novelty

1. INTRODUCTION

In the previous chapter I established the existence of a special class of indefinite NP's. I showed that these indefinites, in one of their readings, do not have existential force and presuppose rather than assert existence. I argued that such indefinites are not necessarily in the scope of an operator and, even when they are, they do not inherit the force of the operator but rather affect the domain of quantification in ways consistent with the presuppositional part of their meaning.

In presupposing their descriptive content, such indefinite NP's share a substantial property with definites. On the other hand, they have the whole range of interpretations of standard indefinites, while having in addition the functional reading in contexts with the special properties described in the previous chapter. At the same time, they do not share the full range of readings of definites as they are never anaphoric. The real challenge, therefore, is to account for the properties of the functional reading while maintaining that the bare plural is an indefinite NP. The question then is in what way the theory of indefiniteness should be revised in order to accommodate the functional reading.

Heim (1982) characterizes familiarity/novelty theories of definiteness and indefiniteness as follows: "the label 'familiarity theory of definiteness' [should be] reserved for theories which purport to show that all other systematic contrasts between definites and indefinites are secondary to, if not derivative on, the familiarity-novelty contrast." (pp. 301–302) Can we preserve novelty and familiarity as the fundamental distinction between definites and indefinites and still account for the functional reading? Although it would appear at first sight that indefinites with the functional reading undermine the novelty theory of indefiniteness, it will turn out that they are not only compatible with it but fundamentally support it. The theory already contains the ingredients necessary for an account of the functional reading.

In this chapter, I will develop an analysis of the functional reading within the framework of a novelty theory of indefiniteness. I will argue that the functional reading arises when an indefinite is evaluated with respect to a file entailing its descriptive content, in a sense to be made precise. In order to characterize the distinction between standard indefinites, which exclude the functional reading, and bare plurals which allow it, I will develop a more fine-grained theory of novelty, specified in terms of two conditions: a novelty of index condition and a familiarity of decsriptive content condition. Formally, the distinction between the two types of indefinite NP's will be characterized in terms of the types of felicity conditions they are associated with. *Strongly novel* NP's are indefinite NP's which are associated only with a novelty condition with respect to their index. *Weakly novel* NP's are indefinite NP's which are associated with a novelty condition with respect to their index and a familiarity condition with respect to their descriptive content. Although the domain of indefinites is not uniform, we can still characterize the class of indefinite NP's as those which are associated at least with a novelty condition with respect to their index. Indefinites can, therefore, be distinguished from definites in a principled manner along the lines of the novelty-familiarity theory.

More generally, the proposal can be seen as an argument in favor of (i) a dynamic theory of meaning, as opposed to the classical truth-conditional theory, (ii) a presuppositional analysis of descriptions and (iii) a strong interaction between semantics and pragmatics, whereby background knowledge directly affects interpretation in a way that cannot be factored away as a Gricean effect.

In section 2 I present some of the general characteristics of and motivations for dynamic theories of meaning and outline how theories of assertion and presupposition can be incorporated within them. In section 3 I present the necessary background on the novelty and familiarity theory of definiteness and indefiniteness. In section 4 I propose an analysis of the functional reading and spell out the more fine-grained theory of novelty.

2. THE DYNAMIC VIEW ON MEANING

Heim's novelty/familiarity analysis of (in)definiteness is couched within a theory of meaning in which the meaning of a linguistic element is specified in terms of the effect it has on a given body of information. Extending proposals by Stalnaker and Karttunen, Heim construes this body of information as a file and specifies the interpretation of definite and indefinite NP's in terms of their file change potential. One of the advantages of this conception of meaning is that both the assertive and the presuppositional content of a given element can be formulated in terms of the same theoretical construct, i.e., the file. Assertions update files, whereas presuppositions are checks on files.

The essentials of the dynamic view on meaning can be cast independently of the specifics of the analysis of descriptions. Sections 2.1 and 2.2 establish the following three points, which are central to the discussion in the rest of the chapter: (i) growth of information as elimination of alternatives, (ii) meaning as an operation on information states, (iii) satisfaction of a presupposition as a precondition for such an operation to take place.

2.1 Assertions and Contextual Update

As part of a formal theory of pragmatics, Stalnaker (1972, 1973, 1974, 1976, 1978) developed a theory of assertions and presuppositions incorporating an essentially dynamic view.[1] Assertions are speech acts which have content and which change the context in which they are made by adding to it the information given by their content. The content of an assertion is the proposition expressed in the relevant utterance context.

Stalnaker (1978) emphasizes both the context-dependence of assertions and the effect assertions have on the context. An assertion takes place against a background of mutually held beliefs of some agents (such as the participants in a conversation) and, once accepted, its effect is to increment the background assumptions of the agents. Taking these background assumptions to be information shared by the agents about what the actual world is like, we can see informative assertions as increasing that information by virtue of their content. Uninformative assertions are then the limiting case in which the background assumptions remain the same.

Formally, contexts can be construed as tuples of the form $c = \langle \mathrm{cg}(c), \mathrm{W}(c), \mathsf{s}, \mathsf{n}, \mathsf{h}, w_0, f, \ldots \rangle$, where $\mathsf{s}, \mathsf{n}, \mathsf{h}$ are the individuals corresponding to the speaker, time and place of a given utterance, w_0 the world in which the utterance takes place and f a function assigning values to free variables. I will call these parameters the *Kaplanian parameters* of the context. The common ground, $\mathrm{cg}(c)$, and the context set, $\mathrm{W}(c)$, are among what I will call the *informational parameters* of the context.[2] The common ground is the set of propositions corresponding to the background assumptions the agents are willing to take for granted up to a given point. The context set is the set of worlds in which all the propositions in the common ground are true. In other words, it is the set of worlds compatible with what is assumed by the agents prior to any assertion (assuming, realistically, that the common ground prior to any assertions is, in general, non-empty) and what has been asserted up to that point. Given the information that the agents (presume to) have, any one of the worlds in the context set are candidates for being the actual world. If the common ground and the context set are realistic, as assumed, then w_0 is one of the worlds of the context set. The context set can be defined on the basis of the common ground if we construe propositions as sets of worlds: it is the intersection of all the elements of the common ground. Since the context set rather than the common ground will play the central role in the discussion to follow I include it as a parameter of the context.

Kaplanian parameters fix the interpretation of some context-dependent expressions, such as indexicals, demonstratives and deictics, informational parameters fix the interpretation of others, such as overt and implicit modal operators.[3] Assertions have their *essential* effect on the informational parameters of the context: the way these parameters change as a result of an assertion is a function of the way they were prior to the assertion and of the content of the assertion in that context.[4] The essential effect of an assertion on the common ground and the context set is thus an updating effect. From here on, I will concentrate on the essential effect of assertions.

An assertion updates the context by adding to the common ground the proposition constituting its content and, as a result, by eliminating from the context set those worlds which are not compatible with its content. One of the main insights of Stalnaker was to see information growth as the elimination of alternatives, as narrowing down the possibilities of how things actually are. Gaining information amounts to being able to eliminate possible alternatives which up to that point were still viable candidates for being the way things actually are. As Stalnaker (1978:323) puts it: "To make an assertion is to reduce the context set in a particular way ... The particular way in which the context set is reduced is that all of the possible situations incompatible with what is said are eliminated. To put it in a slightly different way, the essential effect of an assertion is to change the presuppositions of the participants in the conversation by adding the content of what is asserted to what is presupposed." As we will see below, these two ways of formulating the way contextual update works are equivalent only under certain assumptions.[5]

Given this general conception of information and information growth, it is easy to see that the state of having no (contingent) information in a given context c (often referred to as the empty context) is the case where all possible alternatives are still available, hence $W(c) = W$, where W is the set of all possible worlds (in a given model). A state of having maximal (realistic) information in c is the case where all but one possible alternatives have been excluded, hence $W(c) = \{w_0\}$, where w_0 is the world parameter of c. The state of having inconsistent information in c is the case when $W(c)$ is the empty set. Not having information as to whether ϕ holds amounts to including both alternatives (possible worlds) in which ϕ is true and alternatives in which it is false. Having information that ϕ holds amounts to having eliminated those alternatives in which ϕ is not true.

Let us now see concretely how the content of an assertion determines its context change effect. Let ϕ be (the logical form of) a sentence uttered in a given context c. Its meaning, symbolized as $[\phi]$, is a function from contexts to functions from worlds to truth values.[6] Its truth-conditional content relative to c, symbolized as $[\phi]_c$, is a function from worlds to truth values and $[\phi]_{c,w}$ is its truth value in w relative to c.[7] Both $[\phi]$ and $[\phi]_c$ may be partial. $[\phi]$ is defined only for those contexts relative to which ϕ is felicitous, that is for those contexts that provide values for all the context-dependent elements of ϕ and satisfy their contextual presuppositions.[8] $[\phi]_c$ is defined only for those worlds w in which any proposition presupposed by ϕ is true in w. Let us take p to be the proposition expressed by a (felicitous) utterance of ϕ in context c. The updating/context change effect of an assertion can be modelled as a function from utterances and contexts to contexts. Let U be such a function. If $c' = U(\phi,c)$, then:

[160] a. $cg(c') = cg(c) \cup \{p\}$
b. $W(c') = W(c) \setminus \{w \in W(c): [\phi]_{c_w,w} = 0\}$, where c_w is a context exactly like c in its informational parameters but whose world parameter is w (of course, other Kaplanian parameters might be different as a result of this change).

As can be seen by [160a] and [160b], the updating effect on the common ground is incremental—a proposition is added—while the effect on the context set is eliminative—all those worlds incompatible with what has been asserted are removed from the context set. 'Incompatible' here is taken to mean 'false' and not just 'not true,' which would include both false and undefined. In general, ϕ may be felicitous with respect to c but not with respect to some c_w. If, however, ϕ contains no context-dependent elements or if it only contains elements dependent on the informational parameters of the context, then ϕ is felicitous with respect to c iff ϕ is felicitous with respect to c_w, for any $w \in W(c)$. If ϕ has no presuppositions, then $[\phi]_c$ is defined for any world $w \in W$ and therefore ϕ is either true or false in any world.

By definition, U applied to some ϕ and c yields a context c' whose context set $W(c')$ is a subset of the context set of c. Whether the context is updated non-trivially, or whether the resulting context set is empty depends on the information already contained in c and the meaning of ϕ. Let us call an utterance *informative* with respect to a context if it can update the context non-trivially without reaching inconsistency:

[161] An utterance of ϕ is informative with respect to context c iff
$W(U(\phi,c)) \subset W(c)$ and $W(U(\phi,c)) \neq \emptyset$ iff
$cg(c) \subset cg(U(\phi,c))$ and $cg(U(\phi,c))$ is not inconsistent.

Sometimes the context may already contain enough information so that an utterance is either uninformative relative to it or inconsistent with it. We can then say that the utterance is *true in* the context in the first case and that it is *false in* the context in the second case. According to the definition given in [162], ϕ is true in c iff ϕ trivially updates c and ϕ is false in c iff updating c with ϕ results in inconsistency.

[162] ϕ is true in c iff $W(U(\phi,c)) = W(c)$.
ϕ is false in c iff $W(U(\phi,c)) = \emptyset$.

An assertive utterance may be neither true nor false in a context c. This is precisely the case for informative assertions relative to c.

The updating effect, for example, of an utterance of [163] on the context set of a context c is given in [164], taking both *obstinate* and *bill* to be basic expressions and the sentence to have no presuppositions.[9]

[163] Bill is obstinate.

[164] $W(U(obstinate(bill), c))$
$= W(c) \setminus \{w \in W(c) : [\![obstinate(bill)]\!]_{c_w,w} = 0\}$
$= \{w \in W(c) : [\![obstinate(bill)]\!]_{c_w,w} = 1\}$
$= W(c) \cap \{w \in W : [\![obstinate(bill)]\!]_{c,w} = 1\}$

Suppose [163] is informative in c. Then prior to its utterance the agents of c have no information as to whether Bill is obstinate or not. Since ignorance of this kind is modelled as allowing for either possibility, the context set of c contains both worlds in which Bill is obstinate and worlds in which he is not. According to the definition in [160b], the context change effect of the assertion of [163] is to remove from the context set of c all those worlds in which it is not the case that Bill is obstinate. [163] is not context-dependent (abstracting away from tense); hence, it is felicitous with respect to any context. Moreover, because [163] has no presuppositions and is therefore either true or false for all worlds, the resulting set is that subset of the context set of c whose worlds are all such that Bill is obstinate. Since [163] is not context-dependent, its content relative to c is the same as its content relative to any other context. Therefore, the context change effect is equivalent to intersecting the context set of c with the content of [163] relative to c.

In general, however, the three ways of defining contextual update given in [165] are not equivalent.

[165]   a. $W(c') = W(c) \setminus \{w \in W(c): [\![\phi]\!]_{c_w,w} = 0\}$
      b. $W(c') = \{w \in W(c): [\![\phi]\!]_{c_w,w} = 1\}$
      c. $W(c') = W(c) \cap \{w \in W: [\![\phi]\!]_{c,w} = 1\}$

The reason may be infelicity of an utterance with respect to some c_w, or undefinedness of $[\![\phi]\!]_c$ for some world in the context set, or non-constancy of the content of ϕ relative to different c_w's. If ϕ is infelicitous with respect to some c_w, where $w \in W(c)$, then $w \in W(c')$, by [165a] but $w \notin W(c')$, by [165b]. Similarly if $[\![\phi]\!]_c$ is undefined for some $w \in W(c)$. To see that the non-constancy of content makes [165a] and [165c] non-equivalent, consider a context c with w_0 as its world parameter and $W(c) = \{w_0, w_1\}$ as its context set and some (context-dependent) ϕ whose meaning is such that $[\![\phi]\!]_{c,w_0} = 1$, $[\![\phi]\!]_{c,w_1} = 1$, $[\![\phi]\!]_{c_{w_1},w_0} = 1$, $[\![\phi]\!]_{c_{w_1},w_1} = 0$. Then, as shown in [166], the updates as defined by [165c] and [165a] are not equivalent.

[166] a. $W(U(\phi, c)) = W(c) \cap \{w \in W : [\![\phi]\!]_{c,w} = 1\} = \{w_0, w_1\}$
      b. $W(U(\phi, c)) = W(c) \setminus \{w \in W(c) : [\![\phi]\!]_{c_w, w} = 0\} = \{w_0\}$

In order to connect the information available in a context, the content of an assertion and its context change effect, Stalnaker (1978) postulated the following three principles as governing assertions:

P1: A proposition asserted is always true in some but not all of the possible worlds in the context set.

P2: Any assertive utterance should express a proposition, relative to each possible world in the context set, and that proposition should have a truth value in each possible world in the context set.

P3: The same proposition is expressed relative to each possible world in the context set.

Stalnaker motivated these principles on intuitive grounds of how contextual update should be regulated and used them to connect semantic and pragmatic presuppositions and to account for the informativeness of necessarily true or false propositions. Pragmatic presuppositions are requirements that utterances of sentences place on the informational parameters of the context in which they occur: the proposition presupposed by the utterance must be information already present in the context, in other words, it must be true in every world of the context set of the context.

In more formal terms, these principles guarantee the felicity of assertions, the constancy of their content across different contexts and a truth value in each world of the context set, all necessary for the three definitions of contextual update to be equivalent. They can be reformulated as in [167] and contextual update should then be formulated as a partial function.

[167] ϕ is assertable in c only if:
  P1: ϕ is informative with respect to c
  P2: For any $w \in W(c)$, (a) ϕ is felicitous with respect to c_w and (b) $[\![\phi]\!]_c$ is defined for w
  P3: $[\![\phi]\!]_{c_w} = [\![\phi]\!]_{c_{w'}}$ for any $w, w' \in W(c)$.

[168] U is defined only for those ϕ and c such that ϕ is assertable in c.

Since the world parameter of c is in $W(c)$, if ϕ is assertable in c, then it is felicitous with respect to c and $[\![\phi]\!]_c = [\![\phi]\!]_{c_w}$, for any $w \in W(c)$. P2 is necessary in order for [165a] and [165b] to be equivalent.[10] P3 is necessary for the equivalence between [165a] and [165c] to hold. P1 plays a different role: it is invoked by Stalnaker in order to account for the informativeness of necessarily true or false propositions. Violation of P2 or P1 leads to readjustment of the context, violation of P1 and P3 to reinterpretation of the sentence.[11]

Contextual update relies on the, independently defined, truth-conditional content. Moreover, at least as standardly assumed, in determining the content of a complex assertion relative to some context each one of its constituent parts is evaluated relative to that same context, which is not updated in the compositional determination of the content of the assertion.[12] Stalnaker thus maintains the standard truth-conditional view of meaning and the traditional division between semantics and pragmatics.[13] The dynamic effect of an assertion on the context is a pragmatic matter, while the proposition constituting the content of an assertion is determined independently by the semantics. The conceptual innovation of dynamic semantics, which I will adopt in my analysis of the functional reading, is to make the updating effect on context the central aspect of meaning.

Before going on to elaborate on this view, let me point out briefly that the notion of contextual update presented above is crucially tied to particular assumptions about the range of context-dependency and rests on a semantics that associates truth conditions with individual sentences. As a consequence, it is inconsistent with certain semantic theories and problematic in view of certain empirical facts. It is inconsistent with semantic theories that assign truth conditions to entire texts (Heim 1982, Ch. II) or to DRS's in the manner of Kamp (1981) because in such theories there is, in general, no way to extract truth conditions for individual sentences. A related point is that since intersentential anaphora with indefinite antecedents or the implicit dependence of NP's on a set of individuals introduced in prior discourse (discussed in the previous chapter) fall outside the assumed range of context-dependency, a solution conforming to this idea of contextual update will have to rely on an E-type strategy. Finally, although this notion of contextual update already makes a distinction between the Kaplanian and the informational parameters of a context in that the latter but not the former are updated as a result of an assertion, the difference between the two appears to be more fundamental: the informational parameters of a context are updated in the compositional interpretation of the content of a complex assertion. Presupposition projection phenomena, which make a compelling case for a recursive contextual update (Karttunen 1974, Stalnaker 1974), have to be relegated to pragmatics. Evidence which bears directly on semantic interpretation can be found in the interpretation of conditionals, modals and generics.[14] Consider, for example, [169].

[169] It is raining today and if it rains tomorrow, there will be a flood.

Relative to a context where it has been established that if it rains for two days in a row, there is a flood, and that if it rains only for one day, there might be a flood but where it has not been established that it is raining today, [169] is judged to be true. However, if the conditional is evaluated relative to the same context as the first conjunct, [169] is predicted to be false assuming Kratzer's (1979, 1981) analysis of conditionals and taking the modal base of the implicit operator of indicative conditionals to be the context set and the ordering source to be trivial in this case.[15] Of course, this case relies on a particular analysis of the conditional but it is an analysis that has otherwise been useful in a variety of phenomena relating to conditionals.

In dynamic semantics the meaning of a sentence is determined on the basis of the effect it has on a given body of information, what has been called an *information state* (see Groenendijk & Stokhof (1990, 1991a, 1991b), Veltman (1991), Dekker (1993), Beaver (1992), Rooth (1987), Chierchia (1992)).[16] Its truth-conditional content can then be determined on the basis of its informational updating effect. Meaning is thus an operation on information states. However, it cannot be identified with the contextual update function U because that already presupposes a way of defining meaning, namely in terms of truth-conditional content. If the operation on information states is the basic notion of meaning, then meaning should be defined recursively in terms of updating operations on information states.

Specifically, meaning can be construed as a function from information states to information states. Let us take s to be an information state and $+\phi$ to be the (dynamic) meaning of a sentence. $+\phi$ is then a function from information states to information states; $+\phi$ applied to s, symbolized as $s + \phi$, yields an information state s' that has at least as much information as s, if not more.

The informational parameters of a context are thus a special case of the more general notion of information state and the meaning of a sentence relative to a context is specified in terms of the way the sentence updates the context's informational parameters.

If we take information states to be sets of possible worlds, then the meaning of a sentence will be specified in terms of update conditions on information states, determining a way for eliminating worlds from a given set of possible worlds. For example, the meaning of [163] would be specified as in [170], taking both *obstinate* and *bill* to be basic expressions, s to be an arbitrary information state and a model to be a triple $\langle D, W, I \rangle$, where D is a set of individuals, W a set of possible worlds and I an interpretation function for the basic expressions of the language.

[170] $s + obstinate(bill) = \{w \in s: I(bill)(w) \in I(obstinate)(w)\}$

The meaning of a complex sentence ϕ should be determined compositionally in terms of the update conditions of its constituent parts.

Instead of first determining compositionally the truth-conditional content of a sentence and then on the basis of that the change that it brings about to an information state, we first compositionally determine the change that the sentence brings about to an information state. Its truth-conditional content can then be recovered from its information change effect:

[171] ϕ is true in w relative to a non-empty information state s iff if $w \in s$, then $w \in s + \phi$.
ϕ is false in w relative to a non-empty information state s iff if $w \in s$, then $w \notin s + \phi$.

The dynamic perspective brings along a major change in the way context is supposed to determine truth-conditional content (the proposition expressed). In the standard picture, context affects content to the extent that it supplies values for context-dependent expressions in the sentence. In the dynamic view, truth-conditional content is context sensitive in a more fundamental sense: the proposition expressed is a contextually restricted proposition, that is, a function from worlds to truth values defined at most on the worlds in the context set of a context. If we construe a propositions as the set of worlds in which it is true, then the proposition expressed relative to a given context is a subset of the context set of that context.

[172a] and [172b] specify the truth-conditional content of a sentence relative to a given context under the standard and the

dynamic perspective, respectively ($[\![\phi]\!]_{c,w} = 1$ in [172a] is determined by the standard interpretation rules, $[\![\phi]\!]_{c,w} = 1$ in [172b] is determined according to [171]).[17]

[172] a. $[\![\phi]\!]_c = \{w \in W: [\![\phi]\!]_{c,w} = 1\}$
  b. $[\![\phi]\!]_c = \{w \in W(c): [\![\phi]\!]_{c,w} = 1\}$
    $= \{w \in W(c): w \in W(c) + \phi\}$

Clearly, [172a] and [172b] determine distinct truth-conditional contents. For instance, according to [172b], ϕ expresses no proposition relative to a context c whose $W(c) = \emptyset$, but ϕ may express a proposition relative to such a context according to [172a].

The contextual update function U is partial and is defined only for those ϕ and c such that ϕ is assertable in c. Do any of the conditions determining assertability affect meaning? There is clearly a pragmatic requirement for informativeness: do not assert that which is known (or taken for granted) already and do not assert something which is known (or taken for granted) to be false. Semantically, there should be no general requirement for informativeness. A given expression may be uninformative relative to a given information state, that being the case when the expression updates the information state trivially (i.e., maps it to itself); or it may be uninformative relative to all information states that satisfy certain conditions (purely presuppositional expressions are of that type); or it may lead to inconsistency relative to a given information state (i.e., maps it to the empty set). Felicity (expanded so as to include satisfaction of presuppositions and appropriately reformulated), on the other hand, is crucial for meaning to be defined, as we will see in the next section.

2.2 Presuppositions and Contextual Admittance

Heim (1982, 1983, 1992), building on Karttunen (1974), has developed an approach to presuppositions that construes them as a component of meaning, unifies them with other types of context-dependency and accounts for their projection properties. It does so by expanding the notion of felicity to cover cases of non-contextual presuppositions and by connecting the need for contextual satisfaction of presuppositions with partiality of meaning.

In general terms, Heim's approach can be characterized as follows: if a sentence presupposes a proposition, then the context in which that sentence is uttered must contain the information corresponding to the presupposed proposition in order for the utterance to have meaning in that context. It thus incorporates both the informational perspective of Stalnaker—a proposition presupposed in a context is information already available in the context—and the Strawsonian perspective—truth of the proposition in the world parameter of the context is necessary for the meaning of the sentence in that context to be defined.[18]

Karttunen (1974) took the relation of admittance between a sentence and a context as central for an analysis of presuppositions and presupposition projection phenomena: felicity of an utterance relative to a context is dependent upon its admittance in that context and admittance in a context depends upon the presupposition's contextual satisfaction. He provided a recursive definition of admittance but the admittance conditions associated with particular linguistic expressions did not relate to other aspects of interpretation, such as truth-conditional content.

Taking meaning to determine update operations on information states, Heim specifies admittance as a relation between an information state s and a sentence ϕ that is interdependent with the definedness of the meaning of ϕ for s:

[173] s admits ϕ iff $s + \phi$ is defined.

Presuppositions are then conditions that information states must satisfy in order to admit some ϕ, or looking at it from the opposite side, in order for some ϕ to successfully update them. Taking presuppositions to be relations between sentences and propositions and information states to be sets of possible worlds, the relation of presupposition holds between a sentence and a proposition if and only if any information state that admits the sentence entails the proposition.

[174] A sentence ϕ presupposes p iff any information state s that admits ϕ is such that $s \subseteq p$.

Since meaning is specified in terms of $+$ and presuppositions as conditions that must be satisfied in order for $+$ to be defined, presuppositions become part of the meaning of a linguistic expression (in the technical sense). A recursive definition for $+$ determines the local information states that are updated by the constituent parts of some ϕ and must therefore satisfy the presuppositions of those parts. The solution to the projection problem is part and parcel of compositional interpretation and no separate recursion is needed to calculate the presuppositions of a complex expression in terms of the presuppositions of its parts (as in, e.g., Karttunen & Peters (1979)).

To see how this works in a simple case consider [175]. [175a] presupposes the proposition expressed by [175b] since factive predicates presuppose the truth of their complement.

[175] a. John knows that Bill is obstinate.
       b. Bill is obstinate.

The meaning of a sentence like [175a] is specified in such a way that it is defined only relative to information states that entail its presupposition, as in [176].[19]

[176] $s + knows(john, obstinate(bill))$ is defined only if
$s \subseteq \{w \in W: \text{Bill is obstinate in } w\}$

In this case, it is easy to see that presuppositions can also be construed as relations between sentences.[20] The meaning of [175a] is defined only for those information states s such that $s + obstinate(bill) = s$, that is, only for those information states such that updating with $obstinate(bill)$ would result in no more information than that already contained in s. In general, the presupposition relation between sentences is characterized in terms of their meaning: the meaning of the presupposing sentence is defined only for those information states that are fixed points for the meaning of the presupposed sentence, as in [177].

[177] A sentence ϕ presupposes a sentence ψ iff any information state s that admits ϕ is such that $s + \psi = s$.

Formally, presupposition failure leads to undefinedness of meaning for a particular information state. Although, practically, presupposition failure should consequently lead to a breakdown of communication, not all cases of (at least apparent) presupposition failure make a conversation come to a halt. Presupposition failure can be avoided by accommodation, a process by which the information necessary for the information state to satisfy the presupposition is added to it (Lewis (1979), Stalnaker (1978)).

[178] If ϕ presupposes p and some s does not admit ϕ, then enrich s with the necessary information so that the new information state s' is such that $s' \subset p$ and therefore admits ϕ.

Given our assumptions so far, informational enrichment amounts to removing from s those worlds in which p is not true. That is, s' is informationally richer than s iff $s' \subseteq s$. It is clear that accommodation can only work if p is not false in s since accommodation is enrichment of information, i.e., elimination of alternatives, not revision.

Since admittance is a relation between sentences and information states, when we take contexts into account it is primarily a relation between utterances and context sets and derivatively a relation between utterances and contexts.

[179] ϕ is felicitous with respect to c iff c provides values for all context-dependent expressions in ϕ and c admits ϕ.

[180] c admits ϕ iff $W(c)$ admits ϕ.

In order to take into account dependency on the Kaplanian parameters of a context, dynamic meaning has to be construed as a function from contexts and information states to information states. This also allows us to generalize felicity so as to account both for contextual and non-contextual presuppositions.[21]

On various accounts of (various types of) presuppositions, the existence of presupposing expressions in a language results in partiality—partiality of meaning, content, or contextual update.

[181] If ϕ presupposes a proposition p, then:

Strawsonian Contextual Presupposition: $[\phi]$ is defined for some c only if $\{w_0\} \subseteq p$, where w_0 is the world parameter of c.

Fregean Semantic Presupposition: for any c, $[\phi]_c$ is defined for some w only if $\{w\} \subseteq p$.

Stalnakerian Pragmatic Presupposition: U is defined for ϕ and some c only if $W(c) \subseteq p$.[22]

Heimian Semantic Presupposition: $+\phi$ is defined for some information state s only if $s \subseteq p$.

Within a dynamic system of interpretation, presuppositions result in both partiality of meaning *and* truth-conditional content. In order for ϕ to be true or false in w relative to c, w must be in $W(c)$ and $+\phi$ must be defined for $W(c)$. Hence, $W(c) \subseteq p$ and since $w \in W(c)$ it follows that $\{w\} \subseteq p$. Moreover, if an assertive utterance of a sentence ϕ is to increment the set of background assumptions of the agents in some context, the meaning of ϕ must be defined for the information state corresponding to the conversational background of that context. If $+\phi$ is undefined for that information state, no incrementation takes place. So if ϕ semantically presupposes a proposition p, an utterance of ϕ pragmatically presupposes p. Thus, Heimian semantic presupposition brings together the other three types and results in a more radical partiality of meaning.

To appreciate the way in which presuppositional expressions result in a more radical partiality of meaning, let us compare Stalnaker's and Heim's approaches with respect to [182].

[182] a. John is not married.
       b. John's wife is tall.

Let c be the context in which the (true) assertion that John is not married has been made. Let us assume that [182b] does not have a truth value in worlds in which John is not married, taking the definite description to be associated with a presupposition of existence (and uniqueness). Then the context set of c consists of worlds for which the proposition that John's wife is tall has no truth value. For Stalnaker, [182b] is *not* context-dependent since meaning is relativized to context only to the extent that context provides values for context-dependent expressions. [182b] expresses a proposition relative to c but it is not assertable relative to c. [182b] is not assertable relative to c because such an assertion would violate P2b (given in [167]). For Heim, on the other hand, [182b] expresses no proposition relative to c, since the update of $W(c)$ with [182b] is not defined. The truth-conditional content of [182b] relative to c, according to the definition of truth in [171], would be that subset of the context set of $W(c)$ which is identical with the context set of the context resulting from updating $W(c)$ with [182b]. But since this update is not defined, no such context and therefore no context set of such a context exist either.[23]

Both theories are coupled here with the standard presuppositional (existence and uniqueness) analysis of definites. The difference between the two conceptions regarding [182] does not rely on the familiarity theory of definiteness but rather on the more general dynamic view of meaning. In general, for Stalnaker, any ϕ has a truth value in w relative to c if ϕ is felicitous with respect to c (in the sense of section 2.1) and the propositions presupposed by ϕ are true in w. This is so even if ϕ violates P2b (given in [167]), that is, even if ϕ has no truth value in all worlds of the context set of c. For Heim, by contrast, ϕ has no truth value in w relative to c if not all worlds in the context set of c satisfy its presuppositions.

3. THE NOVELTY-FAMILIARITY THEORY OF DEFINITENESS AND INDEFINITENESS

3.1 Files as Information States

In section 2 we saw how meaning can be seen from an information-based perspective. The assertive part of the meaning of a linguistic element is formulated in terms of an updating operation on information states and its presuppositional part is formulated as a definedness condition for that operation.

Heim's analysis of definite and indefinite NP's takes the dynamic view of meaning as basic. It, moreover, incorporates Karttunen's (1976) notion of discourse referents as an essential ingredient of the theory. The main points about the theory can thus be summarized as follows.

- Information states relevant for natural language interpretation are constructs that contain information about what the world is like and the value of discourse referents. Therefore, they are not just sets of worlds but richer constructs that also keep track of assignments to variables. Such information states are called *files*.
- Information growth is modelled as the elimination of possible alternatives and as the incrementation of the set of discourse referents.
- Meaning is specified compositionally in terms of updates on files. Such updates are called *file change potentials*.
- File change potentials are possibly partial functions from files to files. Partiality is the characteristic feature of the meaning of presupposition triggering elements.

These points should be familiar from the discussion so far except for the enriched concept of information state and the renewed view of information growth as comprising both elimination and incrementation, necessitated by the addition of discourse referents.

Specifically, files are construed as pairs consisting of a set of natural numbers, called the domain of the file and symbolized as Dom(F), and a set of assignment-function/possible-world pairs, called the satisfaction set of the file and symbolized as Sat(F). Models M are taken to be triples of the form $\langle D, W, [\ ]\rangle$, where D is a set of individuals, W a set of possible worlds and $[\ ]$ a basic interpretation function, assigning to each n-place predicate a function from W to D^n. Files can thus be specified as in [183].

[183] $F = \langle \text{Dom}(F), \text{Sat}(F) \rangle$, where
$\text{Dom}(F) \subseteq N$ and
$\text{Sat}(F) = \{\langle f, w \rangle : w \in W \text{ and } f \text{ a total function from variables } x_i, i \in N, \text{ to } D\}$

Discourse referents correspond to variables whose index is in the domain of the file.

The information contained in a file may be in accord with the facts of a possible world or not. In the former case, the file is true in that possible world, in the latter, the file is false in that possible world. For a file to be true in a world, each discourse referent must be matched up with at least one individual in that world with properties corresponding to the conditions imposed on the discourse referent. The formal definition is given in [184].

[184] F is true in w iff there is some f such that $\langle f, w \rangle \in \text{Sat}_w(F)$;
F is false in w otherwise.

As can be seen from [184], a file is either true or false in a possible world. Every file, therefore, determines a set of worlds in which the file is true. This set is called the *world set* of the file and is symbolized as W(F).[24]

[185] $W(F) = \{w \in W : \text{there is some } f \text{ such that } \langle f, w \rangle \in \text{Sat}(F)\}$

From the satisfaction set of a file we can extract its satisfaction set relative to a given world w, which is symbolized as $\text{Sat}_w(F)$. Such a set will be a set of assignment functions, as specified in [186].

[186] $\text{Sat}_w(F) = \{f : \langle f, w \rangle \in \text{Sat}(F)\}$

The file change potential of a formula ϕ, symbolized as $+\phi$, is a function from files to files defined only for those files that admit ϕ. A file that admits ϕ is thus in the domain of $+\phi$; I will call such files *admissible for* $+\phi$. Felicity of a formula relative to a file, admittance of a formula by a file and admissibility of file for the file change potential of a formula are interdependent:

[187] ϕ is felicitous with respect to a file F iff
F admits ϕ iff
F is admissible for $+\phi$.

Therefore, each one of the following types of conditions is defined in terms of any one of the others: felicity conditions of ϕ, definedness conditions for $+\phi$, admissibility conditions for F with respect to $+\phi$.

In section 2.2 we saw that the felicity conditions of a linguistic expression depend on the presuppositions it is associated with. The two notions of the presupposition relation formulated in [174] and [177] can be transported in a file-based system as in [188] and [189], respectively.

[188] If ϕ presupposes a proposition p, then ϕ is felicitous with respect to a file F only if $W(F) \subseteq p$.

[189] If ϕ presupposes ψ, then ϕ is felicitous with respect to a file F only if for every $\langle f, w \rangle \in F$ there is some f' such that $\langle f', w \rangle \in F + \psi$ (i.e., $W(F) = W(F + \psi)$).

However, given the richer structure of files, felicity of a formula relative to a file may depend on properties of the file other than the information contained in its world set. This richer structure is exploited in the analysis of the semantics of NP's, as we will see in section 3.3.

Updating a file F with some ϕ adds new information and results in a more informative file or adds no new information and results in the same file F. Adding information amounts to either specifying extra conditions on the available discourse referents, which would exclude pairs in the satisfaction set of a file, or introducing a new discourse referent fulfilling certain constraints, or both. Applying $+\phi$ to a file, therefore, has the effect of incrementing the domain or keeping it the same and of reducing the satisfaction set or keeping it the same. File change potentials, and hence linguistic meaning, have the property in [190], which, following Veltman (1991), we can characterize as the *update property*.

[190] For any formula ϕ and any file F, $\text{Dom}(F) \subseteq \text{Dom}(F+\phi)$ and $\text{Sat}(F+\phi) \subseteq \text{Sat}(F)$.

In other words, the information we get by updating F with ϕ is at least as specific as that contained in F. Given [190], we can refer to the file that is the value of applying $+\phi$ to F as the *update of F with ϕ*.

The proposition expressed by ϕ relative to F corresponds to the world set of the file that is the update of F with ϕ.

3.2 *Informativeness of Files*

Files encode factual information and information about discourse referents. Discourse referents mediate in incrementing factual information since they are matched with actual referents, i.e., entities in a possible world.[25] The factual information a file contains is compatible with all worlds in which the file is true. The kind of information a file may contain about a discourse referent includes whether that discourse referent has been set up or not, the range of its values (entities it is matched with) in each possible world of the world set of the file, and whether it is uniquely matched with an entity in each world of the world set of the file or not. The first type of information is encoded in the domain of the file, the other two in its satisfaction set.

Changes of factual information and of information about discourse referents go hand-in-hand. Gaining factual information with respect to a file F by the elimination of certain assignment function/world pairs from its satisfaction set that results in a smaller range of values for some discourse referent means that information has been gained about that discourse referent. Setting up a new discourse referent results in a larger domain and may result in the elimination of assignment function/world pairs from the satisfaction set and hence in growth of factual information.

Since files encode both factual information and information about discourse referents, the notions of minimal and maximal informativeness have to be appropriately relativized. [191] defines various absolute and relative notions of minimal and maximal informativeness.[26]

[191] a. A file F is minimally informative iff $\text{Dom}(F) = \emptyset$, $W(F) = W$, and for any world $w \in W$, $\text{Sat}_w(F) = \{f: f(x_i) \in D, \text{ for any } i \in N\}$.
 b. A file F is factually minimally informative iff $W(F) = W$.
 c. A file F is minimally informative with respect to a set of variables A iff for every $w \in W(F)$, for every $x_i \in A$ and every $d \in D$, there is $f \in \text{Sat}_w(F)$ such that $f(x_i) = d$.
 d. A file F is maximally informative with respect to a set of variables A iff for every $w \in W(F)$, for every $x_i \in A$ and for any $f, f' \in \text{Sat}_w(F)$, $f(x_i) = f'(x_i)$.
 e. A file F is factually maximally informative iff $W(F) = \{w\}$, for some $w \in W$.
 f. A file F is maximally informative iff $W(F) = \{w\}$, for some $w \in W$, and F is maximally informative with respect to $\{x_i: i \in \text{Dom}(F)\}$.

If a file is minimally informative (simpliciter), then its domain is empty, its world set is the entire set of possible worlds W, and for each $w \in W$ all possible assignment functions are in $\text{Sat}_w(F)$. The minimally informative file has no (contingent) factual information and no information about any discourse referents. A factually minimally informative file has no (contingent) factual information but may have information about some discourse referents. If a file is minimally informative with respect to a set of variables, then it excludes no possible assignments for these variables, that is every entity in the domain of the model is a possible value for each one of these variables.[27] If a file is maximally informative with respect to a set of variables, then each variable in that set is matched with exactly one individual. If a file is maximally informative (simpliciter), then it is maximally informative with respect to the set of variables whose indices are in the domain of the file (i.e., it is maximally informative with respect to the discourse referents present) and all possible worlds but one have been excluded. If a file is factually maximally informative, then all possible worlds but one have been excluded but discourse referents may still be matched with multiple entities.

As we will see in the next section, in order for a file to participate in semantic interpretation (that is in order for a file to be admissible for any file change potential at all), it must be minimally informative with respect to the set of all variables whose indices are not in the domain of the file.[28]

Some of the information contained in a file is what I will call *modalized information*. For instance, a file may contain the information that a discourse referent satisfying certain constraints *could* be set up if the file were to be updated in a certain way or that such a discourse referent *would* be matched up to appropriate entities for all worlds in the world set of the file. Modalized information will play a crucial role in the analysis of the functional reading.

Files also stand in relations of relative informativeness with other files. One such relation, symbolized as $\sqsubseteq$, is defined in [192].

[192] $F \sqsubseteq F_1$ iff $\text{Dom}(F) \subseteq \text{Dom}(F_1)$ and $\text{Sat}(F_1) \subseteq \text{Sat}(F)$.

If F_1 is the update of F with some ϕ, then, by the update property stated in [190], $F \sqsubseteq F_1$.

Two files may have the same world set without having the same satisfaction set. For instance, if ϕ_1 is the logical form of [193a], ϕ_2 the logical form of [193b], F a file that contains no information about John's marital status, $F_1 = F + \phi_1$ and $F_2 = F + \phi_2$, then $W(F_1) = W(F_2)$ but $Sat(F_1) \neq Sat(F_2)$.

[193]   a. John is married.
       b. $\phi_1 = john(x_j)$ & $married(x_j)$
       c. John has a spouse.
       d. $\phi_2 = john(x_j)$ & $spouse(x_i)$ & $has(x_j, x_i)$

For all $\langle f, w \rangle \in Sat(F_2)$, $f(x_i)$ must be the individual that is John's spouse in w, whereas F_1 places no restrictions on the value of x_i since i is not in its domain. In that sense, F_2 is more informative than F_1 and, in fact, $F_1 \sqsubseteq F_2$. In other words, F_1 is minimally informative with respect to $\{x_i\}$ but of course F_2 is not. Although F_1 is minimally informative with respect to $\{x_i\}$, it contains modalized information about x_i, namely that x_i could be matched in every world of $W(F_1)$ with an individual who is John's spouse if F_1 were to be updated appropriately.

3.3 The Felicity Conditions of Definites and Indefinites

In the familiarity theory of definiteness developed by Heim (1982), definite and indefinite descriptions have identical logical forms: they both correspond to an open formula. The burden of the semantics of definites and indefinites descriptions and hence of their differences is carried by the felicity conditions they are associated with.

For example, the sentences in [194a] and [194b] have the logical form given in [194c].

[194]   a. The man came in.
       b. A man came in.
       c. $man(x_i)$ & $came\text{-}in(x_i)$

Applying the file change potential of $man(x_i)$ to some admissible file F yields a file whose domain includes the index i and whose satisfaction set consists of $\langle f, w \rangle$ pairs such that $f(x_i)$ is a man in w. Let $F_1 = F + man(x_i)$ & $came\text{-}in(x_i)$, where F is an admissible file for that file change potential. Then both [195] and [196] hold:

[195] For every $w \in W(F_1)$: if $f \in Sat_w(F_1)$, then
     $f(x_i) \in [man]_w \cap [came\text{-}in]_w$.

[196] For every $d \in D$: if $d \in [man]_w \cap [came\text{-}in]_w$, then
     $\exists f \in Sat_w(F_1)$ such that $f(x_i) = d$ (assuming that F

contains no more information about x_i except possibly that it must be mapped onto a man).

Although the formula $man(x_i)$ may correspond either to a definite or an indefinite NP, the felicity conditions depend on the definiteness of the NP and, therefore, the set of admissible files as well as the truth conditions for that NP will turn out to be different.

The felicity conditions associated with definite and indefinite NP's are covered by the Extended-Novelty-Familiarity-Condition, given in [197] (Heim 1982:369-70).

[197] *Extended-Novelty-Familiarity-Condition:*
For ϕ to be felicitous with respect to a file F,
for every NP_i in ϕ it must be the case that:
  a. if NP_i is [–def], then $i \notin \text{Dom}(F)$
  b. if NP_i is [+def], then $i \in \text{Dom}(F)$ and if NP_i is a formula,[29] F entails NP_i.

The novelty condition in [197a] is a definedness condition for the file change potential of an indefinite and consists only of an index condition. The familiarity condition in [197b] is a definedness condition for the file change potential of a definite and consists of both an index condition and a descriptive content condition. Index conditions and descriptive content conditions are conditions of a different type and, in general, independent of each other.

The entailment relation between a file F and a formula ϕ is defined in [198] and amounts to the following: the update of F with ϕ contains no more information than F itself.

[198] F entails ϕ iff $\text{Sat}(F) \subseteq \text{Sat}(F + \phi)$.

Given the update property of file change potentials (stated in [190]), if F entails ϕ, then $\text{Sat}(F) = \text{Sat}(F + \phi)$.

Definites are thus purely presuppositional: applying the file change potential of some definite NP with logical form $\alpha(x_i)$ to a file F consists of checking whether i is in the domain of F and whether F entails $\alpha(x_i)$ and then mapping F onto itself, if these two conditions are satisfied, or not mapping it onto anything, if any of these two conditions are not satisfied, since in that case the file change potential is undefined. The descriptive content condition that is part of the familiarity condition captures the intuition that definites presuppose their descriptive content.

What kind of presupposition does the familiarity condition correspond to? According to the familiarity theory, definites presuppose that there are individuals satisfying their descriptive content and, moreover, that the range of values for their corresponding discourse referent is among those individuals. Thus the familiarity presupposition consists of an existential presupposition and, what we might call, an anaphoricity presupposition. As a result, there is no proposition that corresponds to the familiarity presupposition. Although existence of an individual satisfying the descriptive content of the NP is a consequence of the familiarity presupposition, neither the simple existential presupposition in the manner of [188] in [199] nor the file-sensitive existential presupposition in [200] capture the full extent of the familiarity presupposition.

[199] a. Definites of the form $\alpha(x_i)$ presuppose the proposition corresponding to the set of worlds $\{w \in W$: there is an individual d who is α in $w\}$.
    b. F $+\alpha(x_i)$ is defined only if W(F) $\subseteq \{w \in W$: there is an individual d who is α in $w\}$.

[200] a. Relative to a file F, definites of the form $\alpha(x_i)$ presuppose the proposition $\{w \in$ W(F): there is an individual d who is α in $w\}$.
    b. F $+\alpha(x_i)$ is defined only if W(F) $\subseteq \{w \in W$: there is an individual d who is α in $w\}$, i.e., only if $\{w \in$ W(F): there an individual d who is α in $w\}$ = W(F).

The familiarity presupposition imposes requirements on the satisfaction set of a file that cannot be reduced to requirements just on its world set.[30]

Indefinites are purely assertive: applying the file change potential of some indefinite NP with logical form $\alpha(x_i)$ to a file F consists of checking whether i is in the domain of F and mapping F onto a file which contains the information that x_i is matched with an individual having the property corresponding to α, if $i \in$ Dom(F), or mapping it onto nothing, if $i \notin$ Dom(F). Indefinites assert the existence of individuals satisfying their descriptive content and, moreover, assert that the range of values for their corresponding discourse referent is among those individuals. The novelty condition guarantees that indefinites will be assertive in this second sense since if a file already has some information about their corresponding discourse referent, it is not an admissible file for their file change potential.

Since the novelty condition requires that a file *lack* certain information while the familiarity condition requires that a file *contain* certain information, the set of files that are admissible for the file change potential of an indefinite NP with logical form $\alpha(x_i)$ and the set of files that are admissible for the file change potential of an definite NP with logical form $\alpha(x_i)$ are disjoint. Moreover, accommodation can render a definite NP felicitous, since it would *add* the necessary information to a file, while it can never render an indefinite NP felicitous, since that would require *revising* the information available in a file.

A file that is admissible for the file change potential of an indefinite is minimally informative with respect to the variable corresponding to the indefinite. This follows from the novelty of their index, given a general condition that Heim imposes on files, Condition B, which is stated in [201] (Heim 1982:304).[31]

[201] For every file F, any world w and every $n \notin \text{Dom}(F)$: if f and g are two assignment functions that are alike except insofar as $f(x_n) \neq g(x_n)$, then $f \in \text{Sat}_w(F)$ iff $g \in \text{Sat}_w(F)$.

Condition B is an intuitively well-motivated condition on files, ensuring that a file does not cross-reference to discourse referents not already introduced, or, in somewhat more technical terms, that a file does not impose conditions on a variable whose index is not in the domain. As no file change potential is ever defined for files violating it, it introduces partiality that is not due to presuppositions. Condition B has as a consequence that a file must be minimally informative with respect to any set of variables with indices not in the domain of the file:

[202] For any world w and every file F true in w, F is minimally informative with respect to $\{x_n: n \notin \text{Dom}(F)\}$.

Given [202], a file F that is admissible for the file change potential of some indefinite with logical form $\alpha(x_i)$ does not entail $\alpha(x_i)$ unless α happens to correspond to a necessary property, that is a property that any individual whatsoever has in any world.

Coupled with the definition of truth and the novelty condition associated with indefinites, [201] predicts that an indefinite not in the scope of an operator will always have existential force, as we will see in the next section.

3.4 The Truth Conditions for Definites and Indefinites

This dynamic view on definite and indefinite descriptions accounts for their anaphoric potential and can be used to derive their intuitively perceived quantificational force under a quantifier-free analysis. As Heim (1982:332–33) puts it: "Indefinites need not be bound in logical form for them to receive what strikes us as existential readings. How is this possible? The answer lies basically in the way the notion of truth is defined for files: a file is true iff *there is* a sequence that satisfies it. So, in a manner of speaking, existential quantification is built into the truth definition and therefore need not be explicitly expressed in logical form. Still—and this is just as important a point—we do not want to predict an existential reading for just *any* free variable, but only for those that are novel w.r.t. their file of evaluation, which means—thanks to the Novelty-Familiarity-Condition—only to those which are indefinite."

The truth conditions of a given sentence and, therefore, the truth-conditional content of a definite or indefinite NP within that sentence are derived from the file change potential of the sentence, which makes crucial reference to felicity conditions, and the general definition of truth given in [203].

[203] ϕ is true in w with respect to a file F that is true in w and admissible for $+\phi$ if F $+\phi$ is true in w;

ϕ is false in w with respect to a file F that is true in w and admissible for $+\phi$ if F $+\phi$ is false in w.

According to the definition in [184], in order for a file to be true in a world, there has to be an assignment function in the satisfaction set of the file relative to that world; that is, there has to be at least one way of matching up the discourse referents in the file with appropriate individuals in that world. Appropriate individuals are those that have all the properties corresponding to the conditions imposed on the discourse referents.

In order for a given ϕ to be true in a world w relative to a file F, it is necessary and sufficient that certain facts obtain in w. These facts depend on the information contained in F, since F has to be true in w to assess the truth or falsity of ϕ, and on the information change brought about by ϕ. The felicity conditions of ϕ place constraints on the information contained in F and hence play a crucial role in what such facts should be. Consequently, felicity conditions affect truth conditions.

Let us now see how these general considerations apply to derive the existential force of indefinites and the non-existential force of definites. The existence of an individual in a world w that is a man and that came in is necessary and sufficient for the truth of sentence [194b] in w relative to a (true and admissible) file F. Sufficiency relies on the novelty condition associated with indefinites and Condition B. To see the need for Condition B consider some file F such that for all $\langle f,w \rangle \in$ Sat(F) $f(x_i)$ is not a man in w. Now assume further that $i \notin$ Dom(F) and that F is true in some world w in which there is a man that came in. Then F is admissible for $+man(x_i)$ and therefore for $+man(x_i)$ & $came\text{-}in(x_i)$ but sentence [194b] is false in w relative to F. Because F violates Condition B, the existence in w of a man that came in is not sufficient to guarantee the truth of the sentence.

On the other hand, the existence of an individual in world w that is a man and that came in is not sufficient for the truth of sentence [194a] in w relative to a (true and admissible) file F. Since definites are associated with the familiarity condition, an individual that verifies [194a] has to be within the set of individuals that are men *and* have all the properties established by the file to be the properties of the values of the discourse referent corresponding to the definite NP.

The truth conditions of associative anaphoric definites, which are the same as those of other definites, demonstrate an important fact about accommodation: accommodation is not minimal. Accommodation works in such a way as to link an accommodated dicourse referent to an already existing discourse referent. For instance, if the existence of individuals of a certain type is required for felicity, the information actually accommodated is somewhat richer; it is the information about the existence such individuals that are moreover connected to another entity that has been established by the file to be a value of some discourse referent. If accommodation were minimal, then associative anaphoric definites would have the truth conditions of indefinites: the existence of an entity satisfying the overt descriptive content of the NP and the main predicate would be sufficient to verify the relevant sentence. However, not any entity satisfying the (overt) descriptive content of the NP and the main predicate is sufficient but one that is connected to another entity that is itself a value of some discourse referent. For example, suppose [204] is part of a discourse in which the first appearance of an NP with the common noun predicate *garden* is in [204b]. Then (the logical form of) [204b] is infelicitous with respect to the file that is the update of a file with (the logical form of) [204a].

[204] a. John bought a house.
       b. The garden was spectacular.

If we simply accommodated the information that there was a garden, then [204b] would be felicitous relative to the resulting file but it would be true as long as some garden or other was spectacular. However, in that context [204b] is true if the garden of the house that John bought was spectacular. The requirement for richer than minimal accommodation stated above leads to accommodation of the information that there was a garden in the house John bought and therefore to appropriate truth conditions for [204b]. This general requirement on accommodation will be important in the account of the functional reading presented in the next section.

4. THE FUNCTIONAL READING

In this section I will propose an analysis of the functional reading without positing any quantifier or making any appeal to degenerate genericity. The functional reading of bare plurals in English is due to their ambiguity as standard indefinites, on the one hand, and as indefinites with an additional felicity condition, on the other. The additional felicity condition requires familiarity of a special kind and thus captures the intuition that bare plurals on their functional reading presuppose their descriptive content. Because of this felicity condition, a bare plural need not be in the scope of any operator in order not to receive an existential reading.

The ambiguity of the bare plural resides precisely in the felicity conditions it is associated with. It is associated with a novelty condition for its index on one interpretation, and with both a novelty condition for its index and a familiarity condition for its descriptive content on the other interpretation. These felicity conditions taken together delimit a wider range of contexts in which the bare plural is felicitous and result in a wider range of readings. Like standard indefinites, a bare plural is felicitous in contexts that correspond to files lacking information about its descriptive content and discourse referent; in those contexts it receives the regular interpretation of indefinites. Unlike standard indefinites, it is also felicitous in contexts that correspond to files lacking information about its discourse referent but containing information about its desciptive content; in those contexts the functional reading arises.

4.1 Weakly and Strongly Novel NP's

The novelty-familiarity theory presented in section 3 makes the following two predictions about inherently non-quantificational NP's not within the scope of any operator: (a) an NP asserts existence iff it introduces a new discourse referent, (b) an NP presupposes existence iff it is anaphoric on an already existing discourse referent. The evidence from the functional reading argues that we must allow for NP's which do not assert existence but introduce a new discourse referent.

As we saw in the previous chapter, a central fact about the functional reading is that the bare plural presupposes existence without being anaphoric. Within the file change framework, this means that the file prior to the update with the bare plural must entail the descriptive content of the NP, while, however, being minimally informative with respect to the variable corresponding to the NP. Therefore, we should first make precise how exactly the entailment of the descriptive content is to be formulated and then we should specify how the analysis of indefiniteness should be revised.

The familiarity condition for the descriptive content of definites in [197b] makes reference to the entailment relation between a file and a formula. The situation obtaining with definites can be characterized more generally with respect to a file F and a formula ϕ as follows. To determine whether F is admissible for $+\phi$ what is checked is whether the file already contains the information that would be brought about if it were to be updated with ϕ. The specification for the file change potential $+\phi$ thus includes the definedness condition in [205].

[205] F $+\phi$ is defined only if F $+\phi$ = F.

In order for the definedness condition in [205] to be satisfied, F must contain the same factual information and the same information about discourse referents as its update with ϕ. This means that F must entail the proposition determined by the update of F with ϕ, that no matchings of discourse referents to referents are allowed by the information in F but excluded by the information in the update of F with ϕ, and that ϕ must contain no variables with novel indices with respect to F. If the definedness condition in [205] is satisfied, applying the file change potential $+\phi$ to F will result in trivial updating of information.

Clearly, in order to account for NP's that presuppose their descriptive content but introduce a new discourse referent we must appeal to a weaker notion of information containment. If the NP has a novel index with respect to a given file, then the file cannot contain exactly the same information that is contained in its update with the NP. By Condition B, the file must be minimally informative with respect to any set of variables with novel indices, as discussed in section 3.3, whereas its update with the NP will not be minimally informative with respect to the variable with the index of the NP (except if the common noun predicate of the NP corresponds to a necessary property).

The new notion of information containment that we need in order for a file F to entail the descriptive content of an NP while being minimally informative with respect to the variable corresponding to the NP is this: the file should entail that some individual has the property given by the common noun predicate of the NP without requiring that that individual be matched with any discourse referent in F. In more technical terms, all the worlds in the world set of F should be such that they contain some such individual but that individual need not be the value of a variable with an index in the domain of F. For a file F to have this property it should satisfy the condition in [206], taking the CN of the NP to be a simple predicate.

[206] For every $\langle f, w \rangle \in \text{Sat}(F)$ there is some f' agreeing with f on $\{x_j: j \in \text{Dom}(F)\}$ such that for some $k \notin \text{Dom}(F)$, $f'(x_k) \in [\![CN]\!]_w$.

More generally, this conception of information containment can be characterized as a relation of *weak entailment* between files.[32] The relation of weak entailment, symbolized by $\leq$, is defined in [207]. See also Heim (1987, fn. 4), where a relation of entailment between files is defined in order to characterize in the framework of file change semantics weak and strong NP's, in the sense of Milsark (1974) and Barwise & Cooper (1981).

[207] $F \leq F'$ iff for every $\langle f, w \rangle \in \text{Sat}(F)$ there is some f' agreeing with f on $\{x_j: j \in \text{Dom}(F)\}$ such that $\langle f', w \rangle \in \text{Sat}(F')$.

Then the file change potential of some ϕ might be such that it checks whether a given file contains enough information so that it weakly entails its update with ϕ. The specification for the file change potential of such a ϕ will include the definedness condition in [208].

[208] $F + \phi$ is defined only if $F \leq F + \phi$.

A ϕ that requires of its file of evaluation F to weakly entail F $+\phi$ may contain variables with novel indices with respect to F. If F weakly entails F', then F and F' determine the same proposition, i.e., $W(F) = W(F')$, but may differ with respect to the variables they have a fixed assignment for, i.e., $\text{Dom}(F) \subseteq \text{Dom}(F')$ and $\text{Sat}(F) \not\subseteq \text{Sat}(F')$. Although $\text{Sat}(F) \not\subseteq \text{Sat}(F')$, since $W(F) =$

W(F'), Sat(F) has the following property with respect to Sat(F'): if Sat(F) is partitioned into classes of assignment-function/possible-world pairs such that the assignment functions in each class agree on the values they assign to the variables with index in the domain of F, then each class has a survivor in Sat(F').

If an NP with logical form $\alpha(x_i)$ introduces a new discourse referent but presupposes its descriptive content, then its file change potential would be defined only for those files whose domain does not include i and which entail its descriptive content in the sense specified above:

[209] F $+\alpha(x_i)$ is defined only if:
(a) $i \notin \text{Dom}(F)$, and (b) F $\leq$ F $+\alpha(x_i)$.

Such an NP is felicitous only relative to files that contain the following kind of modalized information: a discourse referent satisfying the descriptive content of the NP will successfully be set up if the file is updated with that NP, and, moreover, such a discourse referent would be matched up with appropriate referents in all worlds in the world set of the file. Updating a file F that satisfies the definedness condition in [209] with $\alpha(x_i)$ will then result in no addition of factual information, that is no elimination of worlds and no exclusion of matchings to referents for the discourse referents in F. The effect of applying $+\alpha(x_i)$ to F will simply be to fix the assignment for x_i, which will result in the elimination of any $\langle f, w \rangle \in \text{Sat}(F)$ such that the individual $f(x_i)$ does not have the property corresponding to α in w.

Indefinites may then be distinguished in terms of the felicity conditions they are associated with. I call those indefinites that are associated only with a novelty condition with respect to their index *strongly novel* and those indefinites that are associated both with a novelty condition with respect to their index and a familiarity condition with respect to their descriptive content *weakly novel*. The familiarity condition is equivalent to the definedness condition in [209b]. The felicity conditions of strongly and weakly novel NP's with corresponding logical form $\alpha(x_i)$ are given in [210] and [211], respectively.

[210] For a strongly novel NP to be felicitous with respect to a file F it must be the case that: $i \notin \text{Dom}(F)$.

[211] For a weakly novel NP to be felicitous with respect to a file F it must be the case that:
(a) $i \notin \text{Dom}(F)$, and (b) F $\leq$ F $+\alpha(x_i)$.

Bare plurals in English are ambiguous: they are both weakly and strongly novel. The standardly recognized interpretations of a bare plural arise when it is interpreted as a strongly novel indefinite. The functional reading arises when it interpreted as a weakly novel indefinite, in which case it is felicitous only relative to files entailing its descriptive content.

4.2 Contextually Salient Functions

What gives rise to files entailing the descriptive content of some indefinite NP? More concretely, let us see how the functional reading arises for the bare plural in the familiar example from chapter 3, repeated below.

[212] a. In 1985 there was a ghost haunting the campus.
       b. Students were aware of the danger.

Let [213a] and [213b] be the logical form representations of [212a] and [212b], respectively, and F a file obtained by applying the file change potential of [213a] to some file that contains just enough information to satisfy the felicity conditions of [213a].

[213] a. $ghost(x_m)$ & $campus(x_j)$ & $haunt(x_m,x_j,x_l)$ & $in\text{-}1985(x_l)$
       b. $students(x_i)$ & $be\text{-}aware(x_i,\phi)$

Since we are now dealing with plural NP's, let us assume that the assignment functions in the satisfaction set of a file assign sets of individuals rather than individuals to variables (i.e., they are total functions from variables to the power set of D).

The bare plural NP *students* is ambiguous between a weakly novel and a strongly novel construal. The strongly novel construal is disallowed in this case because the predicate is individual-level. (I will not discuss here what the reasons for this prohibition are; see section 4.4 for some pertinent remarks). In order for the bare plural on its weakly novel construal to be felicitous with respect to a file, its index must be novel with respect to the file and the file must entail its descriptive content. By assumption, F satisfies the index condition of the bare plural but not its descriptive content condition. If felicity is to be satisfied, accommodation must take place.

Given that it is part of general background knowledge that campuses have students, we can assume the existence of a function $s^{student}$ which assigns to each pair of a world and a singleton set consisting of an individual that is a campus in that world a set of individuals who are students on that campus in that world (let us assume that it is undefined for campuses that do not contain any students in some world). Contextually salient functions of this type have been invoked for the analysis of E-type pronouns (Cooper 1979, Heim 1990, Chierchia 1992), interrogatives (Engdahl 1986, Ginzburg 1992), and indefinite NP's with the modifier *certain* (Hintikka 1986). Given the existence of such a function, the file F may be updated as in [214].

[214] $\text{Dom}(F_1) = \text{Dom}(F)$
$\text{Sat}(F_1) = \{\langle f, w \rangle \in \text{Sat}(F)$: there is some g agreeing with f on $\{x_n : n \in \text{Dom}(F)\}$, some $s^{student}$ and some $k \notin \text{Dom}(F)$ such that $g(x_k) = s^{student}(w, f(x_j))\}$

The update in [214] constitutes genuine increase in information. As long as some campus that is the value of x_j has students in some world of the world set of F, $\text{Sat}(F_1)$ would be non-empty. If $\text{Sat}(F_1)$ is non-empty, F_1 contains the information, not contained in F, that any campus verifying [213a] relative to F_1 has students. Since for all worlds in the world set of F_1 and any campus that is matched with the discourse referent x_j, it holds that there is some set of individuals who are students on that campus, F_1 entails the descriptive content of the bare plural *students* (i.e., $F_1 \leq F_1 + students(x_i)$) but it does not entail $students(x_i)$ since F_1 is minimally informative with respect to $\{x_i\}$. In fact, F_1 entails the descriptive content of the bare plural plus its implicit contextual restrictions (i.e, $F_1 \leq (F_1 + students(x_i)) + be\text{-}on(x_i, x_j)$), hence the positive contextual sensitivity of the functional reading. F_1 can then be updated with [213b], as in [215].

[215] $\text{Dom}(F_2) = \text{Dom}(F_1) \cup \{i\}$
$\text{Sat}(F_2) = \{\langle f, w \rangle \in \text{Sat}(F_1): f(x_i) = s^{student}(w, f(x_j))$ and $f(x_i)$ is aware of the danger in $w\}$

The kind of accommodation involved in the update from F to F_1 is the result of *informational accommodation*. It is the kind envisaged by Lewis (1979) and Stalnaker (1978) and advocated by Heim (1982, 1983). It should be distinguished from *representational accommodation*, which involves the addition of a certain piece of structure into a given representation, such as an LF structure or a DRS. Representational accommodation has been proposed by several recent works, such as Kadmon (1987, 1990), Roberts (1989), Kratzer (1995), Berman (1990), Diesing (1990, 1992a), van der Sandt (1992), and has been claimed by some to be the only type of accommodation needed to account for the semantics of linguistic expressions. The functional reading crucially shows the need for informational accommodation.

In chapter 3 I argued that examples such as [216b] or [216c] are infelicitous if uttered in the context of [216a], assuming it is known that Yale has no fraternities, and are, therefore, neither true nor false in the actual world.

[216]   a. A ghost was haunting Yale last year.
        b. # Fraternity members were aware of the danger.
        c. # Fraternity members were not aware of the danger.

The analysis of the functional reading I am proposing captures both the infelicity and the lack of a truth-value for [216b] or [216c]. The functional reading is associated with a Heimian semantic presupposition and, as discussed in section 2.2, semantic presuppositions imply pragmatic presuppositions and presupposition failure results in truth-value gaps.

4.3 Negative Contextual Sensitivity

The negative contextual sensitivity of the functional reading is due to the non-anaphoricity of the bare plural, a consequence of the novelty of its index. Let us consider the discourse in [217].

[217]   a. There is a ghost haunting the campus.
        b. There are 500 students in this dormitory.
        c. Students are aware of the danger.

If the NP *students* in [217c] is assigned the same index as the NP *500 students* in [217b], then [217c] would be infelicitous relative to any file that is the result of an update with [217b]. In order for the novelty condition with respect to its index to be satisfied, the bare plural in [217c] must be assigned an index distinct from the index of any NP preceding it.[33]

Similarly for deictic examples, as in [218], where the bare plural is not presumed to be identical with the perceptually salient students.

[218]   Context: We know that there is a ghost haunting the campus. We are standing in front of the library and we can both see several students.

        Students are afraid to enter the library.

I am assuming that in this case the file of evaluation for the bare plural contains information about the perceptually salient individuals; in other words, it contains a discourse referent that is matched with the individuals that are perceptually salient.[34]

It is important to note that the novelty of the index excludes *presupposed coreference*. If it so happens that some dormitory verifying [217b] relative to the file of evaluation of [217c] turns out to contain all the students on campus, we will have *accidental coreference*.[35] [217c] can be uttered felicitously in contexts where, for all that is known (or taken for granted), the 500 students in this dormitory may or may not be identical with the totality of students on campus. As discussed in section 2.1, lack of information amounts to allowing for both alternatives in this case. An utterance following [217c] may, in fact, subsequently *assert* the identity of the 500 students in this dormitory with the totality of students on campus, thus providing additional information. To exclude presupposed coreference and hence the anaphoric reading for the bare plural, it suffices that some world in the world set of its file of evaluation contain a set of individuals satisfying the descriptive content of the NP and are distinct from those individuals verifying [217b] relative to that file.

The explanation for the negative contextual sensitivity analysis offered here contrasts with the account that would be necessitated by the type of analysis proposed in chapter 3. In order to capture the negative contextual sensitivity of the bare plural, we would have to impose a disjointness requirement between the discourse referent corresponding to the summation of the elements in the restriction of the degenerate generic operator (see Kamp & Reyle (1993) on summation) and that corresponding to any preceding NP. While the analysis proposed in this chapter relies on *non-stipulated coreference* in its account of negative contextual sensitivity, the analysis of chapter 3 would have to rely on *stipulated non-coreference*. As discussed above, an analysis relying on non-stipulated coreference is empirically superior since it allows for subsequent utterances to assert identity. An analysis relying on stipulated non-coreference makes exactly the opposite prediction since subsequent assertion of identity would lead to inconsistency.

4.4 Strong and Weak Novelty and NP Strength

In chapter 2 we saw that individual-level predicates select for a special class of NP's. Milsark (1974) called those NP's that co-occur with individual-level predicates *strong* and those NP's that do not *weak*. Since then there have been a number of attempts to characterize the distinction either semantically or syntactically.

Here I will adopt Heim's (1987) proposal for capturing the weak/strong distinction in a file change framework. This proposal imports the characterization offered in Barwise & Cooper (1981) into the familiarity theory of definiteness. In our terms, it amounts to the following for an NP with logical form $\alpha(x_i)$:

[219]   a. An NP is strong iff every file admissible for $+\alpha(x_i)$ is such that $F \leq F +\alpha(x_i)$.
        b. An NP is weak otherwise.

Given the notion of NP strength in [219], weakly novel indefinites are obviously strong, while strongly novel indefinites are weak. To see that strongly novel indefinites are weak consider the indefinite *a pomegranate* with corresponding logical form $pomegranate(x_i)$ and a factually maximally informative file F (in the sense of [191e]) such that $i \notin \text{Dom}(F)$ and the sole world in W(F) does not contain any pomegranates. Such a file is admissible for $+pomegranate(x_i)$ but $F \nleq F +pomegranate(x_i)$ since $F +pomegranate(x_i) = \emptyset$.

Strength of an NP in these terms is a sufficient condition for co-occurrence with individual-level predicates so it is unsurprising that bare plurals on their functional reading can co-occur with individual-level predicates. Is it also a necessary condition? Given the proposals in this chapter, the answer is no. Strongly novel indefinites are weak NP's and yet they can combine with individual-level predicates if they are in the restriction of a generic operator or adverb of quantification.. Offering a positive suggestion about what a necessary condition would be goes beyond the scope of this work.

Some recent works, such as Diesing (1990, 1992a) and de Hoop (1992), propose to connect inherently strong NP's and NP's with a so-called strong reading to presuppositionality. They claim that NP's with a strong reading have an existential presupposition but do not formulate the presupposition explicitly so it is hard to compare their proposals with the proposals made here. In any case, given the differences between weakly novel NP's and strongly novel NP's in the restriction of generic operators and adverbs of quantification, discussed at length in chapter 3, it is doubtful that association with an *existential* presupposition suffices to characterize the weak/strong distinction. Strongly novel NP's in the scope of adverbial operators do not exhibit any of the properties attributable to an existential presupposition. This is not to say that the distinction cannot ultimately be captured by appealing to some type of presupposition, just that an existential presupposition is not the right concept involved.

4.5 Existential Force and Strong vs. Weak Novelty

Under the theory of indefinites presented in section 3, novelty of the index of an NP with respect to a file was necessary and sufficient for that NP to get an existential reading. As long as indefinites are associated only with an index felicity condition, novelty of their index with respect to a (true) file is sufficient for them to get an existential reading if they are outside the scope of any operator. Given the revised theory of novelty I have proposed, an existential reading is *not* predicted for any free variable that is novel with respect to its file of evaluation. Rather an existential reading is predicted for those free variables that are novel with respect to their file of evaluation and for which the choice of their value does not depend on the value of some other variable for which the file already has more than minimal information.

For instance, let us consider the truth of [213b] relative to a world $w \in W(F_1)$, where F_1 is as defined in section 4.2. Is the existence of some students who are aware of the danger in w—any such set of students—sufficient for the truth of [213b] in w relative to F_1? The answer is no. Because of the felicity condition requiring the familiarity of the descriptive content of the bare plural and the manner in which the necessary information has been accommodated, via some contextually salient function $s^{student}$ relating campuses and students, in order for a set of individuals to verify [213b] relative to F_1, it must consist of students who are associated with some campus verifying [213a] relative to F_1.

Thus, weakly novel indefinites share with definites the property that existence of a set of individuals satisfying their descriptive content and the relevant predicate is not sufficient for the truth of the sentence in which they occur, and hence do not receive an existential reading. With weakly novel indefinites we can see more clearly how implicit information[36] contained in a file and necessitated by the requirement for felicity may affect the truth-conditional content of a linguistic expression.

The empirical generalizations following from the more fine-grained theory of novelty are as follows: (a) if an NP asserts existence, then it introduces a new discourse referent, (b) if an NP is anaphoric, then it presupposes existence. This allows for the following three types of non-quantificational NP's: purely assertive NP's, purely presuppositional NP's, and partly assertive, partly presuppositional NP's. Strongly novel indefinites are purely assertive, definites are purely presuppositional and weakly novel indefinites are assertive with respect to their discourse referent and presuppositional with respect to their descriptive content. The table in [220] summarizes the classification of non-quantificational NP's imposed by my analysis.

[220]	NOVEL DISCOURSE REFERENT	FAMILIAR DISCOURSE REFERENT
ASSERT EXISTENCE	strongly novel indefinites	
PRESUPPOSE EXISTENCE	weakly novel indefinites	definites

The box in the upper right-hand corner is predicted to be empty. If the discourse referent of some NP is familiar, any file admissible for its file change potential would have to be non-minimally informative with respect to that variable, hence existence of some individuals satisfying the descriptive content of the NP and the relevant predicate cannot suffice to verify the sentence containing the NP relative to such a file.

4.6 Maximality

Although the bare plural is predicted to have a non-existential reading in its weakly novel interpretation, nothing so far guarantees that it will have universal force. To see that let us assume that in a world $w \in W(F_1)$, where F_1 is as defined in section 4.2, only a proper subset B of the entire set of students on some campus verifying [213a] relative to F_1 were aware of the danger. The existence of B should be sufficient for the truth of [213b] in w relative to F_1. Consider those $f \in \text{Sat}_w(F_1)$ such that $f(x_i) = B$. Then, by assumption, those f's are also in $\text{Sat}_w(F_1 + (\text{students}(x_i) \& \text{aware}(x_i, \phi)))$, hence [213b] should be true in w relative to F_1. But this is in discord with intuitive judgments.

In order to account for the maximality effect, I will adopt a strategy used by Gawron, Nerbonne & Peters (1991) and Chierchia (1992) in order to account for the interpretation of expressions involving contextually salient functions.[37] I have left it open so far whether there is a single $s^{student}$ function mapping worlds and campuses to students or multiple such functions; recall that in specifying the update in [214] I required simply that there be some such function. Let us assume that there is a family of such functions, each mapping a given campus and a world to a different set of students on that campus in that world. (We can also think of $s^{student}$ as a choice function.) One of them will be such that it has as its value the set of all students on a given campus in a given world.

The strategy in effect used by Gawron, Nerbonne & Peters (1991) and by Chierchia (1992) is this: the truth or falsity of what is said should be constant across different values of the functions $s^{student}$ for a given campus and world.[38] As a consequence, the condition in [221] holds for any discourse referent x_j whose values are mediated via a contextually salient function.

[221] For any file F, any world w and any $f, f' \in \text{Sat}_w(\text{F})$ such that $f'(x_j) \subseteq f(x_j)$: if F′ is the update of F with some ϕ, then $f \in \text{Sat}_w(\text{F}')$ iff $f' \in \text{Sat}_w(\text{F}')$.

Given [221], it is no longer possible for any subset B of the type described above to suffice to verify [213b] relative to F_1. If any subset B has the relevant property (i.e, of being aware of the danger), then they all must, and if some subset B does not have the relevant property, none of them should.

4.7 Consequences of the Existential Presupposition

4.7.1 Positive Contextual Sensitivity

In section 3.4, we saw that accommodation works in such a way as to link an accommodated dicourse referent to an already existing discourse referent. This is manifested in the interpretation of associative anaphoric definites. In general, accommodated factual information relates to existing discourse referents. Therefore, although the descriptive content of the bare plural *students* contains no restrictions to the students on a given campus either in its overt linguistic material or in its logical form representation, relative to a file that is admissible for its file change potential it will be interpreted as if it were contextually restricted. Within the novelty-familiarity framework, so-called incomplete descriptions need not be supplemented in their logical form representation with additional descriptive content or another parameter. The reading of a description relative to a file may crucially depend on the information available in that file, as we have seen.[39]

We can now explain the effects of the positive contextual sensitivity of the functional reading. In chapter 3 we saw that the bare plural in the discourse in [222], does not get the functional reading.

[222]   a. Students were roaming the streets.
           b. A school nearby had ended classes early.

In terms of the analysis I am proposing, this is analogous to the lack of a reading for the NP *the garden* in [223a] as equivalent to *the garden of the house that John bought*.

[223]   a. The garden was spectacular.
           b. John bought a house.

If there is no information about an educational institution in a given file, then the bare plural in [222a] cannot be felicitous relative to such a file on its weakly novel interpretation. Since no more than minimal accommodation is possible, the only available interpretation for the bare plural is as a strongly novel indefinite, hence its existential reading in this case.

In chapter 3 I also argued that the implicit contextual restrictions are part of the presuppositional content of the bare plural, since they are not cancellable, as witnessed by [224].

[224]   a. A burglar was roaming Santa Clara county.
           b. Deputy sheriffs were aware of the danger.
           c. #They had been sent from LA county to investigate.

This fact also follows from the general requirement for richer than minimal accommodation. In order for [224b] to be felicitous, accommodation has to take place but accommodated factual information relates to existing discourse referents and therefore has to be mediated by a contextually salient function relating one kind of individual to another. In this case, the relevant functions are those relating counties and deputy sheriffs of those counties. That information, implicit though it may be, is part of the file that results from an update with [224b]. Updating that file with [224c] leads to inconsistency (unless some revisions in the information available take place), hence the perceived contradiction in the discourse in [224].

4.7.2 Dependent Functional Reading

A weakly novel bare plural may of course appear in the scope of an operator. In that case the need for accommodation will arise in the process of evaluating the file change potential of a complex operator-headed formula. This is the case in [225].

[225] a. Ghosts have occasionally haunted this campus.
b. Students were usually aware of the danger.

Here the relevant contextually salient functions map a world, a campus and an occasions of a ghost appearance on that campus to sets of students on the campus during that occasion. Then if F is some file that is the result of an update with [225a], the felicity requirements of the bare plural would be satisfied as long as there is at least one world in the world set of F such that some campus in that world verifying [225a] relative to F had students during at least one ghost appearance. [225b] would then be felicitous either relative to F—if all relevant campuses had students during all ghost appearances—or relative to a file that is the result of an update of F. Hence, the effect of the functional reading on the domain of quantification of operators.

Similarly, a weakly novel bare plural may appear in the scope of a modal operator, as in [226].

[226] a. A ghost may be haunting a campus.
b. Students must be careful.

If the indefinites in [226a] are within the scope of the modal *may*, [226b] is interpreted as modally subordinated. Modal subordination arises in order to satisfy the presuppositional requirement of the bare plural. The bare plural is evaluated not relative to the file that is the output of the update with the previous sentence but an auxiliary file in which the information that there is a ghost haunting a campus is taken for granted.

These informal remarks fall short of an explicit analysis of the functional reading within quantificational contexts but I hope to have shown that such an analysis is possible given my proposals about weak novelty and the functional reading.

5. CONCLUSION

In this chapter I have shown how adopting the dynamic perspective on meaning and the novelty-familiarity theory of (in)definiteness can help us account for the functional reading of bare plurals. The central property of the functional reading is the presupposition associated with weakly novel indefinites and the novelty of their index. The other properties of the reading fell out as a consequence of that presupposition, the novelty of the index, and general priciples governing accommodation and contextually salient functions invoked to guarantee felicity.

NOTES

1. Related are Lewis' (1978) proposals about the conversational scoreboard and its kinematics.

2. Informational parameters also include modal bases distinct from the context set and ordering sources, as discussed in chapters 2 and 3, but these will not figure in the discussion to follow.

3. The common ground and the context set may supply values for the contextual parameters of epistemic modals (Kratzer 1979, 1981) and indicative conditionals (Stalnaker 1976).

4. Non-essential effects include, for example, change of speaker or place, the inevitable change of time as a conversation unfolds, etc.

5. The latter is explicitly formulated in Stalnaker (1976) as intersection of the context set of a context with the content of the assertion relative to that context.

6. It corresponds to Stalnaker's (1978) notion of the *propositional concept*.

7. For the sake of simplicity I have suppressed reference to all other relevant parameters.

8. Contextual presuppositions are presuppositions associated with expressions whose value depends on the context and constrain the relevant value assigments. For instance, *that man* should be assigned as value by the function parameter of the context an individual who is a man (pointed at by the speaker) in the world parameter of the context (see, e.g., Kaplan (1978), von Stechow (1981)) or even in all worlds of the context set of the context (see, e.g., Stalnaker (1972) and Heim (1982, ch. II) on deictic definites). Soames (1989) calls them 'expressive presuppositions.'

9. Relative to a model $M = \langle D, W, I \rangle$, where D is a set of individuals, W a set of possible worlds and I an interpretation function for the basic expressions of the language, mapping individual constants into D and and n-place predicates into D^n, $[obstinate(bill)]_{c,w} = 1$ iff $I(bill)(w) \in I(obstinate)(w)$ and $[obstinate(bill)]_{c,w} = 0$ iff $I(bill)(w) \notin I(obstinate)(w)$.

10. This reasoning for the need of P2 answers Soames' (1989) objection against Stalnaker's (1978) proposal for connecting semantic and pragmatic presuppositions.

11. P1 is a stronger condition than it might appear at first sight. In general, it is violated by any sentence ϕ which is either true or false in a context c. Sentences which are not informative with respect to any context are not limited to those which express necessarily true or false propositions. Indicative conditionals under a particular analysis and choice for their contextual parameters turn out to not be informative with respect to any context: if we follow Kratzer's (1979, 1981) analysis of conditionals as involving implicit necessity and take the modal base of indicative conditionals to be the context set and the ordering source to be, at least in some cases, trivial (see, e.g., Heim (1982) and Roberts (1989)), then for any context c, such a conditional is either false in c (if the context set of c contains world in which the antecedent is true but the consequent is false) or it is true in c (if all worlds in the context set of c in which the antecedent is true are such that the consequent is true as well). Therefore, such an indicative conditional will always violate P1 and will never be assertable in any context. It is unclear what kind of reinterpretation should be invoked in this case.

12. Although much of the discussion in Stalnaker (1978) presupposes that contextual update is globally defined, part of the discussion on reinterpretation, prompted by violation of P3 and P1, and the account of the presupposition projection properties of conjunctions and conditionals in Stalnaker (1974) presuppose a recursive definition of contextual update.

13. Stalnaker (1976) is particularly clear on this issue. He makes the distinction between semantic interpretation and pragmatic interpretation. Semantic interpretation is defined in terms of a static semantics. Pragmatic interpretation is defined in terms of a dynamic semantics. Furthermore, the crux of his solution to problems such as presupposition projection (Stalnaker 1974), reasonable inference (Stalnaker 1976), the informativeness of utterances of necessarily true or false propositions (Stalnaker 1978) is to move the burden of explanation away from semantics to pragmatics.

14. The 'turtle problem' constitutes such a case with regard to genericity, given the $\odot$ operator analysis in the appendix of ch. 2.

15. For instance, let ϕ be the logical form of the sentence 'it rains today', ψ the logical form of 'it rains tomorrow', and χ the logical form of 'there is a flood.' Consider a context c whose $W(c)$ = $\{w_1, w_2, w_3, w_4, w_5, w_6, w_7\}$ and assume that ϕ is true in w_1, w_2, w_3, and false in the remaining worlds of the context set, ψ is true in w_1, w_4, w_5, and false in the remaining worlds of the context

set, χ is true in w_1, w_2, w_4, w_6, and false in the remaining worlds of the context set. Then $\psi \to \chi$ is false relative to every world in the context set because of w_5 and therefore so is $\phi \,\&\, (\psi \to \chi)$. But if $\psi \to \chi$ is evaluated relative to the context that is the result of having updated with ϕ, then $\psi \to \chi$ is true in all worlds of the context set of that context, more in accord with intuitive judgements.

16. Although all of these works develop a dynamic semantic system, not all of these systems are compatible with the version presented here.

17. The relevant definitions are as expected:

ϕ is true in w relative to context c with a non-empty $W(c)$ iff if $w \in W(c)$, then $w \in W(c + \phi)$.

ϕ is false in w relative to context c with a non-empty $W(c)$ iff if $w \in W(c)$, then $w \notin W(c + \phi)$.

18. See Soames (1989) for a useful overview of different approaches.

19. [176] gives just the definedness conditions, not the full meaning specification.

20. See also von Stechow (1981), who defines a notion of presuppositions as a relation between sentences in a truth-conditional framework.

21. These ideas are developed in Condoravdi & Gawron (1996) and are used to give a uniform account for expressions with indexical and anaphoric readings.

22. We can construe pragmatic presuppositions as relations between sentences, in a fashion similar to [177], in terms of contextual update: ϕ presupposes ψ iff for any context c, $U(\phi, c)$ is defined only if ψ is true in c.

23. Ideally, [171] should have been formulated in such a way as to relativize truth or falsity of ϕ in w to a context that admits it. I did not do that because at that point I had not introduced the notion of admittance.

24. The world set of a file corresponds to Stalnaker's context set discussed in section 2.1. However, whereas in that section meaning was taken to operate on context-set-like information states, here it is taken to operate on file-like information states.

25. Heim (1982) reserves the term 'referent' for the case when a discourse referent is matched to a unique entity. I use it to mean any entity that a discourse referent is matched with.

26. The notions defined in [191] are not meant to exhaust all possible notions of relative maximal or minimal informativeness.

27. The variables in A may or may not have indices in the domain of the file.

28. It would seem that the domain of a file could be derived in a complementary fashion: using the notion of a minimally informative file with respect to a set of variables, one would then derive the domain of the file as the set of natural numbers such that the set of variables A indexed to them is such that the file is not minimally informative with respect to A:

For any $i \in N$ and any file F: $i \in \text{Dom}(F)$ iff $\exists w \in \text{W(F)}$ and $\exists d \in D$ such that $\forall f \in \text{Sat}_w(F), f(x_i) \neq d$.

The domain of the file can be so defined only under an additional assumption, namely that for each discourse referent introduced we have predicated a property that does not necessarily hold of every individual in the model. This assumption is necessary; for instance, suppose we start with the minimally informative file and update it with 'some entity$_i$ is an entity', this assertion would not be sufficient to give us the domain (assuming no possible worlds in entirely devoid of individuals). Then the domain of the resulting file cannot be derived on the basis of the definition above. According to the definition, the domain of the file is the empty set, whereas the domain of the file should be $\{i\}$. In any case, I will not accept this derivative definition of the domain of the file for a different reason: I want to have available a way of defining file change potentials in terms of minimally informative files with respect to a given variable whose index may belong in the domain of the file.

29. This is to distinguish between pronouns, which correspond to variables, and descriptions, which correspond to open formulas.

30. The brief treatment of definite descriptions in Heim (1983) assigns to them an existential presupposition as opposed to (the stronger) familiarity presupposition. It seems that the criticisms advanced by van der Sandt (1992) against the Karttunen/Heim account are really criticisms of that version of the presuppositional account of definites rather than of the familiarity theory, which incorporates the anaphoricity presupposition.

31. [201] is a slightly modified version of the condition given in (Heim 1982:304), so as to accord with the construal of the satisfaction set of files as a set of assignment function/possible world pairs.

32. I call this relation weak entailment because other notions of information containment yield stronger notions of entailment. For instance, we can define a notion of entailment in terms of the

relation $\sqsubseteq$, given in [192], as follows: F entails F' iff F' $\sqsubseteq$ F. See Beaver (1992) and Dekker (1993) for various notions of information containment. Dekker (1993) also investigates the algebraic structure characterizing the relations of information containment on information states.

33. Simplifying somewhat; inherently quantificational NP's or NP's within the scope of some quantifier would not result in infelicity for the bare plural even if they are co-indexed with it.

34. This is regardless of whether deictics are treated descriptively, as in Heim (1982, ch. III), or as directly referential, in the manner of Condoravdi & Gawron (1996).

35. See also Heim (1982) for the distinction between presupposed and accidental coreference and Dekker (1993) for discussion on partial objects.

36. By 'implicit information' I mean information that does not correspond to any information change brought about by overt linguistic material.

37. Gawron, Nerbonne & Peters (1991) use contextually salient functions to account for singular E-type pronouns, and Chierchia (1992) for donkey-pronouns. Gawron, Nerbonne & Peters (1991) then need a strategy to get variable quantificational force for singular E-type pronouns, Chierchia (1992) to get the universal reading of donkey-pronouns.

38. Chierchia (1992) treats contextually salient functions as free variables in a logical form representation and assumes a definition of truth that makes reference to universal quantification of possible value assignments to all free variables. Gawron, Nerbonne & Peters (1991:25) postulate the following principle:

> The choice function χ used in interpreting E-type uses of singular pronouns is fixed for a discourse and is not under the control of any speakerparticipating in that discourse.

This principle guarantees that the truth of an utterance involving an E-type pronoun cannot depend on the choice χ makes out of the extension of the predicate corresponding to the descriptive content of the pronoun.

39. This is not to say there are *no* phenomena that in fact necessitate supplementation of some parameter in the logical form of a description. Turkish accusative-marked indefinites, as discussed by Enç (1991), may constitute such a case.

Bibliography

Asher, Nicholas and Michael Morreau. 1991. "Commonsense Entailment: A Modal Theory of Nonmonotonic Reasoning." In Jan van Eijck, ed., 1–30.

Asher, Nicholas and Michael Morreau. 1995. What Some Generic Sentences Mean." In Gregory N. Carlson and Francis Jeffry Pelletier, eds., 300–338.

Barker, Chris. 1993. "A Presuppositional Account of Proportional Ambiguity." Paper presented at the Third Conference on Semantics and Linguistics Theory, University of California at Irvine.

Barker, Chris and David Dowty (eds.). 1992. *Semantics and Linguistics Theory, vol. II.* Working Papers in Linguistics, No. 40, The Ohio State University.

Barwise, Jon and Robin Cooper. 1981. "Generalized Quantifiers and Natural Language." *Linguistics and Philosophy* 4, 159–219.

Bäuerle, Rainer and Urs Egli. 1985. "Anapher, Nominalphrase und Eselsätze." Arbeitspapiere des Sonderforschungsbereichs 99, Universität Konstanz.

Beaver, David, I. 1992. "The Kinematics of Presupposition." Institute for Language, Logic and Information Prepublication Series, ISSN 0924-2082.

Berman, Stephen. 1987. "Situation-Based Semantics for Adverbs of Quantification." *Proceedings of West Coast Conference in Formal Linguistics*, vol. 6, 17–31. Stanford Linguistics Association.

Berman, Stephen. 1990. "On Certain Differences Between Wh-Phrases and Indefinites." *Proceedings of the Northeastern Linguistic Society*, vol. 20, 31–45.

Chastain, Charles. 1975. "Reference and Context." In Keith Gunderson, ed., *Language, Mind, and Knowledge*, vol.7 of *Min-*

nesota Studies in the Philosophy of Science, 194–269. Minneapolis: University of Minessota Press.

Carlson, Gregory N. 1977a. "A Unified Analysis of the English Bare Plural." *Linguistics and Philosophy* 1, 413–457.

Carlson, Gregory N. 1977b. *Reference to Kinds in English*. Doctoral dissertation, University of Massachusetts, Amherst.

Carlson, Gregory N. 1979. "Generics and Atemporal *When*." *Linguistics and Philosophy* 3, 49–98.

Carlson, Gregory N. 1982. "Generic Terms and Generic Sentences." *Journal of Philosophical Logic* 11, 145–181.

Carlson, Gregory N. 1987. "Exceptions to Generic Generalizations." Manuscript, University of Iowa.

Carlson, Gregory N. 1988. "Truth-Conditions of Generic Sentences: Two Contrasting Views." In Manfred Krifka, ed., 31–51.

Carlson, Gregory N. 1989. "On the Semantic Composition of English Generic Sentences." In Gennaro Chierchia, Barbara H. Partee and Raymond Turner, eds., 167–192.

Carlson, Gregory N. and Francis Jeffry Pelletier (eds.). 1995. *The Generic Book*. Chicago: The University of Chicago Press.

Chierchia, Gennaro. 1982. "Bare Plurals, Mass Nouns, and Nominalization." *Proceedings of the West Coast Conference in Formal Linguistics*, vol. 1, eds. Daniel P. Flickinger, Marlys Macken, and Nancy Wiegand, 243–255. Stanford Linguistics Association.

Chierchia, Gennaro. 1992. "Anaphora and Dynamic Binding." *Linguistics and Philosophy* 15, 111–183.

Chierchia, Gennaro, Barbara H. Partee and Raymond Turner (eds.). 1989. *Properties, Types and Meaning, Volume II: Semantic Issues*. Dordrecht: Kluwer Academic Publishers.

Clark, Herbert, H. 1977. "Bridging." In Philip N. Johnson-Laird and Peter C. Wason, eds., *Thinking : Readings in Cognitive Science*, 411–420. Cambridge: Cambridge University Press.

Clark, Herbert, H. and S. E. Haviland. 1977. "Comprehension and the Given–New Contract." In Roy O. Freedle, ed., *Discourse Production and Comprehension*, 1–40. Norwood: Ablex Publishing Corporation.

Cole, Peter (ed.). 1978. *Syntax and Semantics, Vol. 9: Pragmatics*. New York: Academic Press.

Condoravdi, Cleo. 1992. "Strong and Weak Novelty and Familiarity." In Chris Barker and David Dowty, eds., 17–37.

Condoravdi, Cleo and Mark Gawron. 1996. "The Context-Dependency of Implicit Arguments." In Makoto Kanazawa, Christopher Piñón, and Henriëtte de Swart, eds., 1–32.

Cooper, Robin. 1979. "The Interpretation of Pronouns." In Frank Heny and Helmut S. Schnelle, eds., *Syntax and Semantics, vol. 10: Selections from the Third Groningen Round Table*, 61–92. New York: Academic Press.

Cooper, Robin. 1983. *Quantification and Syntactic Theory*. Synthese Language Library, volume 21. Dordrecht: Reidel.

Cresswell, Max J. 1990. *Entities and Indices*. Dordrecht: Kluwer.

Croft, William. 1986. "Universal Quantifiers and Generic Expressions." Manuscript, Stanford University.

Dahl, Östen. 1975. "On Generics." In Edward L. Keenan, ed., 99–111.

van Deemter, Kees. 1991. *On the Composition of Meaning: Four Variations on the Theme of Compositionality in Natural Language Processing*. Doctoral dissertation, University of Amsterdam.

van Deemter, Kees. 1992. "Towards a Generalization of Anaphora." *Journal of Semantics* 9, 27–51.

Dekker, Paul J. E. 1993. *Transsentential Meditations: Ups and Downs in Dynamic Semantics*. Doctoral dissertation, University of Amsterdam. ILLC Dissertation Series, no. 1.

Diesing, Molly. 1988. "Bare Plural Subjects and the Stage/Individual Contrast." In Manfred Krifka, ed., 107–154.

Diesing, Molly. 1990. *The Syntactic Roots of Semantic Partition*. Doctoral dissertation, University of Massachusetts, Amherst.

Diesing, Molly. 1992a. *Indefinites*. Cambridge: MIT Press.

Diesing, Molly. 1992b. "Bare Plural Subjects and the Derivation of Logical Representations." *Linguistic Inquiry* 23, 353–380.

Dowty, David and Belinda Brody. 1984. "The Semantics of 'Floated' Quantifiers in a Transformationless Grammar." *Proceedings of the West Coast Conference in Formal Linguistics*, vol. 3, 75–90. Stanford Linguistics Association.

van Eijck, Jan. 1983. "Discourse Representation Theory and Plurality." In Alice G.B. ter Meulen, ed., *Studies in Modeltheoretic Semantics*, 85–106. Dordrecht: Foris Publications.

van Eijck, Jan. (ed.) 1991. *Logics in AI: Proceedings of the European Workshop JELIA*. Lecture Notes in Computer Science, 478. Lecture Notes in Artificial Intelligence. Berlin: Springer-Verlag.

Enç, Mürvet. 1986. "Toward a Referential Analysis of Temporal Expressions." *Linguistics and Philosophy* 9, 405–426.

Enç, Mürvet. 1991. "The Semantics of Specificity." *Linguistic Inquiry* 22, 1–25.

Engdahl, Elizabet. 1986. *Constituent Questions*. Dordrecht: Reidel.

Evans, Gareth. 1977. "Pronouns, Quantifiers, and Relative Clauses." *Canadian Journal of Philosophy* 7, 467–536.

Farkas, Donka F. 1985. *Intensional Descriptions and the Romance Subjunctive Mood*. New York: Garland.

Farkas, Donka F. 1993. "Modal Anchoring and NP Scope." Manuscript, University of California, Santa Cruz.

Farkas, Donka F. and Yoko Sugioka. 1983. "Restrictive If/When Clauses." *Linguistics and Philosophy* 6, 225–258.

Fodor, Janet D. and Ivan A. Sag. 1982. "Referential and Quantificational Indefinites." *Linguistics and Philosophy* 5, 355–398.

Gabbay, Dov M. and Julius M.E. Moravcsik. 1973. "Sameness and Individuation." *Journal of Philosophy* 70, 513–526.

Gärdenfors, Peter (ed.). 1987. *Generalized Quantifiers: Linguistic and Logical Approaches*. Dordrecht: Reidel.

Gawron, Mark, John Nerbonne, and Stanley Peters. 1991. "The Absorption Principle and E-Type Anaphora." CSLI Report No. CSLI-91-153 RR-91-12.

Gerstner, Claudia and Manfred Krifka. 1987. "Genericity." To appear in Joachim Jacobs, Arnim von Stechow, Wolfgang Sternefeld and Theo Vennemann *Handbuch der Syntax*. Berlin: W. de Gruyter.

Ginzburg, Jonathan. 1992. *Questions, Queries and Facts: A Semantics and Pragmatics for Interrogatives*. Doctoral dissertation, Stanford University.

Groenendijk, Jeroen A.G. & Martin J.B. Stokhof. 1990. "Dynamic Montague Grammar." In László Kálmán and László Pólos, eds., *Papers from the Second Symposium on Logic and Language*, 3–48. Akadémiai Kiadó, Budapest.

Groenendijk, Jeroen A.G. & Martin J.B. Stokhof. 1991a. "Two Theories of Dynamic Semantics." In Jan van Eijck, ed., 55–64.

Groenendijk, Jeroen A.G. & Martin J.B. Stokhof. 1991b. "Dynamic Predicate Logic." *Linguistics and Philosophy* 14, 39–100.

Hawkins, John A. *Definiteness and Indefinitess: A Study in Reference and Grammaticality Prediction*. London: Croom Helm.

Heim, Irene R. 1982. *The Semantics of Definite and Indefinite Noun Phrases*. Doctoral dissertation, University of Massachusetts, Amherst.
Heim, Irene R. 1983. "On the Projection Problem for Presuppositions." *Proceedings of the West Coast Conference in Formal Linguistics*, vol. 2, 114–125. Stanford Linguistics Association.
Heim, Irene R. 1987. "Where Does the Definiteness Restriction Apply? Evidence from the Definiteness of Variables." In Eric J. Reuland and Alice G. B. ter Meulen, eds., *The Representation of (In)definiteness*, 21–42. Cambridge: MIT Press.
Heim, Irene R. 1990. "E-Type Pronouns and Donkey Anaphora." *Linguistics and Philosophy* 13, 137–177.
Heim, Irene R. 1992. "Presupposition Projection and the Semantics of Attitude Verbs." *Journal of Semantics* 9, 183–221.
Heyer, Gerhard. 1985. "Generic Descriptions, Default Reasoning, and Typicality." *Theoretical Linguistics* 12, 33–72.
Hinrichs, Erhard. 1985. *A Compositional Semantics for Aktionsarten and NP Reference in English*. Doctoral dissertation, Ohio State University.
Hintikka, Jaakko. 1986. "The Semantics of *A Certain*." *Linguistic Inquiry* 17, 331–336.
de Hoop, Helen. 1992. *Case Configuration and Noun Phrase Interpretation*. Doctoral dissertation, Rijksuniversiteit Groningen.
Horn, Lawrence. 1972. *On the Semantic Properties of Logical Operators in English*. Doctoral dissertation, UCLA.
Horn, Lawrence. 1989. *A Natural History of Negation*. Chicago: University of Chicago Press.
Kadmon, Nirit. 1987. *On Unique and Non-Unique Reference and Asymmetric Quantification*. Doctoral dissertation, University of Massachusetts, Amherst.
Kadmon, Nirit. 1990. "Uniqueness." *Linguistics and Philosophy* 13, 273–324.
Kamp, Hans. 1971. "Formal Properties of *Now*." *Theoria* 37, 227–274.
Kamp, Hans. 1981. "A Theory of Truth and Semantic Representation." In Jeroen Groenendijk, Theo Janssen, and Martin Stokhof, eds., *Formal Methods in the Study of Language*, 277–321. Mathematisch Centrum, Amsterdam.
Kamp, Hans and Uwe Reyle. 1993. *From Discourse to Logic*. Dordrecht: Kluwer Academic Publishers.

Kanazawa, Makoto, Christopher Piñón, and Henriëtte de Swart (eds.). 1996. *Quantifiers, Deduction and Context*. Stanford: CSLI Publications.

Kaplan, David. 1978. "DThat." In Peter Cole, ed., 221–243.

Kaplan, David. 1989. "Demonstratives: An Essay on the Semantics, Logic, Metaphysics, and Epistemology of Demonstratives and Other Indexicals." In Joseph Almog, John Perry and Howard K. Wettstein, eds., *Themes from Kaplan*, 481–563. New York: Oxford University Press.

Karttunen, Lauri. 1974. "Presupposition and Linguistic Context." *Theoretical Linguistics* 1, 181–194.

Karttunen, Lauri. 1976. "Discourse Referents." In James McCawley, ed., *Syntax and Semantics, vol. 7*, 363–385. New York: Academic Press.

Karttunen, Lauri and Stanley Peters. 1979. "Conventional Implicature." In Choon-Kyu Oh and David A. Dinnen, eds., *Syntax and Semantics: Presupposition, vol.11*, 1–56. New York: Academic Press.

Keenan, Edward, L. (ed.). 1975. *Formal Semantics of Natural Language*. Cambridge: Cambridge University Press.

Kleiber, Georges. 1985. "Du Côté de la Généricité Verbale: les Approches Quantificationnelles." *Langages* 79, 61–88.

Kratzer, Angelika. 1977. "What 'Must' and 'Can' Must and Can Mean." *Linguistics and Philosophy* 1, 337–355.

Kratzer, Angelika. 1979. "Conditional Necessity and Possibility." In Rainer Bäurle, Urs Egli and Arnim von Stechow, eds., *Semantics form Different Points of View*, 117–147. New York: Springer-Verlag.

Kratzer, Angelika. 1980. "Die Analyse des Blossen Plural bei Gregory Carlson." *Linguistische Berichte* 70, 47–50.

Kratzer, Angelika. 1981. "The Notional Category of Modality." In Hans-Jürgen Eikmeyer and Hannes Rieser, eds., *Words, Worlds and Contexts – New Approaches in Word Semantics*, 38–74. Berlin: W. de Gruyter.

Kratzer, Angelika. 1988. "Quantificational and Non-Quantificational Forms of Genericity." Paper presented at the LSA annual meeting, New Orleans.

Kratzer, Angelika. 1995. "Stage-Level and Individual-Level Predicates." In Gregory N. Carlson and Francis Jeffry Pelletier, eds., 125–175.

Krifka, Manfred. 1987. "Syntax and Semantics of Definite and Indefinite Generics." Partly in collaboration with Claudia Gerstner. Manuscript, Universität Tübingen.

Krifka, Manfred. 1988a. "The Relational Theory of Genericity." In Manfred Krifka, ed., 285–312.

Krifka, Manfred (ed.). 1988b. *Genericity in Natural Language: Proceedings of the 1988 Tübingen Conference.* Seminar für Natürlich-Sprachliche Systeme der Universität Tübingen, SNS-Bericht 88-42.

Krifka, Manfred. 1989. "Nominal Reference, Temporal Constitution and Quantification in Event Semantics." In Renate Bartsch, Johan van Benthem and Peter van Emde Boas, eds., *Semantics and Contextual Expression*, 75–115. Dordrecht: Foris Publications.

Krifka, Manfred. 1990. "Genericity: An Introduction." Manuscript, University of Texas at Austin.

Krifka, Manfred. 1992. "A Framework for Focus-Sensitive Quantification." In Chris Barker and David Dowty, eds., 215–236.

Krifka, Manfred, Francis Jeffry Pelletier, Gregory N. Carlson, Alice ter Meulen, Godehard Link, and Gennaro Chierchia. 1995. "Genericity: An Introduction." In In Gregory N. Carlson and Francis Jeffry Pelletier, eds., 1–124.

Kroch, Anthony S. 1979. *The Semantics of Scope in English.* New York: Garland.

Lahiri, Utpal. 1991. *Embedded Interrogatives and Predicates that Embed Them.* Doctoral dissertation, MIT.

Lawler, John. 1972. "Generic to a Fault." *Papers from the Eighth Regional Meeting of the Chicago Linguistic Society*, 247–258.

Lewis, David. 1973. "Counterfactuals and Comparative Possibility." *Journal of Philosophical Logic* 2, 418–446.

Lewis, David. 1975. "Adverbs of Quantification." In Edward L. Keenan, ed., 3–15.

Lewis, David. 1979. "Scorekeeping in a Language Game." *Journal of Philosophical Logic* 8, 339–359.

Link, Godehard. 1984. "Plural." English version of paper in Dieter Wunderlich and Arnim von Stechow, eds., *Semantics: An International Handbook of Contemporary Research*, 1991. Berlin: W. de Gruyter.

Link, Godehard. 1988. "Dependency in the Theory of Generics." In Manfred Krifka, ed., 313–335.

Link, Godehard. 1995. "Generic Information and Dependent Generics." In Gregory N. Carlson and Francis Jeffry Pelletier, eds., 358–382.

Löbner, Sebastian. 1985. "Definites." *Journal of Semantics* 4, 279–326.

Löbner, Sebastian. 1987. "Natural Language and Generalized Quantifier Theory." In Peter Gärdenfors, ed., 181–201.

Ludlow, Peter and Stephen Neale. 1991. "Indefinite Descriptions: in Defense of Russell." *Linguistics and Philosophy* 14, 171–202.

McNally, Louise. 1992. *A Semantics for the English Existential Construction*. Doctoral dissertation, University of California at Santa Cruz.

Milsark, Gary. 1974. *Existential Sentences in English*. Doctoral dissertation, MIT.

Moltmann, Friederike. 1991. "Measure Adverbials." *Linguistics and Philosophy* 14, 629–660.

Montague, Richard. 1974. *Formal Philosophy: Selected Papers of Richard Montague*. New Haven: Yale University Press.

Neale, Stephen. 1990. *Descriptions*. Cambridge: MIT Press.

Nunberg, Geoffrey and Chiahua Pan. 1975. "Inferring Quantification in Generic Sentences." *Papers from the Eleventh Annual Meeting of the Chicago Linguistic Society*, 412–422.

Ojeda, Almerindo E. 1991. "Definite Descriptions and Definite Generics." *Linguistics and Philosophy* 14, 367–397.

Partee, Barbara H. 1984. "Nominal and Temporal Anaphora." *Linguistics and Philosophy* 7, 243–286.

Poesio, Massimo. 1991. "Relational Semantics and Scope Ambiguity." In Jon Barwise, Jean Mark Gawron, Gordon Plotkin, and Syun Tutiya, eds., *Situation Theory and Its Applications*, volume 2, 469–497. Lecture Notes No. 26. Stanford: CSLI Publications.

Prince, Ellen F. 1992. "The ZPG Letter: Subjects, Definiteness and Information-Status." In William C. Mann and Sandra A. Thompson, eds., *Discourse Description: Diverse Linguistic Analyses of a Fund-Raising Text*, 295–325. Philadelphia: J. Benjamins Publishing Company.

Roberts, Craige. 1987. *Modal Subordination, Anaphora, and Distributivity*. Doctoral dissertation, University of Massachusetts, Amherst.

Roberts, Craige. 1989. "Modal Subordination and Pronominal Anaphora in Discourse." *Linguistics and Philosophy* 12, 683–721.

Rooth, Mats E. 1985. *Association with Focus*. Doctoral dissertation, University of Massachusetts, Amherst.
Rooth, Mats E. 1987. "Noun Phrase Interpretation in Montague Grammar, File Change Semantics, and Situation Semantics." In Peter Gärdenfors, ed., 237–268.
Rooth, Mats E. 1995. "Indefinites, Adverbs of Quantification, and Focus Semantics." In Gregory N. Carlson and Francis Jeffry Pelletier, eds., 265–299.
Russell, Bertrand. 1919. *Introduction to Mathematical Philosophy*. London: Allen and Unwin.
van der Sandt, Rob A. 1992. "Presupposition Projection as Anaphora Resolution." *Journal of Semantics* 9, 333–377.
Schubert, Lenhart K. and Francis Jeffry Pelletier. 1987. "Problems in the Representation of the Logical Form of Generics, Plurals, and Mass Nouns." In Ernest LePore, ed., *New Directions in Semantics*, 385–451. London: Academic Press.
Schubert, Lenhart K. and Francis Jeffry Pelletier. 1988. "An Outlook on Generic Statements." In Manfred Krifka, ed., 357–371.
Schubert, Lenhart K. and and Francis Jeffry Pelletier. 1989. "Generically Speaking, or, Using Discourse Representation Theory to Interpret Generics." In Gennaro Chierchia, Barbara H. Partee and Raymond Turner, eds., 193–268.
Soames, Scott. 1989. "Presupposition." In Dov M. Gabbay & Franz Günthner, eds., *Handbook of Philosophical Logic, Volume IV: Topics in the Philosophy of Language*, 553–616. Dordrecht: Reidel.
Srivastav, Veneeta. 1991. *WH Dependencies in Hindi and the Theory of Grammar*. Doctoral dissertation, Cornell University.
Stalnaker, Robert C. 1968. "A Theory of Conditionals." In Nicholas Rescher, ed., *Studies in Logical Theory*, 98–112. Oxford: Blackwell.
Stalnaker, Robert C. 1973. "Presuppositions." *Journal of Philosophical Logic* 2, 447–457.
Stalnaker, Robert C. 1972. "Pragmatics." In Donald Davidson and Gilbert Harman, eds., *Semantics of Natural Language*, 380–397. Dordrecht: Reidel.
Stalnaker, Robert C. 1974. "Pragmatic Presuppositions." In Milton K. Munitz and Peter K. Unger, eds., *Semantics and Philosophy*, 197–213. New York: New York University Press.
Stalnaker, Robert C. 1976. "Indicative Conditionals." In Asa Kasher, ed., *Language in Focus: Foundations, Methods, and Systems*, 179–196. Dordrecht: Reidel.

Stalnaker, Robert C. 1978. "Assertion." In Peter Cole, ed., 315–332.
von Stechow, Arnim. 1981. "Presupposition and Context." In Uwe Mönnich, ed., *Aspects of Philosophical Logic: Some Logical Forays into Central Notions of Linguistics and Philosophy*, 157–224. Dordrecht: Reidel.
Stump, Gregory. 1985. *The Semantic Variability of Absolute Constructions*. Dordrecht: Reidel.
de Swart, Henriëtte. 1987. "Phrases Habituelles et Sémantique des Situations." In Georges Kleiber, éd., *Rencontre(s) avec la Généricité*, 261–279. Recherches Linguistiques, XII. Paris: Librairie Klincksieck.
de Swart, Henriëtte. 1991. *Adverbs of Quantification: A Generalized Quantifier Approach*. Doctoral dissertation, Rijksuniversiteit Groningen.
de Swart, Henriëtte. 1992. "Genericity, Conditionals and the Weak/Strong Distinction." *Proceedings of the West Coast Conference in Formal Linguistics*, vol. 11.
de Swart, Henriëtte. 1996. "(In)definites and Genericity." In Makoto Kanazawa, Christopher Piñón, and Henriëtte de Swart, eds., 171–194.
Veltman, Frank. 1991. "Defaults in Update Semantics." Institute for Language, Logic and Information Prepublication Series for Logic, Semantics and Philosophy of Language LP-91-02. University of Amsterdam.
Vendler, Zeno. 1967. *Linguistics in Philosophy*. Ithaca: Cornell University Press.
Verkuyl, Henk J. 1989. "Aspectual Classes and Aspectual Composition." *Linguistics and Philosophy* 12, 39–94.
Wertheimer, Roger. 1972. *The Significance of Sense: Meaning, Modality, and Morality*. Ithaca: Cornell University Press.
Westerståhl, Dag. 1984. "Determiners and Context Sets." In Johan van Benthem and Alice ter Meulen, eds., *Generalized Quantifiers in Natural Language*, 45–71. GRASS 4. Dordrecht: Foris Publications.
Wilkinson, Karina J. 1988a. "Genericity and Indefinite NP's." Manuscript, University of Massachusetts, Amherst.
Wilkinson, Karina J. 1988b. "The Semantics of the Common Noun *Kind*." In Manfred Krifka, ed., 407–429.
Wilkinson, Karina J. 1991. *Studies in the Semantics of Generic Noun Phrases*. Doctoral dissertation, University of Massachusetts, Amherst.

Zucchi, Alessandro. 1989. *The Language of Propositions and Events: Issues in the Syntax and the Semantics of Nominalization*. Doctoral dissertation, University of Massachusetts, Amherst.

Index

accommodation, 40, 43, 63, 64, 114, 126, 127, 154, 165, 167, 168, 172, 173, 177, 179, 180, 182
    global, 93, 95
    informational, 173, 174
    intermediate, 93
    local, 93, 95
    representational, 173
adverb of quantification, 23, 29–32, 34, 36, 39, 40, 46, 52, 53, 57, 60, 64–67, 73, 81–85, 90, 97, 98, 101, 115–117, 121, 129, 131, 133, 137, 138, 176
adverb of quantity, 95–101
anaphoricity presupposition, 164, 185
Asher, Nicholas, 41, 45, 47, 54

Barker, Chris, 133
Barwise, Jon, 170, 176
Beaver, David, 93, 134, 150, 186
Berman, Stephen, 98, 133, 173
Brody, Belinda, 98, 99, 135
Bäuerle, Rainer, 133

Carlson, Gregory, 5, 6, 8–10, 12–14, 16–33, 35, 37–39, 41, 46, 48–50, 52–54, 56, 77, 78, 97, 122, 130, 135
Chastain, Charles, 81
Chierchia, Gennaro, 36, 48, 53, 55, 56, 64, 115, 133, 135, 137, 150, 173, 178, 179, 186
Clark, Herbert, 135
common ground, 70, 94, 110, 113, 137, 144, 146, 182
conditionals, 44, 53, 92, 94, 103, 113, 138, 150, 182, 183
Condoravdi, Cleo, 54, 184, 186
context change effect, 145, 147, 148
context set, 136, 144–148, 150, 151, 155, 156, 182–184
contextual sensitivity, 69, 130
    negative, 67, 78, 99–102, 129, 174, 175
    positive, 67, 100, 102, 114, 123, 124, 128, 129, 179, 180
contextual update, 137, 143, 145, 147–150, 152, 155, 183, 184
Cooper, Robin, 21, 22, 93, 104, 134, 135, 170, 173, 176
Cresswell, Max, 118

Croft, William, 60

Dahl, Östen, 39, 44, 47, 53, 60
Deemter, van, Kees, 107–109, 115, 125, 127, 136, 139
Dekker, Paul, 150, 186
derived kind predication, 7, 14, 16, 28, 37, 38
Diesing, Molly, 4, 35, 37, 46, 48, 49, 53, 116, 122, 126, 127, 138, 173, 176
direct generalization approach to generics, 5, 6, 17, 26, 33, 34, 36, 37
directly referential interpretation, 81, 82, 186
discourse referent, 62, 108–111, 123–127, 137, 157–161, 164–171, 173, 175, 177–180, 184, 185
Dowty, David, 98, 99, 135
dynamic binding, 127, 131
dynamic existential quantifier, 36, 53, 56
dynamic meaning, 150, 155
dynamic semantics, 4, 149, 150, 183, 184
dynamic theory of meaning, 4, 142, 143, 151, 152, 155–157, 165, 181

E-type anaphora, 20–26, 50, 52, 72, 115, 131, 149, 173, 186
Egli, Urs, 133
Eijck, van, Jan, 24
Enç, Mürvet, 107–109, 118, 123–125, 129, 136, 138, 139, 186
Engdahl, Elizabet, 173
Evans, Gareth, 50

existential presupposition, 92–95, 101, 102, 131, 134, 164, 176, 177, 179

familiarity, 102, 136, 141, 168, 177
familiarity condition, 3, 142, 163, 164, 167–169, 171
familiarity presupposition, 164, 185
familiarity theory of definites, 3, 141–143, 156, 157, 162, 163, 168, 176, 179, 181, 185
Farkas, Donka, 14, 17, 36, 37, 39, 50, 53, 54, 118, 119, 134
felicity condition, 3, 4, 102, 120, 124, 129, 142, 158, 162, 163, 166, 168, 171, 177
file change potential, 3, 157–159, 161–166, 169–172, 178, 179, 181
file change semantics, 3
Fodor, Janet, 81, 139

Gabbay, Dov, 9, 48
Gawron, Mark, 178, 179, 184, 186
general proposition, 79, 132
generalization
    accidental, 7, 49, 76
    actual, 7, 8, 16, 28, 42, 44, 59, 62, 75–78, 103, 104, 132
    contextually restricted, 64, 75–77, 132
    descriptive, 6, 16, 40, 42–44, 46, 59, 64, 88, 113, 135
    dispositional, 16, 49, 135

generic, 7, 8, 16, 38, 41,
    44, 59, 64, 75–77, 88,
    103, 107, 131
  degenerate, 103, 107
  habitual, 8, 38, 49, 51
  non-accidental, 6, 44, 57
  normative, 6, 16, 42–44,
    46, 49, 113
  operator, 12–15, 19, 30
genericity, 5–47, 56–59, 63, 74,
    102, 103, 106, 130,
    183
  degenerate, 74, 103, 107,
    121, 122, 129
  implicit, 57
generics, 5–47, 150
Gerstner, Claudia, 5, 23, 33, 56
Ginzburg, Jonathan, 98, 100,
    173
Groenendijk, Jeroen, 56, 150

Haviland, S. E., 135
Hawkins, John, 101
Heim, Irene, 3–5, 33, 39, 53,
    55, 56, 62, 64, 85, 93,
    95, 97, 101, 103, 104,
    107, 132–135, 137,
    141, 143, 149, 152,
    153, 156, 157, 162,
    163, 165, 170, 173,
    176, 182–186
Heyer, Gerhard, 49, 52, 53
Hinrichs, Erhard, 48, 53, 135
Hintikka, Jaakko, 173
Hoop, de, Helen, 81, 132, 176
Horn, Lawrence, 52

implicature approach, 75, 76
indefiniteness analysis of bare
    plurals, 5, 6, 33–46,
    57, 59
inferred generalization
    approach to generics,
    5, 16, 17, 34, 49

Kadmon, Nirit, 85, 133, 173

Kamp, Hans, 4, 33, 55, 56, 62,
    97, 107, 115, 132,
    137, 138, 149, 175
Kaplan, David, 47, 132, 182
Karttunen, Lauri, 62, 89, 94,
    95, 130, 143, 150,
    152, 153, 157, 185
kind analysis of bare plurals, 5,
    6, 9–33, 46
Kleiber, Georges, 53
Kratzer, Angelika, 4, 20, 35,
    37–39, 41, 53, 103,
    122, 133, 135, 138,
    150, 173, 182, 183
Krifka, Manfred, 5, 20, 23,
    33–35, 38–40, 51, 52,
    56, 60
  et al., 5, 39, 41, 45, 51, 56
Kroch, Anthony, 98

Löbner, Sebastian, 98
Lahiri, Utpal, 57, 97–100, 135
Lawler, John, 53
Lewis, David, 33, 55, 97, 135,
    154, 173, 182
Link, Godehard, 7, 20
Ludlow, Peter, 75, 79, 139

McNally, Louise, 52
meaning postulate, 10, 14, 15,
    21, 49, 52
Milsark, Gary, 19, 37, 170, 175
modal base, 41–47, 59, 61, 63,
    65, 66, 87, 88, 94,
    103–105, 111–114,
    119, 131, 134, 137,
    138, 150, 182, 183
modals, 30, 34, 41, 44, 52, 57,
    60, 66, 73, 82, 87, 88,
    110, 116–121, 129,
    131, 137, 139, 150,
    181, 182
Moltmann, Friederike, 20
monster, 47
Montague, Richard, 49
Moravcsik, Julius, 9, 48

Morreau, Michael, 41, 45, 47, 54

Neale, Stephen, 75, 79, 108, 136, 139
Nerbonne, John, 178, 179, 186
novelty, 3, 102, 141, 142, 165, 174, 175, 177, 181, 182
novelty condition, 3, 142, 163–166, 168, 171, 174
novelty theory of indefinites, 3, 141–143, 157, 162, 168, 179, 181
novelty-familiarity-condition, 166
    extended, 163
NP strength, 176
Nunberg, Geoffrey, 48

Ojeda, Almerindo, 48, 135
operator
    adverbial, 30, 31, 33, 36, 102, 103, 109, 113, 115, 120, 137, 176
    deontic, 66, 88
    dyadic, 41, 53, 55, 56
    extensional, 28
    generic, 17, 18, 26, 29–31, 34–36, 38–41, 44–46, 52, 53, 58–67, 72, 81, 82, 103–107, 109, 111, 113, 114, 116, 117, 120, 126, 129, 132, 134, 136, 138, 175, 176
        nominal, 33
    implicit, 58, 102, 103, 106, 115–117, 129, 150, 176
    intensional, 12, 34, 139
    modal, 59, 60, 62, 66, 89, 109–111, 118, 128, 129, 134, 136, 137, 144, 181
    monadic, 47, 53, 98
    nominal, 31
    presuppositional, 134
    sentential, 19, 33, 36, 53
    VP, 31, 98
operator analysis, 102, 103, 129
ordering source, 41–47, 59, 61, 63, 65, 88, 103–105, 137, 150, 182, 183

Pan, Chiahua, 48
Partee, Barbara, 133
Pelletier, Jeffry, 17, 40, 48, 50, 53, 54
Peters, Stanley, 94, 95, 153, 178, 179, 186
Poesio, Massimo, 115
Port-Royal Puzzle, 28, 40
Prince, Ellen, 57, 58, 72, 130
pronoun of laziness, 20–24, 50, 51
proper kind predication, 7, 17, 24, 50

referentiality, 79, 81, 133, 139
referentiality approach, 75, 79, 81
restricting set, 123, 124, 126, 128, 129
Reyle, Uwe, 115, 137, 175
rigid designator, 9, 10, 29
Roberts, Craige, 89, 130, 173, 183
Rooth, Mats, 20, 35–37, 40, 53, 150
Russell, Bertrand, 55, 79

Sag, Ivan, 81, 139
Sandt, van der, Rob, 93, 173, 185
Schubert, Lenhart, 17, 40, 48, 50, 53, 54
semantic partition, 35
singular proposition, 79, 81
Soames, Scott, 182, 184

specificity, 79, 81, 124, 132, 138, 139
Srivastav, Veneeta, 98
Stalnaker, Robert, 52, 135–137, 143–145, 148–150, 153, 154, 156, 173, 182–184
Stechow, von, Arnim, 182, 184
Stokhof, Martin, 56, 150
strong novelty, 175, 177
strong NP, 170, 176
strong reading, 81, 176
strongly novel NP, 142, 168, 171, 172, 176, 178, 180
Stump, Gregory, 37, 53
subordination, 87, 89
    conditional, 134
    modal, 63, 66, 87–89, 113, 118, 130, 181
    quantificational, 87–89
Sugioka, Yoko, 36, 39, 53
Swart, de, Henriëtte, 36, 40, 53, 54, 99, 133, 137

Veltman, Frank, 150, 159
Vendler, Zeno, 135
Verkuyl, Henk, 20

weak novelty, 175, 177, 181
weak NP, 170, 176
weakly novel NP, 142, 168, 171, 172, 176–178, 180, 181
Wertheimer, Roger, 54
Westerståhl, Dag, 107, 108, 136
Wilkinson, Karina, 5, 20, 24, 29, 33, 39, 46, 52–54, 56

Zucchi, Alessandro, 135

For Product Safety Concerns and Information please contact our EU representative GPSR@taylorandfrancis.com
Taylor & Francis Verlag GmbH, Kaufingerstraße 24, 80331 München, Germany

www.ingramcontent.com/pod-product-compliance
Lightning Source LLC
Chambersburg PA
CBHW050555240426
43664CB00049B/2574